P9-CRQ-748

The Equipping Pastor

A Systems Approach to Congregational Leadership

R. Paul Stevens and Phil Collins

An Alban Institute Publication

All Bible references are taken from the *New International Version* except where otherwise noted.

The Publications Program of The Alban Institute is assisted by a grant from Trinity Church, New York City.

Copyright 1993 by The Alban Institute, Inc. All rights reserved.

This material may not be photocopied or reproduced in any way without written permission.

Libraryh of Congress Catalog Card Number 92-85825
ISBN 1-56699-108-0

CONTENTS

87043

LIST OF FIGURES

ACKNOWLEDGMENTS

The authors gratefully acknowledge the following people who have contributed to the crafting of this manuscript: Celia Hahn, our patient editor who supported us through the process; Paddy Ducklow, for reading the manuscript and offering helpful criticism both as a pastor and a counselor; and Gail and Lois, our spouses, who supported us in the project and exemplify much of what we have written.

We also acknowledge with gratitude the following publishers for permitting us to reproduce portions of the work of others and helpful drawings and graphs: Augsburg Fortress, Ave Maria Press, David C. Cook, Eerdman's, Guilford Press, Gulf Publishing, Inter-Varsity Press, *Journal of Marital and Family Therapy, Journal of Psychology and Christianity,* Judson Press, Paulist Press, Prentice-Hall, Science and Behavior Books, Scott, Foresman & Co., Sojourners, S.P.C.K., Word Books, W.W. Norton, and Dr. J. Friesen.

Why the Church Is Stuck

There are no proven systems for the shepherding
of the ministry of the laity in a local congregation.
Davida Foy Crabtree[1]

Why has there been so little progress in the liberation of the laity? For
more than thirty years[2] the Western church has been exposed to a growing number of books and resources focused on the release of every
member of the church for ministry and mission. Seminars, videos, and
tapes abound. The reasons for an equipping approach to pastoral leadership are acknowledged to be convincing: Without every-member
ministry, we have unlived biblical truths, unstrategic leadership deploy-
ment, untapped resources in the congregation, and an unreached world.[3]
A congregation needs more ministry than one person, "the minister," can
give.

But this proliferation of information has produced very little change
in church life. Young theological graduates persuaded about the equipping model of pastoral ministry find their enthusiasm doused to death in
their first pastorate. Active lay leaders, hearts warmed by the biblical
message of universal priesthood, universal giftedness, and universal
service in the body of Christ, feel inhibited in their own congregations.
While laypeople feel underemployed, doing "busy work" in the church,
pastors feel overemployed, trying to shoulder the impossible burden of
being the minister of the church.

The Church as a Stuck System

Getting underemployed laypersons and overemployed pastors together ought to be as easy as falling off a log. But it is not. Releasing the people of God for ministry involves more than distributing the work of the church more equitably. Laypeople have their own ministry. And the reasons for the frustration of pastors are complex. God's frozen people, as described by Gibbs and Morton, will not get thawed by changing one dynamic or by trying one more program. We need a systemic solution to problems such as:

—*Overfunctioning Leaders*. Pastors and lay leaders feel stuck with all the responsibility for the church—from dreaming up new programs to locking the building at night.

—*Unmotivated Laity*. Pastors introduce lay training programs but cannot motivate people to get involved. Laypeople are passive receivers, the object of the pastor's ministry rather than the subject of ministry themselves.

—*Standardized Pastoral Roles*. Churches view pastors as replaceable parts in a machine and compare the incumbent with the previous pastor or measure a pastor's performance by standardized criteria. Many pastors feel called to a congregation even though they can see that it is not a good fit.

—*Leadership Burnout*. Pastors blame themselves when they burn out. Congregations also blame the pastors, but the discouraged pastor may be a symptom of a problem in the church. The pastor has become the "identified burnout."[4]

—*Recurring Problems*. Decade after decade, generation after generation, the same problems surface, even though there has been a change of actors for the play, and "new blood" has been introduced. A church born of a split keeps splitting. The polluting negativism of significant members lingers long after they have left or died.

—*Maintenance Focus*. Most congregations are inward looking, focused on self-preservation rather than mission. Mission is the special interest of a few highly motivated members in the congregation.

The church is stuck.[5] The reason for the unreleased congregational potential is much deeper than the problem of clericalism of pastors protecting their turf. We are convinced that the stagnation of the laity is caused mainly by the frustrating power of a church system that keeps the laity marginalized and prevents the pastor doing the most important work: "equipping the laity for the work of the ministry" (Eph. 4:11-12).[6]

We want this book to be read and digested by both pastors and lay leaders; the church needs a gracious conspiracy of pastor and people to bring about the required systemic change. The church needs conversion, organizational conversion. Toward that end we offer our thinking and experience of a systemic approach to congregational leadership and equipping the laity. We do this together because a systemic approach to ministry means that our joint effort is more powerful than the sum of our individual efforts. We also do this out of our own experience.

The Stevens Journey

It is often said that real learning begins only after graduation from theological college. That was not entirely true with me. I made my first important ministry discovery in 1959 while examining the Greek text of Ephesians 4:11-12 in the reading room of McMaster Divinity College, Hamilton, Ontario.

I discovered that pastors fulfill their calling not by doing the ministry themselves but by releasing others for ministry and mission. God did not give pastor-teachers "*to do* the work of the ministry" as implied in the KJV and the first edition of the RSV and supported by an uninspired comma: "For the perfecting of the saints, for the work of the ministry . . ." (v. 12 KJV). The so-called "fatal comma" in some English translations led to a clerical understanding that pastor-teachers were given by God, first, for the equipment of the saints, and second, to do the work of the ministry. But the comma is supported neither by the text nor the context. Rather, pastor-teachers were given to the church *to equip the saints to do* the ministry.

That day I began to understand pastoral leadership and equipping in a different light. The equipping pastor is not merely one who gets the lay people to assist her or him. No, the equipping pastor assists the people to fulfill their own ministry, a much greater thing.

Upon graduation I determined to be an equipper, not a super solo-performer. In more than thirty years I have never recovered from that paradigm shift. I have taken this as my goal in pastoral leadership, in student ministry, and now in theological education.

A few years ago my determination and reflection drove me to take up the hammer and saw to work as a carpenter for five years. By becoming a tentmaker like Aquila and Priscilla (Acts 18:1-3), I was trying to rediscover the lay vocation in society. I learned some important lessons. The average lay Christian spends most of his or her life earning a living, relating to neighbors, and trying to raise a family. If Christianity does not relate to the realities of Monday to Saturday as experienced by the ordinary church member, then it is just another religion. That tentmaking experience drove me back into pastoral ministry again and eventually into theological education where I teach the theology of work, vocation, and ministry for the laity. It also led to the next discovery, which is the burden of this book.

While I was reading Peter and Brigitte Berger's book *The War over the Family,* a sentence jumped off the page. They showed how, possibly for the first time in history, the individual was becoming the basic unit of Western society. I realized that that was exactly how I had been thinking of the church—as a collection of individuals with gifts that should be released. But how did God view the church? Maybe the basic, fundamental unit of the church to be addressed by pastoral leadership was not the individual member but the church itself, a corporate organism described in the Bible as the body of Christ and the people of God.

It was then that I discovered systems theory, now widely used in family therapy. Virginia Satir, one of the pioneers, counseled whole families when there was a problem evidenced in one member. As counselor she saw herself as the leader of the process not the leader of the people in her counseling context. That gave me a new pastoral image for leadership in the church. Jesus is the true leader, the Head. The systemic, equipping pastor leads the process, not the people. Just as a good spiritual director leaves the directee dependent on God rather than the director, so the equipping pastor works to get the people respondent to God for themselves. Systems thinking also helped me work with the church as a living whole, the body, and not just as a bouquet of Christians.

I wondered why so many programs I had undertaken had hardly made a dent on liberating the laity. All the models have their place: one-to-one discipling, courses and study programs, lay schools, small groups, and target groups. But I found they all got short-circuited unless one worked with the whole life of the church by considering the quality of relationships, atmosphere, goals, priorities, and structure. I began to discover why some churches with many programs produced little leadership and intentional mission, while other churches with fewer programs but a healthier corporate life evoked lay ministry almost without trying.

So now I work with a paradox that runs as a thread through this book: To release individuals I do not concentrate on liberating individual saints. I concentrate on the whole. Then I let the church equip the saints! When the congregation is a healthy system, individual members thrive because of the empowering influence of the life of the body. When the congregation is unhealthy, our efforts to equip a few motivated individuals are usually doomed.

The Collins Journey

I approach the liberation of the leadership and the laity with a special interest in the relationship of leadership style and systems thinking. My convictions were forged in the hammer and heat of pastoral experience, in denominational service, and now in theological education. One of my first pastorates was a cluster of small United Baptist Churches with a total combined membership of less than one hundred. Being basically task-oriented, I was well-suited to the challenge. I was entrepreneurial, and I knew how to use the media. I went from house to house. I'm the type of person who can go into a town and not have one member, and in a few weeks have gathered thirty-five people. I have no trouble walking up to people asking, "Hi, how are you? Can I talk with you for a while?" That was my strength. Now for my weakness. For much of my life, I had a problem keeping relationships because for me people become checkers on the checker board, and I am out to win the game. And if I had to take a checker and jump over another one and throw that checker off the board I could do it.

My spouse, on the other hand, is very person-oriented. It is difficult for her to go out and bang on doors to meet people. But my wife is able to keep friends once she has made them. That game of checkers? My wife could never get rid of anyone, even if she lost the game. For her, having the checkers all on the board is more important than winning the game.

Back on this early pastorate, within three years I had helped the
church grow to seven hundred people—this in a rural town of sixteen
hundred. But I discovered that if I wanted to hold those people, I needed
help in the systemic life of the church. People like my wife had to come
along to relate to all the new people, to build the family, the common
bonds, until the body came together. So I discovered experientially that
it is absolutely essential that task-oriented leaders have person-oriented
leaders working with them.

My contribution to this book is also shaped by twenty years in denominational service. During that time I watched both delightful and
agonizing matches between pastors and churches. I have also observed
that no one leadership style is better than another for equipping the laity.
What seems to be crucial is the match between the leaders and the followers in the systemic life of that particular congregation. As I will
explain later, the issue of pastoral matchmaking is helpfully explained by
systems theory.

One event has burned its way into my mind. As a denominational
representative I visited a church to discover a congregation at war! The
conflagration was over plans to enlarge the church facilities dramatically.
Some families had already left the church. Others were threatening to
follow. The present pastor had only been in the church two years, during
which the once-peaceful fellowship had become dangerously fragmented.
Everyone sensed that something had to be done if the church were to
survive.

I spent two days meeting with individuals and participating in two
congregational meetings. One message came through loud and clear:
The leadership given by the pastor was the primary focus of the conflict.
One group in the church fully supported him, while another stood in
solid opposition to him. The first group said he was hard-working, effective, visionary, and sensitive. The other group said he was autocratic,
a poor listener, power-hungry, insensitive, and self-centered. How is it
possible for two groups in the same fellowship to view the pastor's
leadership so differently?

In vain I looked into the pastor's history for some hint that he would
create such a problem. He had served three churches prior to this one.
His previous pastorates had been long, and under his leadership the congregations had done well. But unfortunately the pastor had not changed
when he took his place in this new congregation. He relied on the same

leadership style he had used successfully for many years. Although his style had attracted quite a number of new people to the church, the laity who had worked to build up the congregation clashed with the new members (one of whom was a retired, fractious pastor) and fought the pastor for leadership of the church.

The pastor was involved in an immense misunderstanding. He failed to recognize that the leadership needs and expectations of this congregation were very different from the three churches he had pastored previously. He was out of "sync." He had failed to join the church in a systemic way (the subject we will explore in the next chapter).

From experiences like this and intensive research, I concluded that an understanding of leadership styles as a theory, and one's own leadership styles as an insight, can be of immense help in becoming effective as a pastor and leader. Leadership must be adapted to the specific congregation that one serves.

I have a deep concern for both pastors and lay leaders who feel frustrated. According to one survey, fifty-eight percent of the Protestant clergy in North America have expressed the feeling that their work seems futile and ineffectual.[7] At gatherings of pastors, priests, and lay leaders I have repeatedly been reminded that it was possible to be competent in ministry and yet quite ineffective. This finding is supported by intensive research conducted by the prestigious Association of Theological Schools, funded by the Lilly Endowment a few years ago.[8] A survey of pastors within my own group of churches revealed that at least twelve percent felt a greater sense of fulfillment outside their congregations than within them. They admitted that they got meaning for ministry apart from the people to whom God had called them.[9] The church is a stuck system and the leadership of the church feels equally stuck. The problem is deeper than the pastor, the elders, or the board. It is a matter of the church system.

A Short Primer on Systems Theory

Systems theory expounds the ancient principle that the whole is more than the sum of the parts. The human body is an obvious example of a system. Organs and members stand in specific relationship with other organs and members so that each is dependent on the other, and the health of one member is dependent on the health of another. Kidney disease affects the whole body. The body is a marvelously self-regulating organism that is obviously more than a collection of functioning members.

Systems thinkers use the term *wholism* to describe the family or the social organism as something more than the sum of the members. Feeling that a presenting problem in an "identified patient" is usually a symptom of a family problem, systems family therapists work with whole families.

In the same way, systems pastors work with the whole church, not merely with collections of individuals. The basic unit of the church is not the individual but the church as a whole, even though Western culture contrives to make us believe the opposite. Pastors routinely try to understand their congregations by going through the individual names on the membership lists, but computer print-outs cannot encompass the reality of a whole congregation as a unit.

This fundamental paradox, that the whole is more than the sum of the parts, was expressed by Aristotle ages ago, but it provides the basis of a new way of thinking about reality. In pastoral practice this means that our most productive direction will be to work with the culture and systemic organization of the church rather than to deal exclusively with individuals.

"Do you know your church?" I (Collins) once asked a young man pastoring a church near mine but of a different denomination. Upset by a number of things going on in his church, he sought my help. He commented on this and that individual. He was particularly bitter about the lack of commitment in the church. People came and went, even some who had received significant ministry. They would get in a tiff and not even come to church. "Do you know your church?" It was an odd question to ask a pastor who had served the same people for four years. But I felt that I, having been in the community much longer than he, knew his church better than he did.

He replied, "Yes, I think so."

I said, "If you know the church well, what is the nature of your church?" I did not use the word *culture*, but I was really asking him whether he understood the church's system. "What is different and unique about your church as opposed to the church down the street?"

He had a lot of fine things to say about the church. Even though he was frustrated, he could say he was enjoying the church. He simply was not understanding my question.

So I asked, "Can you tell me in a sentence or two how you would describe your church as a whole?"

He replied, "Uncommitted."

I said, "I would describe your church as a wounded church. It is filled with wounded people, people who need and demand personal ministry. It is not really a question of whether they are committed or uncommitted. They are so wounded, they are not able to commit themselves. If you could see the church as a wounded church, you would change your whole approach to ministry with these people."

It is difficult if not impossible to change individuals directly without changing the system. Systems theory proposes that members of a system are interdependent. Mutual reinforcement, described by the term *synergy*, suggests that more can be achieved by a group than can be achieved by the total efforts of individuals within that group. Synergy describes the effect of taking two medicines together: They may have a powerful hurtful reaction or create a multiple impact for healing. Similarly, synergy describes the multiple impact members of a living system have when they work together. One plus one often makes more than two!

In due course we will have the opportunity to consider Paul's systemic statement about the body of Christ and its members: "The eye cannot say to the hand, 'I don't need you!'" (1 Cor. 12:21). Change in one evokes change in another. We are tied together in family and church like elements in a hanging mobile; changes in one "arm" produce changes in all the others. But this gives rise to two paradoxical needs that collide and interact: the need to be *we* and the need to be *me*. The technical terms for this are *cohesion* (or *fusion*) and *differentiation*.

A simple illustration is provided by marriage. The other day I (Stevens) attended a wedding and watched a man and woman attempt to blow out their own identities! They took their two candles and then lit a third (to symbolize the marriage relationship). So far so good. But instead of expressing the reality of a system (of which intercourse is a powerfully symbolic act) by leaving their own candles burning, they blew out their own candles and symbolically opted for a merger. I felt like jumping up and yelling, "Don't do it! Don't blow yourself out! You will be a better 'you' if you form a system *together*." Of course I kept silent. But one wag, on hearing the phrase "the two shall become one," did not keep silent. He asked insightfully, "Which one?" It is a systems question.

Often the family system and the church system interact so that a poorly differentiated member of a family (a person who cannot leave home psychologically and has not established his or her own identity in relation to other significant "others") is almost incapable of becoming a member of a church. Such people become relationship nomads, moving on when a relationship gets too intense.[10] Some pastors become church nomads and keep "joining" church after church without really joining any of them. Though they claim the reason for their frequent moves is theological conflicts, power struggles, or "the leading of God," the real reason often is related to how they function in a system. When the heat gets turned up, they move on. To stay would require them to address the issues still unresolved in their families of origin. It is a systems problem. And because it is a systems problem it will take the collaboration of *both* the laity and the clergy to work toward healthier membership when pastors first signal that they have "itchy feet."

There is another dimension of systems theory. The term *isomorphism* refers to the structural similarity of fields or systems that may be intrinsically different but behave the same way. Within the church there will be isomorphies: persons and subsystems like families that have a similarity of purpose, motivation, belief, and patterns of behavior. Subcongregations or subsystems in the congregation (small groups, age-group clusters, and families within the church) usually have significant commonalities.[11] Every system has a tendency to return to the "tried and true" (homeostasis) just as the keel in a sail boat forces the boat to return to the upright position after a big blow. A pastor tries to improve congregational participation by changing the order of service to include prepared and spontaneous prayers from the people. But, during the pastor's one-month vacation, the elders leading the service return to the old order. The boat is upright once again! Powerful systemic reasons related to deeply cherished beliefs incline a church to return to the comfortable.

One deacon, when asked by the pastor to close the service with prayer, had the honesty to speak in no uncertain terms to the pastor in front of other parishioners, "Pastor, I will not pray. You are the one to pray because that is what you are paid to do." Understanding the environment or culture of a family, church, or organization is essential in working with that system to bring change to that system and its members to greater maturity. Movement and adjustment in a system are often best accomplished by indirect means. This is a subject to which we will return.

Systems family theory proposes that contemporary family problems often relate to unresolved issues in a previous generation. This also finds congruency with church experience. Sometimes the "ghost" of a previous pastor whose leaving was never properly mourned or a church fight thirty years ago that was never resolved crops up in a church meeting in a seemingly unrelated way. In his ground-breaking book *Generation to Generation,* Edwin Friedman, the Jewish therapist-rabbi explores the multigenerational aspects of church and synagogue leadership.

The Systems Revolution

While more detailed comments on systems theory will be discussed later, we will attempt here to explain how systems theory has developed in the twentieth century. It is one of those things that, once you begin to see things this way, makes you wonder why it took you so long to think systemically.

As early as the mid-1920s Ludwig von Bertalanffy, a practicing biologist, began to understand living organisms in a systems way.[12] He recognized that biological organisms could not be adequately understood by the classical Newtonian method in science,[13] which regarded each object as a collection of distinct and disconnected parts. The assumption of the classical approach was that the whole could be understood by examining each of the parts without considering the relationship of the parts. Bertalanffy concluded that this method neglected some observable features of organisms that were fundamental. Though Bertalanffy recognized that the problems addressed by general systems theory had been noted and discussed for centuries, he was able to articulate systems thinking. The fundamental principle is that neither the whole nor the parts can be understood unless the interrelationships of the parts are understood. Instead of seeing the whole as the *sum* of the parts, we are invited to see the whole as superior to its parts.[14] This means that unity in an organism is a complex whole,[15] an idea we will take up once again when we explore the theology of the body of Christ. Bertalanffy admits that systems theory as he promoted it in the mid 1940s[16] is preeminently a mathematical field, offering partly novel and highly sophisticated techniques of coping with the new and complex problems surfacing in the modern world.[17]

As a new way of thinking about reality, systems theory has recently been applied to a host of other fields including transportation systems, national financial planning, outer space exploration, leadership and management, and large complex organizations. It has penetrated all fields of science and proven to be one of the best ways of understanding and managing large organizations and complex realities. Popular journals such as *Time* routinely use systems terminology without saying so. For example, an article on losses in Japan's stock market says, "The world's financial markets are so intertwined that when one itches, the others scratch."[18] Ministers of finance are now painfully aware that the economic health for their country cannot be achieved by tinkering with only one factor, such as the prime lending rate for banks, but is the result of many complex factors, most of which cannot be controlled. Quite recently a few authors have applied systems theory to pastoral care and leadership in the church, though only one known to us has the liberation and empowering of lay ministry as its focus.[19] Even spirituality[20] and the interpretation of Scripture has been approached systemically. Of direct relevance to the theme of this book is the recent application of this ancient principle to family therapy.[21]

Great strides have been made in the social sciences through a systems approach, especially in the field of family therapy.[22] Family systems theory was developed in the 1950s and early 1960s. The difference made by this theoretical breakthrough is precisely this: While psychoanalytic theory previously interpreted what transpired in relationships as the result of what people in the family contributed as autonomous individuals, systems theory viewed the family as an emotional unit so that the behavior of individuals was related directly to the relational system of the family itself.[23] Clinical and pastoral counselors now routinely receive training in family systems theory and learn to "think systemically." Not only therapeutic work with families is informed by this insight but a basic Christian text on *preventative* family ministry[24] relies heavily on this theoretical structure. This approach to family ministry is an important corrective to the granular individualism of Western society.

Beyond Systems Theory

Recently systems theory itself has come under fresh revision by therapists who are concerned that "traditional" systems thinking puts the therapist "outside" the system as an objective observer, a management-consultant, an expert who "tinkers" with the system, rather than the therapist being a participant-facilitator who collaborates with the client in constructing new realities in a nonhierarchical relationship.[25] Later, we will make some comment on this "poststructural" approach to family therapy but a few preliminary comments bear on our subject.

First, the pastor (or therapist) *is* part of the system and therefore will be influenced by others as much as he or she is a "change agent" of the system, although some therapists question whether a therapist can be a change agent. It is helpful to think of pastor and laity as *copastors* of a church and *coequippers*.

Second, the emphasis of this new generation of systems thinkers on intrapersonal (what is going on inside the leader-facilitator) and not just on the interpersonal relationship conforms more exactly, as we shall see, with the biblical understanding of persons, of relationships, and of the internal and relational sources of ministry. This means that pastors (or lay leaders) who wish to influence churches toward the release of every-member ministry must reflect on what is happening inside themselves in the process.

Finally, by considering the multiple systems (family, church, extended family, neighborhood, workplace, community, society, etc.) these systems thinkers[26] help church leaders understand that what is happening in the church system is profoundly related to what is happening at home, in the workplace, and in society at large. The church is an open or at least a partly open system that interacts with other systems for good or ill.[27] Friesen, Grigg, and Newman, psychologists at the University of British Columbia, summarize their approach with these words:

> Therapy is viewed as a shared journey in which therapist and client collaborate in an I-Thou encounter which involves mutual trust, respect and caring. The therapist is a guide to the intrapersonal and interpersonal process, and as such must be flexible and respond genuinely as listener, coach, teacher, choreographer, advocate, and confronter as required.[28]

Substitute "pastor" for "therapist" and "congregation" for "client," and one has a challenging definition of an equipping church leader. Such a leader establishes deep interpersonal allegiance with the members of the congregation and with the whole congregation and functions as a primary (though not the only) guide to evoking health and life through coaching, playing, defending, and sometimes confronting. Clergywomen may help clergymen discover this new style of leadership, as women are less likely to remain "above" or to see themselves as engineers "tinkering" with the church system. Mansell Pattison, a psychiatrist who was one of the first to explore a systems approach to pastoral leadership, ably expresses (in negative terms) this tendency to stay outside the system:

> The Pastor does not operate from outside the system. The pastor does not speak to the system . . . On the contrary, the pastor can present himself or herself as simply one member, with assets and limitations, who will contribute to the whole.[29]

This is the subject of the next chapter.

The Big View

In the first few chapters of this book we will deal with the pastor and lay leader's relationship with the system as a whole: joining the church, cultivating interdependence, leading the cultural process, matching leadership styles, and shepherding the subsystems. Then, in the chapter titled "Discerning the Body," we ask the theological question of whether systems thinking is parallel to the message of the Bible. In "Becoming a Christian Leader," we ask the spirituality question of what kind of Christian person makes a systems leader. Finally, we summarize all we have explored in ten systems principles for equipping the laity and illustrate these by exploring the theme of equipping the laity for mission. In the epilogue we evaluate more deeply the presuppositions of systems thinking in the light of the Bible. But it all starts with joining the system, the subject to which we now turn.

CHAPTER I

Joining Your Own Church

From a systems view, one may say, 'It is more blessed to give *and* to receive.'

E. Mansell Pattison[1]

Every leader gets the system he or she deserves. And every system gets the leader it deserves.

E. Mansell Pattison[2]

Pastoring a Toronto church for twelve years was definitely the highlight of John's career.[3] In First United, John and his family felt loved; leadership just "happened." There was almost nothing John wanted to do that he could not do at First. He thrived on being loved. Who doesn't? On Valentine's Day in his tenth year, John was given a love-gift from the congregation—a red compact car. But by the twelfth year John felt he was losing steam. Though he was not burned out, he felt he needed a sabbatical or a change. At that precise time a church in Vancouver called him.

Grace Community Church believed that John's creative leadership demonstrated in Toronto was exactly what they needed. The church was small but on the verge of realizing its potential. They wanted someone with proven leadership, and John was their person. John did not realize that search committees almost never tell the truth. They do not intend to lie, but they usually do not know their own church any better than pastors know themselves.

John moved to Vancouver and settled in to Grace Community, but he never really joined the church, though he did go through the motions. He and his family stood at the communion table in their second month to be welcomed by the session. There was an induction service. John's name went on the membership roll, the pastor's study door, and the outdoor sign. But in his heart John was still in Toronto, as was the heart of his family. When things got rough, they would think of the good old days at First United, and every time John stepped into his red car, he was at least subconsciously aware of the love he did not yet feel at Grace, and probably never would.

Understanding Church Membership

Every pastor-people relationship is like a marriage. And every marriage requires "leaving" and "cleaving" (Gen. 2:24 KJV). Without leaving there can be no cleaving, and John had not yet left First United. His successor at First realized this when one after another of the members flew John back to officiate at the marriage of their children. John's successor at First could not seem to win the hearts of his flock. (Often a church looks at a prospective pastor with the ghost of a former pastor in mind.[4])

As for John at Grace, because he was always making comparisons with his Toronto parish, he could not become an effective equipping pastor. Why? Because he did not join his own church. This insight is essential to understanding the pastor's role systemically. John did not leave First United, and the people *would not let him leave*.

Covenant Membership

The hire-and-fire mentality of the North American society has reduced the pastor's ministry to a buy-and-sell commodity. A pastor with a vision to equip all the members for ministry, as proposed in Ephesians 4:11-12, is apt to run into the mentality, "We hired *you* to do the ministry." Quaker Elton Trueblood gave his life to promoting the radical idea that pastors are not called to get the people to assist them with their ministry; rather, the pastor is called to assist the people, the laity, with *their* ministry both in the church and in the world.[5] It will take a gracious conspiracy between pastor and people to bring this change about. But the change will not even begin unless the pastor joins the church (or becomes an element of the system, to use systems terminology). *The people must perceive that the pastor is really part of the system.*[6]

Pastors themselves are not free from the seductions of a commodity society. It is all too easy to consider being a pastor as "my job" and to bring to a pastoral assignment a predetermined set of role expectations, sometimes reasonable expectations negotiated during the search process. When things do not go the pastor's way or the people do not seem to want to change, the pastor can struggle with flash-backs to a previous better job, begin the search for another church assignment, or be resigned to quiet desperation. But covenant (and systems leadership) requires more. It requires taking the risk of joining the church and taking the risk of being changed by *this church*.

Commitment is a big word these days, but covenant is a bigger word. Covenant implies that relationship is more important than performance, that belonging is more important than succeeding, that being is more important than doing. Contracts are conditional; covenants are essentially unconditional.[7] But continuing "for better, for worse" is not embracing a self-inflicted death sentence or locking oneself in a relational prison. It is an invitation to go deeper with God and God's people. Without saying so most people want contracts—negotiated exchanges of goods and services—that can be broken if one partner breaks the contract. Churches easily fall into the trap of thinking they can define the pastoral ministry contractually, as an exchange of services in return for remuneration. But Christian ministry is essentially covenantal. There is a "for better, for worse" about it, a bonding and binding agreement to work this thing out for God's glory and for the upbuilding of the body of Christ because we *belong together.* As we shall see, biblical covenant corresponds to the modern understanding of systems theory.

Nontransferable Membership

Neither leadership nor membership is fully transferable from church to church. When John moves from one church to another, he is essentially the same person in each place, but his leadership and ministry will result from all the relational, spiritual, and systemic factors in each situation.

Leadership must be negotiated in each new church. That is one of the great insights of situational leadership theory. Indeed we could say that one never joins an *old* church because it becomes a new one when one joins it. Just as a new baby defines a new family and does not join an old one, so a new member defines a new church by joining it.[8] It becomes a new church, at least in a limited sense.

One cannot merely replace one's membership in an old church with membership in a new one. It is similar, once again, to a marriage. A remarriage will never be successful until a person genuinely "mourns" the loss, whether through death or divorce, of the first partner and embraces the new marriage as a *new* marriage. In the case study at hand, John tried to recycle his membership from First United to Grace Community, *and his membership did not "take."* The reason is not hard to discover. Each local church is a unique system, and leadership is something that emerges and happens in the unique systemic situation of a particular church. Leadership cannot emerge until a person has taken his or her place in the system both to influence and be influenced by the system.

Systemic Membership

Three dynamic principles of a living system are involved in joining a new church: wholeness, synergy, and isomorphism.

The principle of wholeness relates to the basic systems idea that the different parts that compose the system form a single organic whole that can be seen as such even though the parts are still distinguishable. As a whole unit a family can be described: humorous, serious, hard-working, playful. Similarly, a local congregation can take on a corporate life that can be defined: casual, formal, playful, or wounded. Imagine a formal, superserious and patriarchal pastor trying to join a church that is informal, playful, and egalitarian. In joining a church, leaders must attend to the whole and not merely the individual members. The identity of the system must be developed and the purpose of the system be carried forward by a new leader. Leaders must join groups not to tell them what to do but rather to help them fulfill their own missions.

Leaders are also subject to the principle of synergy. As we have already seen, synergy describes the powerful interaction of members when they are working harmoniously. Two people often can accomplish together more than the sum of their individual efforts. Because families and churches can take on a life greater than their members, families and churches have historically had an awesome influence on society. Synergy is at work.

Synergy is a profoundly biblical concept. Paul in his pastoral letters repeatedly exhorted the church using the term *one another*. He uses that term twenty-four times, nearly always giving ethical instructions to the community of believers—to submit to one another, to agree with one another, to bear one another's burdens, and to live in harmony with one another. For synergy between pastor and congregation to occur, a pastor must interact with the people so they can work together, support one another, avoid unhealthy conflict, and realize their potential as the people of God. Leaders can influence and persuade only if there is harmony between the actions of the leader and the needs of the group. This means that groups must allow leaders to change them, and leaders must allow groups to change them.

A new pastor and the church must also join forces in terms of the principle of isomorphism. Just as there are structural similarities between systems and within systems, so there must be a commonality of purpose, vision, and style between a new pastor and the congregation. The term *isomorphic fit* is sometimes used to describe the way a family's identity and way of relating may be well expressed, for example, in its home environment. *Complementary fit* describes a balance of opposites between members of the family and their home environment. Some blended families eventually view their experience as a complementary fit.

Because leaders normally have a unique, symbolic identity in the body of Christ, it is crucial that there be an isomorphic fit with their congregations. But this can happen only if pastor and people have shared common goals, a shared way of relating, a shared view of the outside world. Leaders thrive and effectively lead precisely because they are *like* the system, like the people. I (Collins) have seen this over and over again in my experience of "settling" of pastors in congregations. Sometimes pastors have short-lived pastorates because they do not fit. Their presence violates the systems theory of commonality. Rather than being an isomorphic fit, they prove tragically to be "nonfit." So using the systems ideas of wholeness, synergy, and isomorphism, we conclude that a systemic approach to church leadership implies that a pastor can never make a difference in the system if the pastor is outside the system or attempts to make the system fit him or her. Jesus addressed this issue when he spoke about the good shepherd (John 10:1-18). The stranger does not even know the sheep. He is outside the system. The hired hand acts as though the sheep are not his. The thief is bent on his own purposes with the sheep. He uses "my sheep" to express ownership rather than belonging. Both the hired hand and the thief pretend to be inside the system. But the good shepherd can speak honestly of "my sheep" because such a shepherd profoundly belongs and will not leave when there is trouble.

Some congregational leaders stay outside even though they say it is "their" church and speak about "their" people. The reason for the incongruity of speech and reality is subtle and profound: It is the only way they can maintain their own positions and their own views of ministry. Intuitively, they know that if they join the system, *they* will have to change. They may have to relinquish their agenda and their freedom to do what they want. But to equip the church, equipping pastors must join the church that exists; they must hold their own agendas lightly and join with the people in discovering what is God's agenda for the people.

One significant reason for the nonliberation of the laity is that pastors accept calls to churches and move in with specific agendas—to equip the saints for the work of the ministry. They preach it. They organize small groups, run programs, set up institutes within the church, and conduct seminars and training programs. They say, "We're going to release lay ministry here. I've got a program for starting lay pastoral care, one for lay evangelists, one for lay counseling."

The people reject the programs and the pastors feel rejected, when in actual fact it is they—the pastors—who have rejected the new churches. Pastors may end up judging the churches as being intransigent, inflexible, and unresponsive to the Holy Spirit; they may leave. The programs did not fail as programs. They failed because the new leaders did not join the churches. Joining makes one a part of a living organism and whatever emerges—for the system is prior to the programs—has to come out of the systemic life of the church.

The Unconnected Leader

Pastor Samuel is a tragic example of an equipping pastor who never joined. He views himself as the chief executive officer of the congregation and leads the church from behind the pulpit and behind his desk. In his office he sends out directives. He once said to a business executive in his church, "Ernest, you are not the CEO. I am the CEO, and you will do what I say!" Yet the search committee felt they had found the right person for the job because in his prime years Samuel had enjoyed two successful pastorates. He had demonstrated leadership. He was a good preacher. He was a person who loved God and wanted to see people come to personal faith. What was not apparent to the search committee was that the preceding congregation was not as strong as it was when Samuel first went there. He had lost the warm-hearted appreciation of his people to the point that when he left most people were secretly relieved.

Though Samuel wanted to do the right thing in this new church, he again lost the affection of the people. The reason? He never became a member of that congregation. And the longer he stayed, the worse it got.

If we took this pastor aside and told him what we are discussing, he would probably say, "What do you mean? You're crazy. I was so much joined to them that—well, in the five years I was there, I visited every person who went to the hospital. When they got sick, when they got married, I was there for them. When they died, I was there for their families." If he did all these things, even if he had some friends in the parish, how is it possible that he was not a member? (Task-oriented people always have a small circle of supportive people with whom they are "members." Their circle of friends is their "church.")

We are considering something that is really quite subtle. It is not a question of roles; it's a matter of the heart. It also relates to one's understanding of the church. If you have an institutional view of the church, as Pastor Samuel had, then you can fail to give leadership because you are not joined. Ironically, if you view the church with this systems theory, if you have a body-life view of the church as a living organism, you can see that the pastor influences a church only if he or she joins it and then renounces a will to influence it in the sense of accomplishing personally set goals.

Understanding the Leader's Membership

The pastor's membership in the church is, in one sense, different from
that of other members because the pastor enters the church as a potential
leader. Once again it is similar to marriage, when someone who is not a
blood relative becomes next-of-kin and a family member. This new
person enters the extended family with a special relationship and a
unique role. But pity the bride or groom who immediately tries to lead
the family she or he has joined!

Our discussion of the pastor's membership is complicated by the
ambivalence our society feels toward leadership. Some say we are suf-
fering a famine of leadership and, as William Stringfellow says, technical
managerial proficiency "has resulted in the erosion of strong leadership
wherever one looks."[9] Others are so fearful of leadership that they want
societies in which there are either no leaders or everyone is equal in
leadership. As Robert Greenleaf has said, this is the "day of the antileader."[10] So in this day of fear of and fascination with leadership, it is
more important than ever to define what we mean.

Defining Leadership Systemically

The following are some representative definitions of leadership in secular literature: "leadership is the process of influencing the activities of an
individual or group in efforts toward accomplishing goals in a given
situation";[11] "a learned behavioral skill which includes the ability to help
others achieve their potential as individuals and team members";[12] "the
activity of influencing people to strive willingly for group objectives";[13]
and "an interpersonal influence exercised in a situation and directed,
through the communication process, toward the attainment of a special
goal, or goals."[14]

From these and other academic definitions of leadership, three elements keep emerging: ability, activity, and influencing. A synonym for
these three words could be *persuasion*. From these elements, one could
say that leadership comprises qualities and skills in the leader's actions
and behaviors that cause people to respond. Norman Shawchuk has
framed a very simple definition of leadership: "Leadership is the ability
and the activity of influencing people and of shaping their behavior."[15]

To lead is to possess a vision and to carry responsibility for an organization's program and purpose. But—as systems theory teaches—to lead is to depend upon the cooperation of other persons. It raises questions about how people are motivated and what might be the most effective way to work with a group.

To be effective as a leader requires understanding how one's leadership behavior affects the people to be led—the followers. One needs to know one's preferred leadership style and one's back-up styles, a subject we will explore in a later chapter. Further, a leader *in a system* must recognize multiple sources of influence upon the members of the group: family, vocation, wife or husband, events in society—all are forces that influence, for good or ill. The leader must consider the behavior of individual group members and the *situations* in which *the followers* carry out their work.

Leadership can be described as a function of the leader, the followers, and other situational variables. This concept of leadership can be formulated under the following equation:

$$L = (L, F, S)$$

The equation means, "Leadership equals the function of the leader, the followers, and the situation." Anytime someone attempts to influence, or persuade, the behavior of another person or group, regardless of the reason, he or she is exercising leadership. The pastor then is obviously only one of the leaders of the church. This is one reason for our addressing this book to all the people of God.

The motive for influence may be entirely within the leader, or it may be shared by the followers being persuaded. An assumption also needs to be made (to which we will return later in this book) that Christian leadership is motivated by servanthood as suggested by Mark 10:35-45. So we propose an expanded definition to include the Christian leader: Christian leadership is the ability and the activity of various styles of leadership, motivated by the biblical concept of servanthood, with the purpose of influencing people, persuading them, and shaping their behavior.

The function of the pastor-leader in the living system of the church is to direct the whole body to the end that the parts of the church mesh with one another and exercise mutual care and help so that in the interaction the whole body grows. Within the church system this results in an important paradox: The most effective leader will become increasingly less visible as the functioning of the system becomes more effective and manifest. What is happening? The leader is moving from task orientation to a more integrated involvement. And why? Because the leader is a part of, not apart from, the whole system.

But the Christian leader can never assume she is an integral part of the group (system) until she has passed through several stages of negotiating acceptance by the congregation. In our experience this takes a minimum of three years in a local church, and no one should seriously consider moving from a church until three years have passed. Many pastors leave too soon, often on the very edge of blessing, not recognizing the process we are describing!

Group Acceptance

In one of the very few books that explores a systems approach to pastoral leadership, Mansell Pattison outlines four stages of acceptance in which the leader will negotiate acceptance in the group and an appropriate leadership style at each stage in the development of the group. The key word is *negotiation*, a word that represents the intricate nature of the unending interaction between a pastor and congregation that results in leader-acceptance. Pattison's four stages of acceptance are pictured in terms of a movement from "storming," to "forming," to "norming," to "performing."[16] Pattison's drawings of these four movements are found in Appendix 1.

Stage 1: Storming. In this stage you have a group of individuals not yet systemically related to one another, except on an ad hoc basis. They are just getting together. The pastor is off to one side existentially and emotionally. The group may have called the pastor to serve it or to serve with it. Acceptance is pending. The system is not yet for the leader. The group has not yet given the leader full authority. The congregation does not yet manifest the properties of wholeness, synergy, and isomorphism. Basically the pastor is functioning to bring the group together at stated times—for Christian service, a Bible study, prayer, or worship. That's all that is happening. A pastor in this new position should listen, observe, and not start many new things. It is probably wise for a pastor to do little that is new in a first year of ministry, except that which the people themselves might want to initiate.

This stage has been called storming because the new pastor-leader is a "disturbance" in the group. The pastor's presence introduces new dynamics that have yet to be processed by the church. If the new pastor initiates a new action, its acceptance may not be forthcoming or may come very slowly.

Stage 2: Forming. In this stage the congregation moves toward forming its own identity and purpose. Having a new leader, the congregation is moving toward the formation of a new system. Between pastor and people there is a growing sense of common identity and shared goals, yet the pastor-leader is still perceived as an outsider, as a person negotiating the way "in." It is a strange paradox: The church is forming as much by the leader's function as by its own, yet, it is still holding the pastor at arm's length.

As similarity (commonality) develops, both pastor and congregation begin to say, "We are alike." Oddly, the congregation may be unaware of the pastor's part in all of this forming, which eventually leads to some recognition of the pastor as leader.

Stage 3: Norming. Problems in the journey to commonality become evident. What happens? The shared identity and common purpose require each person to contribute more or less in the same way. This has the effect of blocking individuality, an often stressful experience for many Western people. As the congregation gets down to work, members feel a heightened tension between personal self-fulfillment and the church's corporate achievement. Some members, protesting against the "tyranny of the group," assert their individual identity. Some of these "deviants" may withdraw from the church to protect their own individual freedoms. Sometimes the church excludes them and conflict ensues.

Pastor-leaders are very vulnerable at this stage of leader-group development. Though they might think of trying to exercise stronger leadership, it is too soon for this. The pastor who asserts leadership will be seen as threatening the identity of the group.

An example of this happened in a church that had two Sunday morning services: an early service, attended by an easily defined group in the church, and a more traditional eleven o'clock service. The earlier service featured guitars and chorus singing. They sat around in a cosy circle in the lounge. A new pastor came and, in her second year, wanted to close down the early service. The "early" people bristled with resistance to the idea, and their leader even interrupted the "traditional" service during communion to castigate the members and pastor for attempting to threaten the smaller group's identity. He did not use these exact words, but that was what he meant.

This is a critical stage in the pastor's path to acceptance. Here the pastor-leader needs a good understanding of conflict management and problem solving. The pastor's task at this point is to identify the tension, confront the conflict, and enable the church to grow beyond this stage toward group maturity. During this stage the pastor is gradually moving steadily toward full acceptance by the church. She will soon be able to persuade, to influence, and to change behavior—soon able to lead!

Stage 4: Performing. In this stage the system achieves "resolution" or at least considerable reduction of the conflict between individuals and the church as a whole. The tension—inevitable and often fruitful—never quite disappears. Out of this comes mutual recognition of, and commitment to, the congregation. Everyone's unique individuality is recognized and accepted. Some of the most awkward people in the church become warmly accepted. The pastor-leader is recognized as a member of the group, a full-fledged partner in the common enterprise. Once the church both recognizes and gives the pastor authority, that pastor has awesome influence and power. Remembering that the power is symbolic, such a pastor-leader must never abuse it or, for that matter, deprecate it.

The pastor must perform as a pastor-leader, motivated by servanthood, allowing his or her style and learned styles to meet the situation. As a community of faith is formed, embodying God's character and distributing justice fairly, all can be free to both serve and love.

Let us review Pattison's four stages in the light of Pastor John's experience. How did John turn his situation around and eventually become an effective leader at Grace?

Stage 1: storming—individual autonomous behavior. John gradually understood that a church changes when a new pastor arrives; it was unrealistic to expect a church to have a mature systems development, as he remembered First United to have had. When John began the process of joining Grace, he perceived that everyone was "doing his own thing" just as he had been! The congregation was in stage 1 of system development.

Stage 2: forming—developing a common identity. In this stage John devoted a lot of time to asking questions of key leaders. He led a major church retreat in which the whole church considered its vision and identity. John gave an "I have a dream" speech at that conference, being careful to work with the church toward a vision that was the church's vision and not merely his.

Stage 3: norming. This stage is more complicated. As a system matures and deepens, as contract gets increasingly replaced by covenant, and as members increasingly "own" the church's vision, individuals begin to worry about losing their own identity, their own missions and ministries. John remembered feeling this way back at First United, when he felt he no longer had any interests in life outside the church. Edwin Friedman speaks of this as the paradoxical need to be both "we" and "me." John was losing the "me" in the "we." But with the help of someone who understood what was happening, he remained in the church and "joined" the church once again as the system moved to the fourth stage.

Stage 4: performing. Pattison describes this as the dialectical tension between individual identity and system identity.[17] It had now been five years since John had come to Grace Community and it looked as if he had finally achieved the ultimate connection with the church—perhaps with even deeper satisfaction than he had experienced at First United. But if John remains at Grace Community, he will have to keep changing and keep joining because a system is never static. Change in the church requires change in the pastor and vice versa. For that reason we need to get inside the delicate process of negotiation.

The Process of Negotiation

Ministry and leadership are a continuous process of negotiating with a variety of significant people, including the congregation, family, peers, denominational and organizational executives, and community. Out of these negotiations will emerge the realities of one's leadership—its style, its significance, and its effectiveness. These negotiations can be conscious or subconscious, satisfying or frustrating, serendipitous or planned, informed by vision or aimless, effective or ineffective. Through such negotiation, whatever the character, issues are being identified for the leader and the followers; expectations are discovered. These greatly affect one's leadership.

Some leaders refuse to negotiate because they think it denies their God-given authority, their giftedness, or their competence. Management conflict theory[18] can help us understand this reaction. Management conflict theory says that the one who takes a position of special authority "from above" operates from a win/lose position. The implicit message communicated is that the leader does not trust anyone else. Understanding leadership from the perspective of negotiation communicates that we recognize the Christian community as a system that should be taken seriously and that God's leadership is expressed not only through leaders but through the systemic relation of leaders and people.

To negotiate with sensitivity, leaders need to hold the people in high esteem. They do this for many reasons, one being that they should never assume that they have a following that is loyal no matter what. As church leaders and in terms of negotiation, holding people in high esteem involves two things: (1) negotiating by making appeals to the biblical values of our understanding of God's mission, which we trust our followers will affirm, and (2) negotiating for the existence of our ministry on the basis of the *felt* importance of our leadership by the people. The followers must sense that both their felt and real needs are being considered and some of them met.

The leader's "call" should be a living, Spirit-led, continuing process of negotiating with people in terms of their felt needs and their spiritual potential. Theologically speaking, leaders are called to be cocreators with God and God's people, for accomplishing God's purpose and mission in the world. They are not called to be "competent authority figures." But this "cocreator call" calls for leaders who know who they are. Followers respond more affirmatively to Christian leaders who have a sense of direction, vision, and clarity of purpose than to leaders who try to do everything because they are confused about who they are, what they can do well, and even what they want to do. A growing self-awareness is continually developed as leaders allow people to negotiate with them. The people will affirm, instruct, guide, correct, and support. To negotiate successfully, the systemic leader must be willing to risk this ever-growing self-awareness.

Pastor and people are co-equippers, just as pastor and people are members together.

The Lost Art of Joining

We will now summarize what we have learned about joining the church, both from the point of view of the pastor's progressive membership, and from the perspective of what a community can do to accept new members, including the new pastor.

Davida Foy Crabtree, pastor of Colchester Federated Church, insightfully remarks that "membership affiliation is an important component of a management system because it is the entry point, determining the way the member will relate to and understand the church in future years."[19] Here are some steps churches can take to evoke deeper membership at the point of entry, ways that are consistent both with systems theory and biblical truth:

1. Give the new member time to join. Crabtree advises not rushing people into membership and, when people are ready for formal membership, requiring participation in several membership class sessions. It occurs to us that many churches treat membership as a marriage without engagement, without premarital counseling, and without much forethought. No wonder there are so many church membership divorces! Such hasty marriages may be stimulated by anxiety. Trust will allow people to take their time. Similarly, the congregation needs to give a new pastor time to join.

2. Offer members the opportunity to think systemically about the church they are joining. Crabtree offers an outline of four themes she used in premembership classes: (1) our church's way of work; (2) gifts identification, not only for in-church ministry but for all of life; (3) introduction to the ministry of the laity; and (4) frank talk about faith and money, including our tradition, denominational relationships, and our setting in Christian history.[20] Because true covenantal membership is mutual and bilateral, the process of receiving a new member is also an opportunity to expound the implications for the other members. Remember the image of the mobile; when one member moves, all the other members must adjust. *Explain to the congregation how the church itself changes when a new member is added. A new gift calls forth maturity in others.*

3. Make the membership specific, concrete, and covenantal.
Symbols are important to this process. Offering "the right hand of
fellowship," as it is called in some churches, or a similar ritual has a
powerfully evocative impact on both the new member and the church
(really the "new" church), just as the vows "for better, for worse," in a
wedding service can hardly be witnessed without tears. If new members
are welcomed "officially" by several representatives of the church, the
act symbolizes joining the church, not joining the pastor. Thoughtfulness
about the symbols of joining can make a lasting impression. Similarly,
the pastor who is joining the church can create meaningful symbols of
his own deepening covenant with the people.

4. Make joining a continuous process. The church you join to-
morrow will not be the church you joined yesterday. A systemic approach to church membership will involve more than passing on information gained in a membership class. Members who have been leaders
in other churches and some who have not yet been leaders will have to
find a new leadership role in this new church just as pastors do. Each
local system is unique and neither members nor pastors are interchange-
able parts in standardized machines. Joining a church takes time, and
church leaders will care for and support people through a process that
may take months, possibly even years, through which a person finds his
or her own "place" in the new church. And if we have learned anything
from systems theory, *remaining* a member means participating in a
continuous process of renegotiating one's place in the system. In a
sense, the whole corporate life of the church—teaching, worship, fellowship, adult education, governmental meetings, and structures—must be
understood as one continuous ministry of empowering people to *become*
members of this living organism called the local church. The pastor is
not exempt from this process.

**5. Be aware of the dangers of membership and encourage
healthy membership.** Some people are all too ready to join—indeed to
become addicted—to the church. Some churches are addictive organizations requiring a total commitment that should never be demanded. Like
marriage, church membership should be social intercourse but not a
merger with the attendant blurring of emotional boundaries. In unhealthy membership, one's personal emotional stability and the church's
well-being are inseparably tied. For these people, expectations of the

church are the sum of what a healthy person should expect from family, church, neighborhood, school, extended family, friends, self, and God. Family systems therapists Bowen and Kerr explain the process of addictive relationships in terms of poor differentiation. People who have not established their own identity are more prone to becoming addicted, and, at the same time, may be prone to flee from others.

> This addiction can feel just as physical as the addiction of a drug. A person's sense of emotional well-being becomes dependent on how he perceives himself to be thought about and responded to by another [in this case, how one is thought about by the church].[21]

Tragically, we must confess that some churches particularly love such members because they "do all the work." And some churches love the pastors who will "have an affair with" the church; they think that the best church leaders are workaholics. The problem is systemic; it is not just the pastor's problem.

What does a "good" member look like? Michael Kerr gives a fascinating and highly suggestive description of a well-differentiated family member.[22] It also opens up for us the issues in the next chapter— the systemic life of the whole and how this relates to the individual believer. We would like to adapt Kerr's description of a well-differentiated person and describe a good church member in systemic terms:

— needs people but not excessively;
— is able to hear strong messages from others without merely reacting;
— enjoys other members and can receive their ministry without requiring to be with them all the time;
— is not dependent on the praise and approval of other members;
— does not need to be in leadership and in any particular situation may be at the top or the bottom of the hierarchy;
— is sure of personal beliefs but is able to hear and learn from differing viewpoints;
— in discussions and conflict is usually able to see both sides of the argument; and
— feels that he or she has a contribution to make but does not feel ultimately responsible to keep the church going.

6. Make membership prayerful, an opportunity for spiritual formation, because membership evokes deep issues of faith, especially for pastors like John and Samuel. The moment when they feel like leaving can be the most important moment of spiritual growth. I (Stevens) remain moved by a confession made by Kefa Sempangi, a church leader nurtured during the East African Revival:

> Hardly any of us can go to his own Christian community and say: "This is my body which is broken for you. I am laying all my professional skills, abilities, and economic resources at your disposal. Take them and use them as you see fit." We cannot say this because we are not broken. We are too proud to give our lives away to people who are not perfect. We don't want to lose ourselves for sinners. We want to find the perfect person and the perfect community, but we never find them. So, like Judas, we make only a partial commitment to the body of believers to which we belong, and we find our identity in our rebellion from them.[23]

When first I read these words I was about to leave a pastoral role because I felt "unfulfilled" and "unappreciated." But at this point I discovered that I had not yet joined the church. I repented in tears and joined my own church! The people felt the difference and reciprocated. For the pastor and the people to be well-connected, the people must also "join" the pastor. This mutual membership and mutual negotiation is a spiritual ministry in which pastor and people equip each other and so liberate all the people of God for ministry and mission in the church and the world.

CHAPTER II

Cultivating Interdependence

The goal of pastoral work is to build the people of God.
Stephen B. Clark[1]

In Christ we who are many form one body, and each member belongs to all the others.
Paul, Romans 12:5

Much that passes for pastoral care does not build up the body of Christ. Instead it strengthens the pastor-people dependency. For example, an outstanding pastor in his farewell sermon to a church made a remarkable confession. He was deeply loved by the people he had served for many years. No one would deny the integrity with which he cared for the people. He was widely regarded as "successful." But as he reflected on the result of his pastoral ministry, he made a revealing comment. "I know every one of you. And every one of you knows me. But you do not know each other!" It was simultaneously an admission of failure and a breathtaking systemic insight. In that moment he saw what few church leaders understand: The goal of Christian leadership is not to get people to follow the pastoral leader but to relate together as they follow Jesus. Systemic leadership is concerned with interdependence. It is a complex though important concept.

For example, in the human body interdependence is expressed in the way white corpuscles multiply and rally to combat an invading infection, while the same corpuscles diminish in number when the infection subsides. Change in one part of the body requires change in the nature of the relationship to others. In the church, members function together in such a way that, for the proper functioning of the body, they express interrelationship and constantly adjust the equilibrium. Speaking to the issue of interdependence in the body of Christ, Paul observed that "the eye cannot say to the hand, 'I don't need you!' " (1 Cor. 12:21). But the equipping pastor must be able to distinguish between healthy and sick "need" and cultivate the former.

In this chapter we will look into the body of Christ and not merely at it. We will explore how it is put together and how it works. We will discover how the members relate, and how, as equipping leaders, we can equip the saints "so that the body of Christ may be built up until we all reach unity in the faith" (Eph. 4:12-13). We will explore how things happen in a system and how people function when they get close to one another. Then we will deal with some problematic issues in building community: the overfunctioning leader or member, addictions, the influence of relational triangles, and the tyranny of the weak. Finally we will take a systemic approach to discovering and deploying spiritual gifts.

But first we must understand that interdependence is neither dependence nor independence. Expressed on a continuum, the two extreme possibilities of relationships in the system are independent (autonomous and disconnected) and dependent (fused and compliant). But relational health and growth into maturity is found in the middle: interdependent.

INDEPENDENT   INTERDEPENDENT   DEPENDENT

Understanding Togetherness and Diversity

"In Christ we who are many form one body, and each member belongs to all the others" (Rom. 12:5). Paul's systemic statement about the church holds in dynamic tension two essential dimensions of the church: unity (togetherness) and the unique existence and function of each member (diversity). When these are dynamically balanced, the church functions fruitfully in a life-giving way to its members and the world. But unity without diversity leads to the formation of a monolithic organization, a sect that swallows up the individuality of its members. In the drawing below we call this the "melting-pot church." It makes everyone look the same. On the other hand, diversity without unity leads to rampant individualism and the loss of corporate life. The church would then be merely a bouquet of individual believers. Members of the "bouquet church" use the church as a resource to facilitate their own ministries and missions. When there is low unity and low diversity, we have the "seed package church"—a loose collection of people who have almost no reason to be together but great potential. But when unity and diversity are held together in dynamic tension, we experience body life, and the church functions as a healthy, interdependent system.

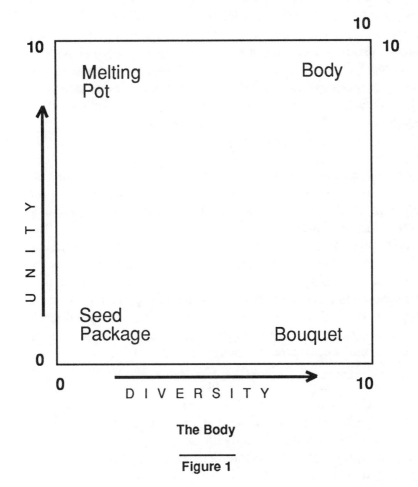

The Body

Figure 1

Interdependence is the dynamic balance of unity and diverse gifting, togetherness and differentiation. Family life gives us the best illustration of this principle. Virginia Satir[2] has pictured the family as a mobile in which any movement by one member causes a movement by other members as they adjust themselves to the changes in their interdependent relationships. Contrary to what one might think, interdependence does not mean that members of a family are victims of the actions of other family members. They all "pull their own strings" and must take responsibility for their own participation in the system. But each is affected by each of the others and the group as a whole.

As we've mentioned earlier, family therapists have discovered that the identified patient (the one who is perceived to have the problem and comes for counseling) may be a symptom of a family problem. Sometimes a family has an unhealthy need for a black sheep, just as the spouse of an alcoholic *needs* an alcoholic mate. A husband and wife may *need* a son or daughter to be sick to help them maintain their marital relationship. In fact, they may unconsciously undermine the healing and maturity of their child to avoid change in themselves.

It's a real chicken and egg situation. Which comes first, healthy members or a healthy family? We cannot tell, but we know that health will not come to a family until we focus not just on the identified patient but on how each person in the family functions interdependently with other members. Observing this interdependence led Virginia Satir and many other family therapists to work with families as a whole.[3] The whole family becomes the "patient," and the patient is not cured until all the members of the family are able to take responsibility for how they pull their own strings on the mobile. Satir proposes that treatment of a family is completed "when everyone in the therapy setting can use the first person 'I' followed by an active verb and ending with a direct object."[4] This is a worthy goal for an equipping pastor who wants to foster healthy interdependence in the church.

The church, like the family, is very simple and yet unbelievably complex. The unity of the church, like the unity of the family and the unity of God (Father, Son, and Holy Spirit) is a complex social unity. That makes tracking down causes and anticipating effective pastoral strategies very difficult. In family life when someone with little provocation explodes in anger or someone does something "off the wall," we might ask, "Now where did that come from?" We cannot explain an event by a single action or the words of any single member. Why? Because something systemic is happening. The same is true of the church. Leadership strategies in the church do not seem to have a simple cause-effect relationship. So we must begin our exploration of interdependence by examining causation.

Causation: The Way Things Happen in a System

One way of answering the chicken and egg question—which comes first?—is to look for a single direct cause. The chicken produces the egg. This way of thinking, which places cause and effect in a linear relationship, is called classical Newtonian causation—the billiard ball effect. In the drawing, A causes B; B causes C; C causes D; D causes E.

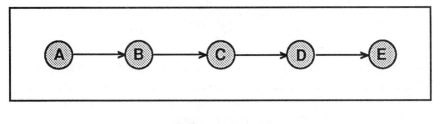

Linear Causation

Figure 2

Almost all scientific endeavor and most pastoral strategies operate on the assumption that the same cause generates the same effects. Most how-to books (on everything from how to make your church grow to how to start a lay pastoral care program) assume this Newtonian causation.[5] An example is the advice sometimes given to pastors to build a larger parking lot, add twenty percent more chairs than you need, and the growth will come. The source of this love-affair with causality is the scientific view of reality that emerged in the seventeenth century.[6] But we are beginning to discover that simple cause-effect does not explain how things work in a social organism. In families, for example, emotional "need" is not a one-way linear cause-effect matter but a complex interrelationship of many factors involving all the members. In the church, good leaders apply how-to manuals but discover they get the opposite effect *in their churches* from the one anticipated. So a more comprehensive view of causation is needed.

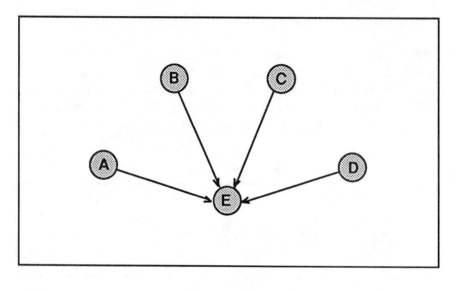

Multiple Causation

Figure 3

ultiple causation is similar. Instead of a sequence of events that form a chain, several, perhaps many, events act independently on the same object. Applied to the task of equipping laity, the concept of multiple causation helps a pastor grapple with multiple strategies that can be used to develop a ministering laity: informational seminars, modeling, skill-oriented seminars, and field educational experiences. But there is more to systemic causation than this.

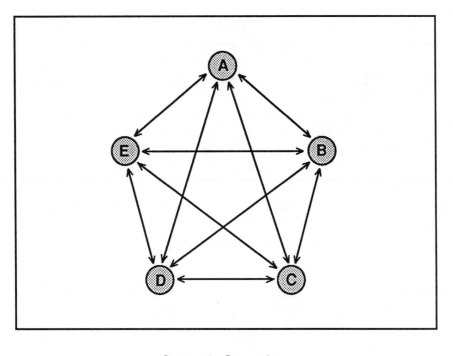

Systemic Causation

Figure 4

In systems thinking the forces involved are understood to be interdependent. The diagram shows all the elements linked in a cause-effect relationship to all the other elements. Movement and change in one element affects all the other elements. Further the behavior or functioning of an element is influenced more by its position in the system than by its inherent "nature." As we shall see, the equipping pastor must "keep on top" of many factors that will produce mature Christians and lay ministry. This requires thriving on a degree of complexity.

The diagrams, adapted from Friedman,[7] do not account for the varying degrees of influence recognized in systems thinking. Nor do they illustrate the feedback process. Finally, the diagrams do not distinguish between interactional patterns and interpersonal patterns; interpersonal dynamics are only a portion of what is happening at any given moment. In a church the interactional patterns include not only the relationships of members but also subsystems (subcongregations), nuclear and extended families, structures, leadership patterns, financial constraints, and cherished values of the community. Since the church is an open system, it is also influenced by the media, politics, schools, and the ethos of its own neighborhood.

In response to the chicken and egg question, we must offer the answer "both." Which comes first, a healthy church or healthy members? Which is more influential, a formed corporate, unified community or the diverse expression of personal gifts in the members? In answering "both," we are inviting attention to the process by which members function together. In practice this involves a balance between the two seemingly contradictory forces that exist in interdependent relationships—*the need to be "me" and the need to be "we."*[8]

"Me" and "We":
How People Function When They Are Close Together

The simultaneous need to be together and to be separate is illustrated by a German fable.

> One very cold night a group of porcupines were huddled together for warmth. However, their spines made proximity uncomfortable, so they moved apart again and got cold. After shuffling repeatedly in and out, they eventually found a distance at which they could still be comfortably warm without getting pricked. This distance they henceforth called decency and good manners.[9]

But there is more to the me-we tension than merely finding a comfortable distance. We are dealing with how people define themselves by the "togetherness force" in a group. Neither the rugged individual (the independent person) nor the compliant person (the dependent person) have found a satisfactory way of relating to the togetherness force because they are merely reacting. But persons who define themselves and remain connected are able to contribute to the group while being true to themselves. Their need for other people is not so strong that it impairs independent functioning. As the therapist John Friesen put it, "In such relationships there is less psychic energy tied up in concerns about whether each person is paying enough attention to the other, being rejected by the other or being understood."[10] Remember our description of a good church member in chapter I.

The word *individuality* needs to be redefined. In systems theory it does not mean "selfishly independent and autonomous," in the sense that is common in Western society. Individuality does not mean independence (as shown on the "independent-interdependent-dependent" scale above). Rather, as Michael Kerr says, "individuality refers to the capacity to be an individual *while part of a group*."[11] The individual is *inter*dependent. In family systems theory, people are considered "stuck" or "fused" when they are very undifferentiated and have little emotional separation.

Bowen used the concept of "differentiation of self" to describe the potential for binding and freeing within the family system. One of the major tasks of parents, say Kerr and Bowen, is to help children grow up to be differentiated from their parents. It must start shortly after birth! In this process children are likely to become more differentiated (and therefore less emotionally fused with one or both of their parents) if their parents differentiate themselves from their children. This means that the parents' and child's work are interdependently related. If differentiation fails the child may be unable to leave home to marry, or, if he does, he will remain dependent upon and fused with his parents. Even running away from home does not solve this problem but merely displaces it; it will likely resurface somewhere else and with someone else.[12] Sometimes the "independent" person is actually emotionally dependent!

According to this understanding of relationships, the very poorly differentiated person has almost no capacity for autonomous functioning.[13] Yet in systems theory "autonomy does not mean selfishly following one's own directives." Rather, explain Kerr and Bowen, "it means the ability to be self-determined" while remaining connected.[14] Poorly differentiated people use the pronoun "I" for narcissistic statements such as "I want; I hurt; I want my rights." The better differentiated person makes statements such as "I believe; I am; I will do."

How does this apply to the church?

Returning to Figure 1 presented earlier in this chapter, we see how the "body" church encourages members both to remain connected and to express their own gifts. Interdependence is a "10" on both the unity and the diversity scales. In the "melting-pot church," fusion (dependence)

takes place among members and leaders or among members. The case
of pastor-people dependency is all too common. Pastors can encourage—unintentionally of course—the immature dependence of members
on the pastor's spirituality. Pastors may regard the equipping task as
getting the members to assist the pastors in their ministry. In the "melting pot" the people take on the pastor's vision, the pastor's spirituality,
and the pastor's ministry. A high-commitment church can add a de-
manding dimension—"the sacrifice of all for the church." This demand
for the betrayal of self in order to preserve harmony and togetherness is
sometimes called "deselfing." It involves failing to be true to oneself
and failing to address issues that are important to oneself. Ironically, in
some people this approach produces rugged individualism—rebels who
are determined "to do their own thing." But it is still a reaction.

Fusion or dependence among members is also common enough.
Members can "feed" on each other, gaining "self" from others, especially
significant others. This is transparently the case with some members
who gain a sense of self by imagining that they have a special inside
track with high-profile leaders. Kerr speaks of this dynamic as using a
relationship available to a poorly differentiated individual, to "complete"
him "by providing an identity and greater sense of worth."[15] In such a
case a person fills his or her tank with togetherness and heads out on the
highway of life. But, Kerr notes, the mileage is always low.

It is truly remarkable that Jesus is able to say, "Feed on me. Eat me
up" (John 6:51 loosely paraphrased). No one else in the universe can
offer self so extravagantly without fear of being "eaten up." And no one
else can offer to be consumed by another and yet leave that person more
self-controlled, more free, more interdependent than before. The gospels
reveal that Jesus wanted neither compliance nor rugged individualism.
He evoked interdependence. And that must be the goal of the equipping
leader. Unfortunately leadership often produces the opposite effect, and
we must explore four dysfunctional patterns in the church.

Discerning Dysfunctional Relationships

The word *enabling* (unfortunately sometimes used interchangeably with
equipping[16]) has come to be used in a specific and negative sense. An
enabler is someone who contributes, often unconsciously, to an un-

healthy dependent relationship. Every alcoholic, it is argued, is linked with an enabler, often a spouse, who makes it possible for the addicted person to continue in a destructive lifestyle. The reasons are often complex. Sometimes the enabler feels he or she is given dignity and worth as a rescuer/helper. *Codependency* is another word that has been used to popularize this dysfunctional relating of people. Instead of being interdependent, such persons are dependent on each other. Oddly, an "equipping" leader who wears him- or herself out trying to mobilize the laity and an "enabling" church find themselves in what can only be called a neurotic marriage!

The Overfunctioning Leader

Overfunctioning leaders have some or all of the following characteristics: They know what is best not only for themselves but for others; they feel they are the answer to most of the problems they encounter; they have difficulty letting others struggle; and they take over quickly when stress hits a community. Overfunctioning leaders are generally described as "always reliable" and "always together." They rarely can reveal their underfunctioning side, especially with "people with problems."

Underfunctioning people tend to have more than one area where they cannot get themselves organized; they invite others to take over in stress situations; they become the focus of concern for the family or the church. They also have trouble revealing their strong, competent side.

From these definitions[17] it is obvious that the hard-working equipping pastor is frequently an overfunctioning leader, and the congregation is composed of underfunctioning members. Behind the pastor's complaint—"I have to do everything around here"—is the shadow of passive, underinvolved lay people whom the pastor would like "to equip for ministry." The pastor often does not realize that his or her overfunctioning and their underfunctioning are systemically related. As Edwin Friedman shows, "what rarely occurs to those in the overfunctioning position is that in any type of family the rest of the system may be underfunctioning as an adaptive response!"[18] Can it be that members of the church are reluctant to get involved in ministry *because the pastor has too great a sense of responsibility for all the ministry, even though he or she complains bitterly about the "noninvolved laity"?*

In contrast Friedman describes how he got the members of his
synagogue to function for themselves: He stayed in touch with the
relational system; he kept defining himself and his own beliefs, and he
labored not to rush in when things faltered.[19] Without using the term,
Friedman describes the equipping pastor who understands and works
with interdependence in the church system and its family subsystems.

The Addictive Church

An extreme example of togetherness at its worst is the addictive church.
In a fine article titled "Is the Church an Addictive Organization?" Anne
Wilson Schaef proposes that as we become increasingly aware of the
addictions in our society—sex, money, chemicals, power, and romance
—we should be willing to ask hard questions about the church's functioning in an addictive way.[20] She sees four levels of addiction.

   1. When an addict is in a key position.   If the pastor is addicted to
work or power, the members will never be able to do enough to please
the pastor, but they will keep trying.

   2. When the church, functioning as an "enabler," supports addicts in
their addictions. Schaef gives an all-too-common example of a church
that had an alcoholic in a key position. The church spent an inordinate
amount of energy trying not to notice that he was doing a poor job on an
important committee.

> They griped and complained behind his back when he did not follow
> through on his responsibilities or when he came to a meeting drunk,
> but everyone covered up for him and did not want to "hurt his
> feelings" by confronting his behavior or asking him to resign.[21]

I (Stevens) read this case study rather clinically until I remembered an
almost identical circumstance in a church in which I have served. In this
case, we refused to confront the alcoholic because we did not want to
hurt the feelings of his wife, who, incidentally, was also covering up for
him! This was one more case of codependent enabling instead of
equipping.

   3. A third level of church addiction is organizational addiction—
when the organization itself provides the fix. People who look to the

church to be "the family they never had" are setting themselves up for disillusionment. In extreme cases, such as in high-commitment missions and parachurch organizations, and sometimes in the process of founding a new work, the mission becomes *too* important. The leaders and members lose their spirituality and their touch with God because of the all-consuming demands of "the work." In founding one church I came close to that myself. I remember the day I discovered that I could not allow myself to fail in this work. It was an important discovery and led to deeper faith in God, whether the work thrived or failed.

4. The fourth level of organizational addiction is when the organization itself functions as an addict. "In these cases," notes Schaef,

> there is an incongruity between what the organization says its mission is and what it actually does. An organization's personnel practices, its emphasis on control, and how it interprets and works with power can all reveal signs of addiction.[22]

Schaef cites the Roman Catholic Church as an example, especially in its handling of sexuality, but we are convinced the problem is universally present in organizational systems, and the church is not exempt.[23]

In each of these four kinds of church addictions, people have a dysfunctional relationship that destroys the dynamic balance of togetherness and diversity. Relational triangles are a common symptom of this.

Triangled Relationships

A triangle is formed when one person in a two-party relationship involves a third party. Triangles are not in themselves bad, but they become negative when they are fixed or stuck and lead to togetherness without differentiation.[24] In a triangle two are usually aligned against a third, who may be used as a scapegoat.

In the Drama Triangle way of looking at relationships, three persons or groups are often organized into a three-role system: victim, persecutor, and rescuer.[25] In a family a son may be using drugs and complaining that he is nobody's nothing ("poor me")—the victim. The father—the persecutor—may punish the son and give authoritarian discipline without affection. And the mother—acting as the rescuer—may keep defending the son to her husband and secretly slip the son money. The father seems to be the most powerful (because he wields the stick). The mother seems to be the good person. But the boy is actually the most powerful, because he has the family organized around his problem. Who is at "fault"? A systems answer: All three.

In churches triangles abound: the pastor, the official board, and the congregation; or the pastor, the pastor's wife, and the congregation; or the youth pastor, the senior pastor (who wants the youth pastor to reach out to kids on the street), and the church parents (who want the youth pastor to save their own children). Pastors can be anywhere on the triangle (though we hope they will soon get off!), but they most commonly function as rescuers. They can get off the triangle by differentiating themselves and by taking actions that exemplify the need for diversity within unity.

Let us give a dramatic example of how a husband and wife formed an alliance against the church: With Gordon and Sonya it was hard to figure out which one made the balls and which one fired them. Gordon appeared to be the emotional component in this twosome, but in church meetings they became a powerful force together—negative synergy. In one meeting in particular, they ganged up against the church. The vote was on the purchase of a new electronic organ to replace the aging pipe organ, but it could have been anything else. In this case Gordon was touched personally because he was a pipe organ buff. He got up and said he simply could not understand how such a motion could be passed and how insensitive the people were. He said, "You are my people. You are those with whom I worship. You are God's people to me." He saw the church in a parental way. But the church that was his family was about to shaft him. While Gordon was excoriating the people, his voice rose in a high tenor pitch.

Sonya was not speaking but it was obvious that she was very upset. She had a heart condition, and when Gordon stopped speaking, she left the meeting, slamming the glass doors behind her. Her husband followed her out. The place was pregnant with silence. Suddenly the door to the room opened, and Gordon stuck his head in and yelled at the top of his voice, "If my wife dies—you know she has a heart condition—you are all responsible, all of you!" Then he slammed the door as his wife had done previously, punctuating the sentence in his own inimitable way. The atmosphere was electric in the face of such emotional blackmail.

The people drifted from the meeting wondering what they had done wrong. Sometime later the pastor understood how the victim—or someone who thinks of herself as the victim—is often the most powerful person in the church. Not until much later did the church leadership have the courage to deal with the triangle that was frustrating the systemic life of that congregation. Without detriangling that couple, the saints could not be equipped for the work of the ministry.

The Tyranny of the Weak

We have been considering various forms of "unity with a vengeance," or unity that does not evoke diversity and differentiation. Kerr and Bowen argue that the "one for all and all for one" consensus approach in leadership or in an organization makes for an unhealthy "unity."

> If one person reneges, the consensus collapses. A togetherness solution makes the integrity of the group dependent on the "weakest link," the first person who gets reactive. An individuality solution, they argue, is much more durable.[26]

Immediately our mind goes to the famous passage in 1 Corinthians 12 where the apostle Paul speaks of the interdependence and the diversity of the members. "Those parts of the body that seem to be weaker are indispensable, and the parts that we think are less honorable we treat with special honor" (vv. 22-23). Does this mean that the weaker member should dominate the church?

In fact many emotionally and spiritually weak people do dominate the church. They often appear emotionally fragile, and people around them "walk on eggshells." Sometimes they dominate the church with their messages: "Poor me" or "The church is not meeting my needs (or saving my children)." But systems theory teaches that the seemingly weak member of a family or a church is the most powerful, organizing everyone around his or her needs.

In the church some people are weaker, some stronger. Perhaps each of us is weak in some areas and strong in others. But Paul's concern is not to get the church organized around weakness. His stated concern is unity and fellowship "so that there should be no division in the body, but that its parts should have equal concern for each other" (1 Cor. 12:25). Some parts, he reminds us, have built-in honor simply because their ministry is high-profile. Pastors usually fall into this category. Paul would say they do not need much public recognition because there is public reward in their daily ministry.

But many members in the body, though important, do not get much recognition. Like the genitals in the human body, they are vitally important even though they are covered and treated with modesty. If we honor the people who deliver casseroles to sick people, those who serve unseen on community action committees, and those who wash the communion cups, every member will feel an equal honor and place, and there will be both unity and mutual respect. Paul would have us defer in love to weak people, as he counsels in Romans 14, especially where there is a weakness in conscience. "Make every effort to do what leads to peace and to mutual edification" (Rom. 14:19). But Paul will not allow us to be bound to another person's weakness. As a systems pastor, Paul wanted every person to take responsibility for his or her own life and yet to remain deeply connected to the entire body of Christ.

We have considered four examples of dysfunctional relationships in the church. It is a tragic irony that some leaders, thinking they are equipping the saints, may be contributing to and appealing to the lowest level of personal maturity. Equipping the laity is not mobilizing the laity to help the pastor but helping people discover and develop their own ministry. They must do this together—be "me" and "we" simultaneously. Independent autonomous behavior is, in a sense, subchristian. So is compliant, addictive, or codependent behavior. What we desire is people responding as fully participant members of a team, but doing so through their own motivation, exercising their gifts and having the time of their lives doing what God intended them to do and be. One way of describing this uses the biblical term spiritual gift.

Giftedness: A Systems Approach

Since the sixties North American Christianity has been fascinated with spiritual gifts. We greet this with mixed joy. On the one hand, the emphasis on spiritual gifts as expressed in scriptures such as 1 Corinthians 12, Ephesians 4, and Romans 12 reflects the joyful rediscovery of the forgotten truth that God works through every member of the body of Christ. On the other hand, it seems that the gift movement has been co-opted by the granular individualism of Western culture and is used as one more way to achieve personal fulfillment. We need a systems approach to gifts as well.

Understood biblically and systemically, gifts are not something we possess, things that are implanted in us when we become Christians or have a deeper experience of God. Instead gifts are simply the persons we are in Christ and in relationships. *We* are gifts.[27] The bottom line is simply this: Gifts are ways in which people express their personhood in love *in concrete relationships*. A systems approach to spiritual gifts suggests that we do not have gifts *in ourselves* but only in relationships. And the relationships in which we become gifts are those where there is both unity and diversity, both togetherness and diversity, both connected-ness and differentiation. No gifts emerge where there is togetherness without diversity nor where there is diversity without togetherness.

A gift of teaching, for example, only "happens" in a learning rela-tionship.[28] The gift is a result of the interdependent relationship of members in the body of Christ. Gifts also change when a person is placed differently in the system. A pastor's "gift" may change as he or she takes different positions of influence as a church matures. (Note Pattison's four stages of group development in chapter 1.) Further, one's "gift" in one church may not be the same as one's gift in another, as illustrated by Pastor John's move from one parish to another.

Joining God and God's People

There are deep theological reasons for viewing gifts as a phenomenon of systemic life rather than as personal possessions. In becoming Christians we do something more than join the church. *We join God* (1 John 1:3). But this joining is not a matter of being merged with God. It is unity with diversity because God insists that we be differentiated as sons and daughters (John 1:12). Then, having joined God who is love and who lives in the relational community of Father, Son, and Holy Spirit, we discover that being in God's image (Gen. 1:27) involves living relationally and interdependently.

Paul demonstrates the mystery of our life of unity and diversity by joining the Greek prefix *sun* ("with" or "together") with a number of key words in Ephesians to show the practical impossibility of being in Christ alone. "Joined together" (2:21) is merely one English phrase among many (2:5; 2:6; 2:19; 2:22; 3:6; 4:16) that, in the original, are single words. Paul crafts new words to express our interdependence in Christ because he is dealing with a new social reality: members together, joined together, knitted together, raised up together, built together, and sharers together.

Further, our study of Ephesians 4:16 reveals that the "joints" (KJV) in the body of Christ are not the pastors trying to link everyone else up. Rather, the "joints" or "ligaments" (NIV) refer to the points of contact and connection at which *every believer discovers mutual growth, love, and ministry.* We live and minister at the "joints." Impersonal, non-relational Christian ministry is unthinkable.

Gifts are ways of expressing healthy interdependence, and it does not matter whether or not we can put a name on "our gift."[29] Perhaps that is why Paul put the chapter on love (1 Cor. 13) between the chapters on spiritual gifts (1 Cor. 12) and prophecy-tongues (1 Cor. 14). If we are confused about gifts, we should simply love.

Inventories that help us catalog our gifts may be of some help. But they can affirm only what we have learned about ourselves in concrete relational experiences. Inventories might even be deceiving. Because one can never discover one's gift alone. So the pastor who wants to lead a process of discerning giftedness concentrates not on categorizing gifts but on building a community in which giftedness will "happen." He or she will also "expound" the interdependence of the community by recognizing how God is at work.

For example, in small groups in which I (Stevens) have been a part, we designate one night each year for affirmation. It takes a whole evening. We agree not to put a label on anyone or even attempt to use the titles given in the three gift-lists in the New Testament. Instead we go person by person around the circle, and each member in the group is asked to finish the sentence (if he or she can), "Colin, you are a gift to this group in the following way . . ." or, "God works through you, Celeste, to minister to us in . . ." Where there is genuine interdependence, this exercise is almost always a relational feast.

Chapter Summary

In conclusion we will summarize what we have presented about equipping in this chapter: (1) Equipping is essentially a relational, rather than a programmatic ministry; this involves building the people of God. (2) Leaders have the challenge of building unity in the people without evoking compliance or autonomy; this involves encouraging people to remain connected and to define themselves and their own ministries rather than merely assisting the leaders in their ministry. (3) Healthy interdependence starts with the leadership; this involves teaching and modeling interdependence and allowing people to minister to the leaders. (4) Leaders should define themselves and encourage others to do so; this involves expressing their own convictions and visions while remaining committed to the community. (5) As relationship shepherds, equippers should be able to discern dysfunctional relationships; this involves taking appropriate actions to deal with over- and underfunctioning, addictions, triangles, and the domination of the weak.[30] (6) Equippers should exegete the community by recognizing giftedness; this involves helping people to "sound" their own dreams and visions, as well as helping others affirm the contributions of each and every member. (7) Finally, equippers should embrace the goal of church growth using a deeper definition of church growth than the one normally used. This final point deserves a further comment.

Sometimes, at the conclusion of a "successful" pastorate, a pastor, such as the one whose farewell message we quoted at the beginning of the chapter, is asked, "Did the church grow under your leadership?" The questioner almost always refers to numerical growth. But the Ephesians passage on equipping gives us a systemic definition of church growth: growth into unity (4:13); growth into maturity as a community (4:13); growth into individual theological maturity so the members are able to distinguish truth from error for themselves (4:14); growth in love-motivated truth-speaking (4:15); growth in dependence on Christ the Head of the church (4:15-16); and growth in mutual enrichment (4:16). The question, "Did the church grow under your leadership?" now takes on a new perspective. It can be argued that a sign of maturity in a church is the existence of great diversity of thought, action, and perspective, *in the context of deep unity*. Christian unity is not uniformity but the enriched social complex of a community in which "each part does its work" (Eph. 4:16). One of the greatest challenges of equipping the saints is to help the church discover itself as a church by cultivating interdependence—togetherness with diversity.

When I (Collins) was a student pastor in a Baptist Church in Maine, all of the people seemed to like Lois and me and our children. They could not do enough for us. Sometimes I would shake hands at the end of the church service and feel something in my hand. It might be a twenty dollar bill to help me out with my studies.

Despite the goodwill, I sensed a deep three-way split in the church. By looking through records and piecing together various conversations, I estimated that the three-way split was a systemic situation that had been in place for eighty years, now in the third and fourth generations. It was getting worse and church meetings were a tragic circus—laughable if the situation hadn't been so serious. It was frustrating both the spiritual life of the church and its mission in the town.

For advice I went to see Dr. Barker, New Testament professor at the divinity college where I was studying. He agreed to talk if I'd buy him a cup of coffee. The eighty-five cents I spent for coffee and a donut was the best investment I have ever made in the practice of ministry. Without using the term, he showed me how both the problem and the solution were systemic. He told me to use the communion table to help these people see themselves and to bring about a change in the life of the congregation. "If you try to work with individuals in these three groupings and try to get them to change, thinking that it will change everything, you are mistaken. You must deal with the congregation as a whole."

In two weeks we had a communion service. Just before we were to partake I said my piece: "You are all wonderful people, and you have been great to me and my family. But you are so hard on each other. I do not want to single out any one person here and say that you are the real problem. I am not even going to call on individuals to make things right. What I want you to understand from Matthew 5 is that if you bring your gift to the altar and have something against your brother or sister, then leave your gift, which is your life, at the altar and go and make it right with your brother or sister and then come to the altar. In 1 Corinthians 11:29 it says that we must discern the body of Christ, which is the physical body of Christ on the cross. But discerning the body also means discerning our relationships in Christ. What I would like us to do, prior to our receiving the bread and wine this morning, is to think of how we could wait on one another and truly be the people of God. That leadership cannot come from the pastor. That leadership has to come from the whole body of Christ."

I just sat there. In the silence Cyril got up and went across the center aisle. Cyril was the treasurer, a leader of the church, and an elder. He went over to Howard, another elder, and said, "Howard I want you to forgive me. For eighteen years I have been on your case. I have tried to thwart things that you are trying to do. I have been a problem for you, and I want to ask for your forgiveness." He spoke only of himself: "I need forgiveness." I sat there holding my breath.

Then Howard said, "Cyril I need to ask your forgiveness. I have been a problem, and I want to make it right with you." Those two men hugged each other and the tears began to flow.

Thirteen of the leaders got up and made it right with others in that meeting. It was wonderful. Tears all around. That church made a permanent systemic change as a result of that meeting. Over the months that followed, without any newspaper advertising or radio announcements, the church grew steadily, not just numerically, but—even more important—in interdependence and corporate dependence on the Lord. When I left that student pastorate, there were no longer three groups in that church but one body with interdependent members.

CHAPTER III

Leading the Process

People would rather have the security of false truth than the
freedom of ambiguous reality.

Eric Fromm[1]

The Disney people (and Maturana) understand that you do not
change organisms—you design an environment in which organisms
thrive, respond, and *change themselves.*

Jay Efran and Michael Lukens[2]

Several years ago I (Stevens) took a course in cinematography. The
professor began his first lecture with a statement meant to get our attention. "A movie," he said, "is like religion. It is based on a lie!" Having
our attention, he continued: "The objects on the film appear to be
moving but in fact the film itself is a collection of still pictures moving
quickly enough to fool the mind." I have forgotten almost everything
else about the course except this opening volley. As I return to it over
and again, I connect it to church leadership, which is composed of a
series of individual strategies, messages, and actions, like the frames of a
movie. But that is not the whole picture. In systems thinking *the process,*[3] the movie itself, is the message and the reality. The content—
individual strategies and initiatives, which are like the frames in a movie
—is not as important as the total influence of the process. But in this
case the impression is not based on a lie or intentional deception. It is
just a different way of looking at reality that systems thinking provides.

In the context of counseling families, Virginia Satir[4] makes a remarkable statement about systems leadership. She says, "I consider myself the leader of the *process* in the interview but not the leader of the people." She continues,

> I am a strong leader for the process. This is based on the fact that I am the one who knows what the process I am trying to produce is all about. I want to help people to become their own designers of their own choice-making.[5]

Church leaders can learn from this. To say "I am not the leader of the people" invites the question of who the leader is! Biblically the church leader must affirm that the ultimate leader of the church is Jesus, called the Head of the church in Ephesians 4:15. In the New Testament no human leader is ever called the "head" of the church. This has incredible implications for the equipping pastor, whose primary responsibility is to facilitate and deepen the dependence—indeed the interdependence—of the members of the church and the Head.[6] To do this a pastor must lead the process by which people find their maturity in their life together in Christ. In the human body the head does not tell the left hand to tell the right foot to move. In the body of Christ, Christ the Head does not tell the pastors to tell the people. Rather, the Head is connected with all of the members, and the pastor's work is to strengthen that connection and to facilitate unity (1 Cor. 12:25) and growth (Eph. 4:13).

So process leadership asks questions, clarifies goals, orients people to their mission, maintains and explains the culture, and helps families and other subcongregations take responsibility for their own systemic life. The most direct way to equip the saints for the work of the ministry is not to devise strategies for equipping individuals but to equip the church (as a system). Then the church will equip the saints. This book is entirely about this principle. In this chapter we will focus on three dimensions of leading the process: envisioning, cultivating the environment, and making changes systemically.

Envisioning: I Have a Dream

Accidentally, I (Stevens) did it right in my first church, a struggling inner-city parish in a Montreal neighborhood where seventeen ethnic

groups were attempting to make their home. In *Liberating the Laity* I
told the story of how I reached the place of total frustration putting out
fires of discontent in the church. During one of my daily coffee breaks, a
deacon, Bill Maxwell, dredged out of me that I was planning to resign.
The fire-fighting was getting to me. "But," he said, "you are the best
damned fire-fighter we have ever had!" We both laughed uproariously.
But in that previous book I didn't tell the end of the story. What Bill
then did was to equip me to equip the church by giving leadership to the
process. He said, "What kind of church do you really want to see? What
do you believe in?" It was the vision question.

The next hour was one of the most important in my life. Sitting
together in Lesters Delicatessen, Bill and I drank coffee and talked. I
wrote down my thoughts on a paper napkin. I believed in a church
where the pastor did not run everything, but served the whole congregation by releasing ministry and mission in every member. I believed that
the church did not "have" a mission as one of many activities in which
interested people could engage; I believed the church *is* mission. The
workplaces, homes, neighborhoods in which people lived from Monday
to Saturday were the primary location for the church's mission during the
week. They did not "go" to church; they were the church wherever they
went. (I got that idea from Elton Trueblood.) I believed that the church
was a rhythm of gathering for worship and teaching, and dispersion for
ministry and mission—both *ecclesia* and *diaspora*. I believed that the
congregation needed both the sanctuary church structure and the house
church structure. Since the church was no longer at the center of the
community—as was the case in rural churches a generation earlier—
people needed to find intersection points in their life together by meeting
in face-to-face communities to pray, read the Bible, and consider how to
live the Christian life Monday to Saturday.

I believed that the church organization should serve the organism of
the church, not vice versa. We had a dinosaur structure of three boards
and thirteen committees designed when the church was four times its
current size. Serving God had come to mean maintaining the church
organization. I believed that leadership should be *plural* and that our
obsolete board structure should be replaced by mature and gifted lay
leaders who would serve together on a Group Ministry—a form of
eldership. I scratched out a diagram of this on the napkin showing a
simple but effective structure. As pastor I would be part of the Group

Ministry with a special assignment and with "the big view." I believed that the future of our church was neither in the preservation of a white Anglo-Saxon ghetto in a multicultural part of the city nor in starting several new ethnic churches. My reading of Ephesians 2:11-22 convinced me that in Christ the wall between Jews and Gentiles, and between ethnic groups, had been broken down. The church should demonstrate the broken wall and the one new humanity (Eph. 2:15). (I had been profoundly affected by Markus Barth's interpretation of this passage in which he says that if people are meeting together because they would be meeting anyway—insiders with insiders—no Christ is confessed![7]) I told Bill that I envisioned Temple Baptist Church becoming a multinational and multiethnic church in one location with subcongregations for evangelism, service, and edification in the appropriate languages of the ethnic groups. The whole church would meet together weekly to experience the supernatural community of Christ. I drew five overlapping circles—the Italian, Spanish, English, Armenian, and Greek congregations—but all within the one church represented by one larger circle. (Eventually this came about, and we had simultaneous translation in the morning service and a monthly combined service using five languages. I was never sure whether it was Pentecost or Babel!) I also told Bill that I believed nobody wanted this. But he said, "I would like to belong to such a church!"

"But no one else would be interested," I protested.

Bill said, "Why don't you share your vision and see what happens?" So I did.

I was now free to explore vision more playfully and less seriously, though this was unknown to all but Bill. Perhaps it was because I had already given up the leadership of the people by writing my letter of resignation and filing it in my office drawer, a highly symbolic act. Ironically, it took my emotional resignation to allow me to join the church in a new way. This vision statement was not a do-or-die attempt at leadership on which my future depended but something from the heart that I could present in faith, trusting that words from God would be planted deeply, while the chaff would be blown away. The process of doing this took almost a year.

I preached an "I have a dream" sermon. It was not couched in "This is what you must do or I will leave!" language. Nor was that message communicated nonverbally. Many of the sermons during these weeks took on this visionary character. My wife noticed that I had stopped preaching on "the demise of the institutional church"! I described the vision in a single printed pamphlet as simply as I could, remembering that some of our members were almost illiterate. The proposal had lots of drawings. I stayed in touch with the relational systems by visiting all the members in their homes, discussing these things freely and openly. We also discussed them in boards and committees and over many more coffees in Lesters.

I listened to all the negative responses and fears expressed. I wrote a weekly pastoral letter in which I tried to answer questions nondefensively. I circulated thousands of mimeographed pages to the congregation. I adjusted the ideas on the basis of what I heard people saying about "their" vision for the church. I kept defining my vision as the pastor while avoiding as much as possible "ought" language. I did not do it perfectly, but I was surprised at the positive response.

At one critical moment, a young man came to me privately. He was one of the most influential in the church and had secretly wanted to be appointed as the pastor. I had known of his leadership aspirations and, while recognizing the complicated sources of his need to lead, I spent a lot of time with him, encouraging, praying with him, discussing books, and doing some service projects together. At the height of this year of envisioning, he made a solemn announcement to me: "I am turning over the pastoral leadership of the church to you!" The official leaders would have been scandalized to hear him say this, and they never knew about it. But it was a significant and symbolic gesture, even if it was a little ludicrous. Ironically, once again, he joined the church by resigning, just as I had!

After almost a year we came to the fateful annual meeting to present to the congregation one single motion we had drafted as pastor and board members. As I now reflect on it thirty years later, it was incredible. It dispensed with the whole existing church structure (three boards and thirteen standing committees) and replaced them with a Group Ministry composed of elected elders from all the congregations that met in the building. The motion passed with only one negative vote! The woman who voted negatively did so in a good-hearted spirit and later became a loyal supporter. Fleshing out the vision, however, took several more years of work. In fact it is incomplete to this day. But nothing would have happened without projecting a vision.

Temple Baptist Church went through an organizational conversion. I have many times asked, how was this possible? It has been said that churches are most ready to change when one of three conditions is met: (1) the congregation is desperate (Temple was that!); (2) it is a new church with few traditions; or (3) it is being affected by a special moving of the Holy Spirit. I do not deny the influence of the first and third factors in our case, but I think there is a fourth. Change takes place when it is not merely programmatic but *on the level of the church's systemic life and through a process consistent with its systemic life.*

One crucial dimension of leading a church "consistent with its systemic life" is understanding and cultivating the culture of a particular local church. Without knowing it, I had projected a vision that was more than a mission statement (why we exist and where we are going). I had also projected a vision about the culture and character of the church (what we believe and the values we hold dear). Only later did I come to understand that *vision includes both mission* (what we should *do) and the culture of the people* (what we should *be*).

When making changes it turns out that culture is a critical factor. We may make changes in what we do but find them reversed later because the culture of the church is opposed to the changes. On the other hand, if the culture supports the changes, or can be changed to be congruent with the proposed direction, major directional changes can be made and sustained. A man in a museum looking at the colossal skeleton of a dinosaur that once roamed the earth triumphantly turned to the woman beside him and asked, "What happened? Why did they die out?" She answered, "The climate changed."

Cultivating the Culture

One way of considering the whole as more than the sum of the parts is to examine the environment or culture.[8] Every church has a corporate "feeling" that communicates to new and old members what is important and what is permitted. Through extensive surveys conducted during his Ph.D. research, Kenneth Van Wyk uncovered what is seldom appreciated: Most churches concentrate on equipping by offering courses that focus on content, but these strategies fail to release significant lay ministry until they consider the environmental factor. Van Wyk writes:

> Every congregation has an attitudinal climate. This "feeling" is a
> powerful determiner of how adequately the ministry of Christ is
> carried out by lay people. A sense of enthusiasm gets people
> unstuck.[9]

An equipping environment is determined by a number of important factors, including verbal and nonverbal clues and symbols that tell a person
whether his or her movement into lay ministry is invited. Experts in
communication tell us that most of our communication is nonverbal! In
a church the environment does most of the talking.

A pastor may facilitate a training program for lay pastoral care
giving, but if the environment communicates that only a professional can
be of any help, the program is undone by the environment. The problem
is systemic. A pastor may equip Christians to discover their ministry in
the workplace, but if the structures and ethos of the church "eat up"
people's time in housekeeping and maintenance tasks, equipping for
diaspora is frustrated. A lay leader may start a discipleship training
program, but if the relationships in the church are impersonal and functional, the training program is at odds with the systemic reality of the
church. A pastor may start a lay evangelism program, but if new Christians are frozen out of the church by lovelessness or driven out by
phariseeism . . . The problem is not programmatic but systemic.

We are too well aware of the heartbreaking tragedy of a pastor who
preaches a high view of married life and runs marriage enrichment programs but finds his own marriage destroyed by the idolatrous demands of
church life. A couple is educated to form an unconditional marriage
covenant during premarital counseling, but "nurtured" in a church that
has low expectations of members and unintentionally encourages throw-
away relationships. The environment has a bigger influence than the
premarital educational program. The equipping pastor needs to be an
environmental engineer, not only because the environment is highly
influential, but also because it affects motivation.

Motivation in a church must be understood systemically. When a
pastor complains that the members are unmotivated for lay ministry or
lay mission, he or she is making a statement not only about the individual
members but also about the system. From family systems theory we have
learned that motivation is a result of a process in a group or system; it is
not just generated from within the individual as an isolated phenomenon.[10]

You may have known of someone who had the time of her life, highly motivated to serve God in the context of one church, but when she moved to another church, she was bored stiff. As we will see, this difference has less to do with the stated goals of each church (often advertised on the sign outside) and more to do with underlying and unconscious factors about essential values, beliefs, and convictions.

As a working pastor I (Collins) was always thinking about how the culture of the church included or excluded young people. One church I served had a marvelous choir. Prior to my coming it had won prizes from various music festivals, even in Europe. But they always sang classical music that did not "catch on" with most of the young people. In the area of music the young people in the choir received nonverbal messages that they did not have a part in the mission of the church.

The young people wanted to sing a song that today would be acceptable almost anywhere: "In His Handiwork I See, The Great Nativity." But the choir director did not want it sung—just because the kids had suggested it. She did everything to block it without ever directly saying that they were not going to sing this song. The young people were losing heart, losing motivation to stay in the choir.

One day I photocopied the song and blotted out the title page and the words. I took it to her and I said, "Would you like to play this? I think it might be very interesting to use it in one of our worship services."

She said she was pleased to try it—on our beautiful pipe organ that is worth a million dollars today. At first she found the five/four time a little difficult, but when she got the rhythm she said, "You know, this is one of the most beautiful pieces of music I have ever heard."

Calling her by name, I said, "Do you know what the name of that music is? 'In His Handiwork I See.'" Her teeth almost fell out.

She said, "You tricked me. That is the song the young people want to sing."

I said, "Yes, but you said it was one of the most beautiful pieces of music you have ever heard. Don't you want to try it with the young people? They feel left out. If we want to keep them involved, especially in terms of the music of the church, we have to create an environment where all good music has a place in ministry. And I really need you to give us leadership and to open up suitable and appropriate music for all age levels. Would you do that for me?"

She said, "Well, I am a little angry at the way you did this, but I will help."

One of the symbolic successes of this change in musical environment for the congregation was that, in six months, we developed three choirs, a senior choir of thirty-five, a teenage choir of forty, and a junior choir of sixty boys and girls. One Sunday evening we packed the sanctuary and lined the walls with all three choirs, more than 125 singers. One of the songs they sang was "In His Handiwork"! The culture had changed a little and the young people felt included.

Defining Culture

The classic study on organizational culture is Edgar H. Schein's *Organizational Culture and Leadership*. His central thesis is that much of what is mysterious about leadership becomes clearer "if we separate leadership from management and link leadership specifically to creating and changing culture."[11] He is using the word *culture* not for countries and ethnic groups but for organizations, companies, and small groups. In his terms, culture is one of the unresearched dimensions of local church life. According to Schein, culture includes each of the following, but is deeper than any one of them: (1) *the observed behavioral regularities* in a group (for example, people do not pray out loud in groups in our church, and they will be embarrassed if you ask them to); (2) *the dominant values* of the group (for example, church attendance is the ultimate expression of spirituality); (3) *the rules or "ropes"* of the group (for example, the usual way to become a member of the session is to serve several years on the finance committee); and (4) *the feeling or climate* that is conveyed (for example, it is also not acceptable to raise one's hands in worship).

Schein says that *culture concerns the underlying assumptions and beliefs that are shared by members of the organization and often operate unconsciously.*[12] These assumptions address fundamental questions such as: (1) What is the "right" way for human beings to relate (cooperatively, competitively, etc.)? (2) What is ministry? (3) What importance does play and worship have in this group? (4) What is our view of human beings—intrinsically evil, intrinsically good, or neutral (think of how this affects the church's handling of sexuality)? (5) What is truth and how does one get to know truth? (6) How should people relate to the created order, and to God?[13] These unspoken assumptions are learned, usually over a long period of time, and come from experiences of the group exploring its unique destiny and coping with challenges.

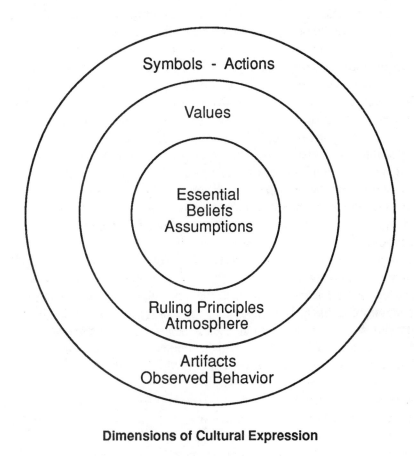

Dimensions of Cultural Expression

Figure 5

In my first church I (Stevens) did not "read" one of the signs of an underlying assumption about the professional ministry. The women of the church had given every previous pastor a clerical gown. I was convinced that my ordination did not set me apart but rather recognized a function among all the people of God (*the laos*), all of whom were set apart by God for the ministry. I asked them not to give me a gown! Fortunately their love and forgiveness overcame my cultural insensitivity, and I recovered from the mistake to deal with culture on a more fundamental level.

Some pastors are put into a bind by the culture of their church. For example, an Occidental pastor serving a Chinese church wants to recommend a change in personnel on a mission committee, but the nominating committee—operating from different fundamental assumptions—cannot agree to the change because the member in question will "lose face" if eliminated from the committee. More to the point of this book, pastors and lay leaders who want to release lay ministry and mission may try programs to equip lay people in the context of a church culture that is opposed to lay ministry. The underlying assumptions of such a culture are (1) that the church is a hierarchical institution with the clergy at the top; (2) that ordination makes the pastor essentially different; (3) that only a professional should do public ministry; and (4) that ministry is what the professional does—preaching, administering the sacraments, conducting worship, and pastoral counseling.

Changing the artifacts—to use Schein's phrase—might involve moving the Sunday service to the church hall where the chairs can be arranged in circles to increase participation. But unless the fundamental assumptions of the church are understood, cultivated, and gradually changed, such equipping initiatives may be as effective as rearranging the deck chairs on the Titanic when the ship is going down. When the leader and the culture collide, the culture will probably win!

The Process of Forming an Environment

Culture is not formed overnight but through a long process. In the church, culture often originates with the founding pastor who projects a personal vision of what is "right" and "valued" and how people are to be treated. The mysterious "charisma" of leadership enables a leader to embed his or her fundamental assumptions into the organization or group. To whom does the leader pay attention? How does the leader react to critical situations? How does the leader intentionally coach other leaders? What criteria does the leader use for praising and rewarding others? On what basis does the leader recruit or reject other leaders? The answers to these questions lay the foundation for the church's culture.

Years before we understood anything about culture, we observed that each church has something like a genetic code embedded at the time of conception that determines most of what the church will become, just as the genetic code of the fertilized ovum determines every detail of the mature person's body. The future of a person is in large measure the unraveling of this code. Something similar happens in churches. This means that the founding moment, the founding person, and the founding principles of a church are exceedingly important. A church that starts with certain assumptions about the nature of the fellowship, style of leadership, the place of ordained and theologically trained leadership, and the mission of the church in society will find it very difficult, though not impossible, to change the genetic code later.

As the group evolves, members take on the founder's assumptions, usually unconsciously. Some groups never allow their founders to die or leave, no matter how many successors have come and gone! Cultures tend not only to incarnate the strengths of founders but also their weaknesses. Some churches would be helped if they could have a once-and-for-all funeral service for their founding pastors! But whoever would try to suggest this will be resisted by the culture. In fact the opposite approach is usually more fruitful: finding out everything you can about the contributions of your predecessors and appreciating their gifts to the church. You might also recognize that the praise people give to your predecessors is not an implicit criticism of your ministry.

Schein's work is extremely helpful in elaborating what happens at various stages in a group's history[14] and the importance of stories (about the "good old days in the past") in transmitting the culture of a group.[15] At an annual fall retreat new students at Regent College and Carey Theological College are enculturated as administration and faculty tell them stories from the past. In doing so we transmit some of the fundamental underlying assumptions about our community. The selection of the stories is critical.

Culture Questions

Here are some questions for an equipping pastor to ask about the systemic environment: Does our environment prize the contributions of

laypeople just as much as visiting or resident clergy? Are people prized
as people, for who they *are* in our community and not merely for the
contributions they can make—what they *do*? What values and beliefs
have been embedded in our community from the founders? Am I willing
to share freely visible roles of leadership in the church with nonordained
people who are gifted and equipped to do so? Why or why not? What
"messages" do people receive about lay ministries that have not been
initiated and approved by the pastor or the official board? Does our
systemic life communicate that a lay person's involvement in society is
less significant than involvement in congregational activities? Who gets
recognition in our community? Who should be recognized? Because
symbols not only represent but convey power, do we have symbols and
signs in our life together that affirm the priesthood of all believers and
not merely the traditional ministry hierarchy (lay and clergy)? What
incongruities do I see between my stated goals in leadership and the
cultural realities of our community? What is my vision for the church's
culture?

Making Changes Systemically

How difficult change is! Imagine trying to change the climate of a whole
hemisphere because dinosaurs were considered undesirable to the human
population of that hemisphere. Schein's research shows that culture-
change mechanisms are at work in every stage of a group's history—
birth, midlife, and maturity (which he calls maturity and/or stagnation,
decline and/or rebirth).[16] He also shows that change becomes increasingly more difficult as a group becomes more established. While all
change is motivated and does not happen randomly, "many changes do
not go in the direction that the motivated persons wanted them to go"
because they were unaware of other forces in the culture that were simultaneously acting.[17] So being the leader of this process is complex indeed.
On the simplest level, a systemic approach to change recognizes that
change in one part of the system requires adjustment in every other. We
will approach this systemic dimension first by looking at change in the
culture.

Changing the Culture

Schein suggests several strategies that we apply to pastoral leadership:

1. Understand the culture before you try to change anything.
Give the culture its due. It influences everything.

2. Recognize that the culture cannot be manipulated. While
you can manage and control many parts of the environmental life of the
church (who leads services, whether the sermon is delivered from a
raised pulpit or from a music stand on the level of the congregation), the
culture itself, with its taken-for-granted underlying assumptions, cannot
be manipulated.

3. Good leadership articulates and reinforces the culture,
especially those parts consistent with the vision of the church. If this is
not done, people will not accept any change in the culture. During a time
of changing culture, leaders have to bear some of the pain and anxiety
felt by the group, while the leaders simultaneously make the members
feel secure.

**4. Sometimes direct change in a culture can be promoted by
introducing new people in leadership,** by promoting "maverick"
individuals from within and especially by bringing in outsiders who hold
slightly different assumptions. The appointment of a new pastor, a new
assistant, or a new board chairperson are all opportunities for culture
change.

5. Change takes time.[18]

One night I (Collins) received a phone call that introduced me to a
crucial learning experience on how culture can change. The caller was
the neighbor of Mrs. McAdam. The neighbor was very agitated and told
me to come over to the McAdam home immediately. Mr. McAdam had
Mrs. McAdam by the throat, against the wall. He was smashing the wall
with a pulp axe on each side of her head and yelling for the guitar. Later
on I found out that he wanted to pawn the guitar to get some money to
buy illegal beer. I went over naively, not knowing the drama that was
soon to overtake me. They did not prepare me for this kind of pastoral
intervention in seminary!

I took my cues from the old cowboy-style, wild-west movies. Slid-
ing along the wall I looked in the window. Tom had Mrs. McAdam up
against the wall, exactly as the neighbor had reported. I was nervous, but

some of my survival forces came to the fore. I crashed through the door, ran across the room, and grabbed Tom around the knees, slamming him on the floor and turning him over, wrapping his arms behind him. I yelled at Mrs. McAdam to get some help because I could only keep him down for so long. Fortunately he was drunk and I was not. Help came, but Tom McAdam went. In fact he never came back. And he left this abused woman and eight children with no income except welfare. Something had to be done.

Prior to this event the leadership of the church was thinking about how we could help people around us. I saw in the McAdam situation a way to encourage systemic change in the church, to make the church as a whole look outward, not only in evangelism but in justice ministry and social responsibility. So I went around to the key people in my church, told my story, and asked people what we could do as a church to help. Within a year-and-a-half, six families took in the eight children so Mrs. McAdam could go to the city for training as a practical nurse. The church paid for her course. Eventually she got a job and was able to take care of her family. With the agreement of Mrs. McAdam, one family took care of the oldest girl, who was fourteen, until she was nineteen years old and through high school. They also paid for the girl's university schooling. Today she has a very good job. Mrs. McAdam and seven of the eight children became Christians and are active in the church. Not only did this family experience change; the church changed. By focusing pastoral leadership on the real mission of the church, a change took place in its very heart and soul.

Bringing about Systemic Change

Edwin Friedman has some additional insights on how a pastor can bring change to a system. He uses the concept of homeostasis, that marvelous capacity of human bodies and social systems to regain their balance after a trauma. Every system has a natural tendency to maintain the status quo (homeostasis) when new response patterns are required through a threat, tragedy, or positive change. The tried and tested are preferable to a revised and even improved basis (morphogenesis).

A negative biblical example of homeostasis (returning to the tried and tested) is the return of converted Jews in the early church to a less than full expression of Christian unity with Gentile believers, a hypocrisy fervently challenged by Paul (Gal. 2:11-21).

A positive example of morphogenesis (feedback leading to constructive change) is the extraordinary resolution of the Council of Jerusalem (Acts 15:1-29) in which the church changed the terms upon which Jews and Gentiles could have fellowship together. On the simplest level homeostasis means that systemic change will be fervently resisted and no program will be adequate to effect a revolution.

To bring about systemic change, leaders must first join the system, becoming an integral part of the whole and negotiating their place in the system. As we have already seen, the pastor must lead the way in this. Pattison's four stages of negotiation are helpful in understanding how a pastor earns the right to influence. Then, suggests Edwin Friedman,[19] the pastor might take an initiative that has a ripple effect throughout the system. Usually a problem will surface without provocation, as in the McAdam situation. But if a problem does not surface, something as inconsequential as changing the order of service will normally suffice. How the pastor responds to the ripple is crucial, because the response of the system will be a reflection of all the systemic factors that make it stable, including the multigenerational influences. The provoked or unprovoked crisis is an opportunity to explain what is going on and to appeal, as did Barnabas, Paul, and Peter in the Jerusalem Council (Acts 15), to the systemic values that can be expressed in a more constructive way. The Chinese word for crisis is composed of two characters, one meaning "danger" and the other "opportunity." The systemic pastor welcomes the opportunity of every crisis. Sometimes he or she will provoke one.

Using family systems theory (really Bowen Theory), Friedman says we bring greatest change in a system not by concentrating on the dissenting or sick member of a system, but by changing the structure or the way people relate. He recommends concentrating on the person or persons in the group that have the greatest capacity to bring change.[20] Finally, the equipping pastor must always remember that the only person she can definitely and immediately change is herself! A systems view encourages us with the view that changing ourselves *can* make a difference to the others with whom we are interdependently linked in a system.

We have explored three arenas in which a pastor or lay leader can give leadership to the process: envisioning, cultivating the culture, and making changes systemically. Without saying so, I have been suggesting that the way a church makes decisions is as important as what decisions are actually made. Decisions can be made in such a way that members are directed to Jesus as Head (Eph. 1:22; 4:15; 5:23) and true leader of the people. The pastor is not the ultimate leader of the people. Indeed, leading the process is challenge enough! But leading the process cannot happen unless there is congruency or a good "fit" between the leader and the people. To that subject we now turn. It is the hidden reason why some equipping pastors thrive and others fail.

CHAPTER IV

Matching Leadership Styles

> Matchmaker, Matchmaker, make me a match; find me a find, catch
> me a catch. Matchmaker, Matchmaker, look through your book,
> And make me a perfect match.
>
> Fiddler on the Roof[1]

Edwin Friedman recounts an ancient story in which a Roman woman
comes up to a rabbi and asks:

> What does your God do now that he has created the world and set it
> in order?
> She is answered: "He tries to match up couples."
> "Is that all?" she says. "Why I could do that myself."
> "Maybe so," she is told, "but for him it is as difficult as splitting the
> Red Sea."[2]

Friedman comments that the antiquity of this story suggests that marriage
failure is not merely a modern phenomenon and that successful mating is
almost never easy. In this chapter we are dealing with another kind of
matchmaking—the leadership style of the leader with the needs and
maturity of the followers in the congregational context. Remember the
formula we used in Chapter I. L (leadership) equals L (the function of
the leader) plus F (the followers) plus S (the situation). Without an
isomorphic "fit" between the leader and the people, leadership is frustrated. Here we are dealing with "fit" in terms of leadership style. It is
another dimension of systemic leadership.

Pastoral Compatibility

We will explore two principles. First, there is no biblical or theological support for one style of leadership over another. Except for the
styles of the dictator, the slave, or the martyr—unacceptable styles we
will discuss later—all leadership styles are appropriate in the church.
Studies done by Robert Tannenbaum and Warren Schmidt led to the
discovery that no one style is better; the most effective leaders are those
who could "match" the leadership expectations of those who are led.[3] It
is a systemic issue: how the leader relates to the whole living organism
of the local church.

Second, our thesis is that neither the people-oriented style nor the
task-oriented style—styles we will explore—is *intrinsically* better at
releasing every-member ministry in the local church. Both styles have
problems and potentials when it comes to equipping the laity. Each
needs to be complemented by the other, and this is a powerful argument
for plural leadership in the local church.

When task-oriented leaders try to empower people for ministry but
do not understand their own style, they tend to function as power-brokers
and use the laity to make their ministry work, instead of assisting the
laity to engage in their own ministry. Person-oriented leaders[4] at the
other end of the continuum will do the same thing for a different set of
reasons. They may be just as interested in *control* as the task-oriented,
often more so, although this is not immediately apparent. Person-oriented
leaders need task-oriented leaders. If a person-oriented leader boasts, "I
am not an administrator," but fails to release administration in the
people, the church may be handicapped even more than with the task-
oriented person. Again, the issue is not whether one style is better than
another—in fact, both are needed. We are convinced that effective
equipping of the saints requires a leader whose style is matched to the
congregation and to the stage of development in that congregation. A
godly pastor with an equipping orientation may utterly fail simply because of a mismatch. The same pastor, well-matched or adjusting her
style to the needs of that congregation, can have the time of her life
releasing others in ministry.

A Pastoral Mismatch

Pastor Andrew moved three thousand miles to Saint James Episcopal, coming from a larger congregation and leaving behind an extensive radio ministry. Prior to his coming, Saint James had been diminishing, some leaving out of explicit anger, but most by quiet attrition. Those who left almost always gave a general statement like this: "I have nothing against the church, the rector, or the people, but I need to be fed." Initially, Pastor Andrew's ministry was relational in style and his work flourished. He had a repertoire of leadership styles but chose in this situation to become a passive "servant leader." His view of this was "Tell me what you want done, and I will do it." However, the majority of the congregation responded by saying in effect that they wanted leadership not just service. Pastor Andrew began to antagonize people, especially an influential couple in the church. This couple had leadership charisma, and Andrew had a serious clash with them. Eventually the couple left the church to the keen dismay and confusion of most of the other members.

Shortly after this, Andrew himself left the congregation psychologically. He pursued his own special ministries unrelated to his people. One of these was a radio ministry. Although he had the blessing of the church in his effort to renew his past radio ministry, this project never became fully operational and did not provide sufficient income for him to live, as he had hoped.

The attrition rate speeded up. The pastor seemed to have no answers, and the church board steadily moved toward pure panic. Although most church members believed the pastor had inherited the situation, an increasing number of people were blaming the pastor, and the pastor began to blame himself. The people were saying, "Our church has the potential of becoming a significant ministry in our city. The municipality is growing rapidly, and we ought to be growing too. What is wrong?"

Many people offered some answers and the church implemented a few new programs. They tried unstructured church services and guitar-playing, but to no avail. The church diminished, from more than two hundred members to seventy regular attenders. The pastoral staff was reduced from two full-time pastors to Pastor Andrew. Finally, with the church's financial and prayerful blessing, Pastor Andrew resigned to become the first full-time chaplain of a parachurch ministry he had brought into being.

Andrew's problem was compounded by the fact that no one understood what went wrong. But the situation could have been helped if
someone had assisted Andrew in discovering the expected leadership
style in the congregation, his own preferred leadership style, and his
back-up styles.[5] The needs of his faithful people and the expression of
this pastor's servant theology did not "match." But notice, we did not
say that the people and the pastor were a poor match. The mismatch was
Andrew's chosen leadership style and the needs of the congregation at
that stage of development.

The Myth of Pastoral Incompatibility

Some research on marriages that succeed and those that fail suggests that
there is little difference between the two! In one sense you might say
that all marriage partners are "incompatible." There is always enough
difference between a husband and a wife to "justify" a divorce and,
viewed from another perspective, hardly enough to explain a marriage
breakdown. Some couples with strikingly different personalities and
backgrounds make it, while others with less "difference" persist in quiet
desperation or split up.[6] Edwin Friedman points out that "incompatibility
in marriage has less to do with the differences than with what is causing
them to stand out at any given moment."[7]

In terms of pastoral incompatibility—or church leadership more
generally—we wish to affirm a crucial principle: *It is generally not that
the people are incompatible but that the styles of leadership are.* We
believe that people like Pastor Andrew could have a long and fruitful
ministry right where they are. If there was a "mistake" made in the original selection, it is like the "mistake" of marrying the "wrong" person.
The best solution is not to eliminate one of the partners! Incompatibility
in leader-follower relationships is a myth. To focus on incompatibility of
the persons directs our focus on the fault of one or both instead of examining the systemic factors that could lead to a harmonious marriage.

Understanding Leadership Style

Our conviction is that leadership is effective when the leader correctly
assesses the needs of the group, understands the *situation* of the group,

and chooses a leadership style and behavior appropriate to the group's level of organized maturity. The Blake-Mouton Managerial Grid reproduced in Appendix 2 expresses this in graphic form.[8] But first we must define what we mean by leadership style.

Two Fundamental Leadership Concerns

Most leadership studies deal with two fundamental concerns about leading: (1) the people who must be led (relationships) and (2) the task that must be accomplished (effectiveness). Effective leadership involves the leader's intentional choice of behaviors that focus on the task or on the people or on some combination of the two. This can be represented simply in the following figure:

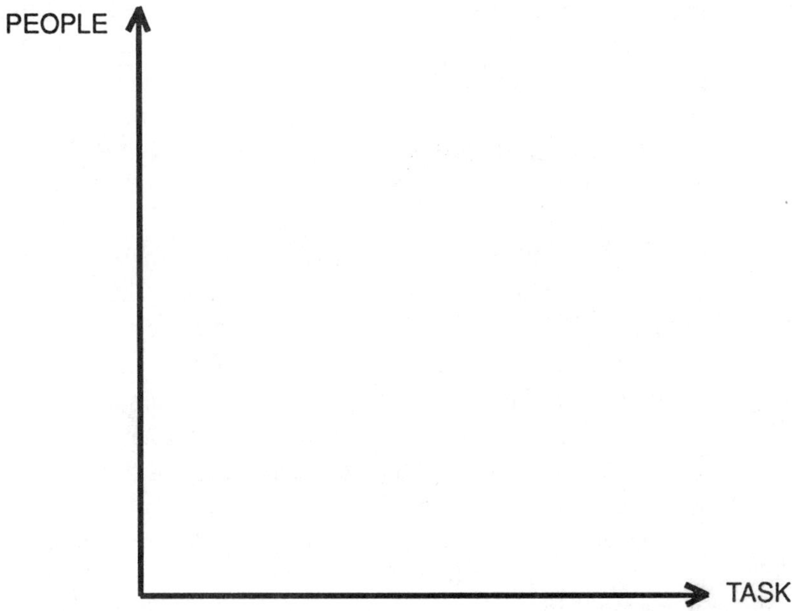

PEOPLE ↑

                                                                    → TASK

Two Fundamental Concerns of All Leaders[9]

Figure 6

The leader's degree of commitment to each of the two basic leadership concerns—relationships and task effectiveness—determine his or her leadership style. For example, a person who is highly task-oriented, but has a low concern for maintaining interpersonal relationships is usually viewed by others as a controlling or directive leader, while the leader having a high concern for relationships but a low concern for programs and tasks is viewed as a relational or person-oriented leader. But people may complain that the relational leader "doesn't accomplish very much and hardly ever finishes a job." The leader having a low concern for both relationships and task effectiveness is seen as a passive leader. The leader having a high concern for both is viewed as a participative or total-involvement leader.

Before we consider which basic leadership styles are effective in the church, we must consider three styles that are never appropriate in a church. One is the *dictator* or dominator. In the Drama Triangle discussed in chapter 2, the dictator sometimes appears as the persecutor. A second inappropriate style, the *slave*, can be found in the Drama Triangle as the victim. Unlike the dictator, the slave appears to be weak. But he or she might be the most powerful person in the church. This is the eager leader who rushes about, keeping extremely busy, doing far more work than is necessary, much of it done poorly. This person is looking for sympathy and the bustling about helps avoid facing tough and difficult situations.

The third unacceptable style is the *martyr*. In the triangle this can be the victim, but with a determination to inculcate guilt in those who do not serve as sacrificially as he or she does. It is an extreme example of the task-oriented leader. Again, the victim, in this case the martyr leader, is very powerful because he or she attempts to control others by producing feelings of guilt and pity. "How can we help but do what John wants us to do? Look at all he's done and all the things he has suffered for us." This is a subtle and effective method, but it is manipulative.

In one of the churches I (Collins) served, Hilda Crosby dominated the church in many ways, even though she was also very dedicated to the church, perhaps too dedicated. It was amazing what this woman could do all by herself. She could organize whole events singlehandedly. For example, when we had a Hawaiian festival, she produced all the material we needed for that event, including awnings and decorations. She taught the women to dress in Hawaiian styles and put on a Hawaiian show. She collected all the food. She did everything. When someone thanked her, she beamed. At first I thought this was wonderful.

But the night we put on a Thanksgiving dinner in our church, I learned that there was an unhealthy control in her apparent sacrificial service. Mrs. Crosby had secured all the turkeys and the trimmings and recruited all the people needed to serve, cook, and decorate. It was great. But when the event was all over and twenty or so people remained milling in the banquet room, Lois, my spouse, commented, "Well, we will have to clean this up."

"Yes," answered Mrs. Crosby.

Lois said, "We ought to get some help."

But Mrs. Crosby said, "No, no, don't do that. You don't need to do that."

"Why not?" Lois asked.

Mrs. Crosby answered, "You and I, we can do it ourselves. They will really appreciate it. Then they can go home. They'll have had a nice evening—not having to do any of the work."

Lois said, "Well, I don't think so."

As pastor I was caught in the middle, but before I could do anything, Lois went into the banquet room and announced, "We need help here to clean up all the dishes, move tables, and put back the chairs. How many people will help us?" She got twenty-one volunteers.

Mrs. Crosby was so angry that she did not stay to help. She got in her car and went home. From that point on we had trouble with Mrs. Crosby. She was a task-oriented martyr type of leader.

A true martyr, however, can be defined differently. Edwin Friedman tells of a minister with an extremely kind, but passive husband. She said, "I used to believe a martyr was someone who went around taking everyone else's pain without complaint and refusing praise for his actions. I now realize that is not a martyr; that's a saint. A martyr is someone who's willing to live with a saint."[10] Perhaps in the light of the foregoing story, we could turn the definition around: a saint is someone who is willing to live with a "martyr" like Hilda Crosby!

The Four Basic Leadership Styles[11]

Having considered three inappropriate styles we can consider four
suitable styles that can be represented on a grid as follows:

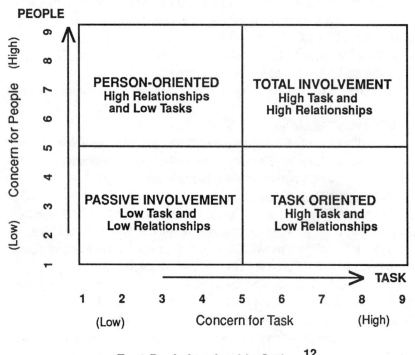

PEOPLE

(High)

Concern for People

(Low)

| PERSON-ORIENTED
**High Relationships
and Low Tasks** | TOTAL INVOLVEMENT
**High Task and
High Relationships** |

| PASSIVE INVOLVEMENT
**Low Task and
Low Relationships** | TASK ORIENTED
**High Task and
Low Relationships** |

TASK

1   2   3   4   5   6   7   8   9

(Low)   Concern for Task   (High)

Four Basic Leadership Styles [12]

Figure 7

Adapted from Robert B. Blake and Jane S. Mouton, *The Managerial Grid* (Houston: Gulf
Publishing, Co., 1964). (Permission Granted)

The Task-Oriented Leadership Style

This style of leadership is characterized by the comment "She gets things done!" The task-oriented leader places a major emphasis on programs. The typically hard-driving leader's motto is "Produce or perish." He already thinks he knows what is best for the people or the institution and so is sometimes willing to damage personal relationships to safeguard the organization's interests and assure the completion of the task. If there is an inevitable contradiction between the need to complete the task (re-solve the issue, serve the organization) and the need to consider relation-ships, the task-oriented person will get the job completed.

As with each leadership style, there is a down-side to this one. Sometimes the source of this leadership style is not merely the high val-ue placed on the accomplishment of the goals of the church, but on a personal need to control. Leaders using this style rarely ask for advice, suggestions, or guidance. To do so would be to admit weakness or incompetence. What matters is to win; being liked is irrelevant. While the picture we have drawn is not uniformly attractive, there are times when almost total power is necessary to resolve a problem and create a favorable outcome. Most churches would never be founded without task-oriented leaders. Every church needs some task-oriented people.

The Person-Oriented Leadership Style

The person-oriented leadership style, shown in the upper left quadrant of the grid, assumes that task completion (concern for structure, resolving issues) interferes with the needs and desires of people. People are never commodities for this person. Seeing the concerns and feelings of people as being of primary importance, this style of leader tries to arrange con-ditions so that personal and social needs can be satisfied both on the job and in terms of the follower's desires.

Leaders using this style actively monitor interpersonal relationships so that a work climate is created in which group members will enjoy working together to accomplish the task. To do this, the leader will, if necessary, relinquish both personal and organizational goals to maintain conflict-free relationships. This is intentional behavior. Believing that camaraderie and friendship characterize the church, the person-oriented

leader may even turn the followers away from a task in the interest of a
congenial atmosphere.

The use of this style requires the leader to be flexible, permissive,
interested in people, and willing to provide social and emotional support
where possible. At the same time, this type of leader places little emphasis on structures and gives few directives.

One of the motives underlying this style is the desire for acceptance
and approval. This person feels secure when relationships are positive.
This requires being kind, "nice," and helpful. Usually the person-oriented
leader fears disapproval or rejection. When rejected, a typical reaction
for this person is flight. To avoid conflict and minimize differences, he
or she might stay in close contact with what others are thinking and agree
with them.

While some persons adopt this style because of their respect for the
group's capabilities of working without much direction, others have a
more nonaffirming view of the group's abilities. These leaders tend to
see individuals in the group as fragile and unable to tolerate conflict or
uncertainty. As leaders they must ensure such situations do not arise,
and, if they do, move quickly to correct them. The person-oriented leader creates what Blake and Mouton call the "country club" atmosphere,
where people can enjoy an easy tempo, without a lot of pressure. (See
the grid in Appendix 2.) But the task suffers and there usually is not
much creativity expressed.

The person-oriented style is exactly what is needed in some situations. For example, Myrna was invited to become pastor of a Congregational Church. In one previous setting she had shown a wonderful ability
for getting people together, drawing them out, and getting them to work
together. She had the grace to make every person in a room believe that
he or she was important. She seldom took direct initiative in a meeting.
She would allow the group to arrange and develop its own family
characteristics. In the new church she needed this skill more than ever.

Why? Before she came to First Congregational more than fifty
people had left in anger. Most had drifted to other congregations, leaving First considerably weakened. Within six months of taking her new
assignment, Myrna met with the congregation several times to help the
remaining people process the situation. Then she met with the people
who had left. She listened, cried, laughed, and made the concerns of
each person uppermost. After several meetings she gained consent to get

the current First people and the former First people together. Her self-effacing manner and genuine graciousness allowed each person to express concerns and to feel valued rather than used. As a result of this meeting and hours of pastoral ministry to individuals, more than forty people returned to First. The church is once again together and growing in all the ways one would hope. A task-oriented person would probably have failed. Yet Myrna will need to draw task-oriented leaders beside her to move the church along to the next stage of growth and effectively to release lay ministry.

The Passive Involvement Leadership Style

The passive involvement leadership style, shown in the lower left quadrant of the grid, experiences little or no contradiction between completion of the task and the needs of people. This is largely due to the leader's uninvolved, withdrawn position in the group. This type of leader will conform to the job description, but do his best to stay out of the limelight. This is often intentional. The leader wants to create a leadership vacuum so group members will assume leadership roles and carry on the work themselves. The classic group dynamic theory behind this strategy proposes that the leader be allowed to move around throughout the group. To gain this silent permission, the leader must become passive. In some cases, he or she may even withdraw from certain group meetings and activities altogether. The use of this style requires that the leader be nondirective in group task-oriented activities and assume little or no responsibility for maintaining interpersonal relationships, making the group members responsible for both task achievement and personal relationships.

The negative side to this style? The motivation behind it is often to avoid being resented. By being visible yet inconspicuous, it is possible to avoid being in controversies, gaining enemies, or getting fired. It's a play-it-safe mode.

Normally, passive involvement might be successfully adopted only from time to time in a group's history, on the rare occasion when a group is "fully capable" and functioning well on its own.[13] There are times when a stance of "benevolent disinterest" can be helpful in a congregation. It can gently push people to make their own decisions and define their own goals. But the pastor who consistently used the passive involvement style would not be able to survive as a long-term leader in a congregation. Not to be deeply interested in either people or tasks is usually fatal, as Pastor Andrew learned, leaving Saint James for a radio ministry.

The Total Involvement Leadership Style

The total involvement leadership style, in the remaining quadrant of the grid, integrates high concern for getting the task completed and high concern for good people relationships. This style of leadership assumes that there is no inherent contradiction between organizational goals and the needs of the people. For this leader, effective integration is possible by involving people and their ideas in determining the goals of ministry and achievement. This leader also invests in establishing sound and mature relationships among the members, as this is essential to accomplishing the organization's task.

The intent of this style is to get everyone fully involved in all phases of the organization's planning and programming, while providing the necessary supervision to safeguard fully the interests of the organization. To do this, the leader puts equal emphasis on maintaining human relationships and organizational structure, equal emphasis on people and task. The leader using this style has a genuine desire to help others reach their highest potential. He or she avoids advancing selfish interests at the expense of others or the organization.

The total involvement leader does not shy away from conflict and tries to reduce or resolve issues by finding sound solutions to the problem without creating animosity. This type of leader tends to use confrontation in the positive sense—involving people in the problem early on, getting differences out into the open, and talking them through. He or she seeks to move people away from the emotional feelings of the participants and toward reflection on the issues or problems. That is, moving people away from asking "*Who* is right?" to asking "*What* is right?" To the extent that this action can be accomplished, the leader believes that conflict can be reduced.[14]

This style of leadership exercises a flexible, strong, pro-organizational manner in terms of attitude, planning, and follow-through to ensure that the organization's goals are achieved. At the same time, person-orientation is developed through active listening, clear separation of fact and opinion, and team-wide decisions, based on understandings and agreements.

With this leadership style, tasks are usually completed, a high level of creativity is maintained, and the leader possesses a great sense of fulfillment. Research indicates that people who adopt this leadership style tend to advance, increasing their responsibility within an organization.

The weakness of this style? Crisis intervention is slow and personal counseling is not in-depth.

Adapting to Systemic Reality

All of these leadership styles are appropriate at some time in the life of the church, provided they are motivated by servanthood and the desire to create a community in which justice and love are experienced by both leaders and followers. That is, not one of these styles is necessarily bad; each can be effective in a specific situation.

All of us have a preferred leadership style and back-up styles to which we turn when our preferred style is not working. Back-up styles provide flexibility, an essential quality in any good leader. An effective leader does not use the same leadership style in every situation. For example, the task-oriented style may work well with the junior boys' group, but be counterproductive in an adult singles' group. The leader must respond to the variables in a particular situation.

A pastor may not be conscious of a personally preferred style, but that pastor's spouse, children, and elders are very much aware of it. Knowing ourselves in this matter is very important. The failure to understand himself was one of the factors in Pastor Andrew's demise. A standard mode of operation has been building since childhood, as my (Collins) own story indicates.

The Leader's Self-Knowledge

I (Collins) grew up in a low-income neighborhood in Toronto. My father often "beat the tar out of me," so I learned to be aggressive and assertive. I also determined that I would not end up as a nonachiever on the streets.

As a result I became task-oriented. I learned to make things happen. I learned how to survive in my environment.

I will never be free of that deeply imbedded learned behavior. In a crisis I revert to it and become an aggressor again. Yet I am learning to strengthen my capacity to be a people-oriented leader. (After all, I do genuinely care for people, and people care for me.) I could not do this without knowing who I am as a person; it is crucial for leaders like me to know ourselves and to learn alternative styles.

Norman Shawchuk suggests that there are at least three ways to gain insight into one's leadership styles:[15] (1) by asking yourself honest questions about the results you have experienced as a leader; (2) by using a survey instrument[16] to identify your leadership behaviors in a variety of situations, measuring your relative effectiveness in each one of them; and (3) by asking others how they view your leadership and its effectiveness. Shawchuk suggests contacting at least five to ten people and then comparing their responses to seek out common themes. It would be good to use a brief questionnaire to assist these people in their evaluation. The best insights will come when you use all three of Shawchuk's methods. Too many of us base our leadership behavior on suppositions of what feels good to us or what has seemed to work in the past. We may then become fixed on our leadership behavior until we run into a frustrating situation and wonder what went wrong. *Since styles of leadership can be learned, we are not trapped in our preferred leadership style. That is why we are convinced that most pastoral mismatches are not the result of incompatible relationships, but the result of the incongruity of a leader's style with the system in which he or she is working.*[17]

Now we must apply these four leadership styles to the task of matching leadership styles and systems. The key word is *adaptability*. Systems thinking requires it. Failure to "read" the situation and to be flexible can be catastrophic, as it was for Pastor Andrew.

Situational Leadership

Take another example, this time of a board chairman in a church in a denomination that stresses lay ministry and is fearful of clergy domination and of being involved in society. Wally is the founding elder. He and his friends, long-time members of this denomination, had wanted to start a new kind of church to reach people in a rapidly growing suburb. They were mavericks and had some splendid ideas. Wally was just right to be a founding elder. He was the CEO and owner of his own business, and his task orientation (with a strong component of personal caring) was exactly what the church needed in the early years. Forming a church with a culture substantially different from the denomination, weathering the storms and hard work of those early months—these required Wally's preferred style of task-oriented leadership.

The elders, under Wally's leadership, developed feedback groups, which met after the Sunday morning sermon, and started a very successful youth ministry in the community. They visited door-to-door and created two very successful service projects in the community. A network of small groups in homes was developed to balance the sanctuary church experience on Sunday with the house church during the week. Women were encouraged to exercise their giftedness despite the fact that other churches in the denomination observed this with raised eyebrows. It is hard to imagine that the forging of this new work could have happened without Wally's dynamic leadership. But eight years later the situation was different.

The church had matured and strong people in the church found little opportunity for leadership working beside Wally. The strongest leaders in the church never were appointed as elders. The eldership was composed of one leader (Wally), five "leaners," and one frustrated staff person. Wally had not changed his leadership style to suit the maturing experience of the church. He continued to hold all the reins himself, but he was getting more and more tired. His task orientation, so necessary in the early days, had not adapted to the need to be more passively involved to draw out other leaders. As the pressure mounted, Wally reacted by taking on even more church work and responsibility "just to get the job done" because he "lacked the energy" to involve others. He still thought of himself as a good equipper of the laity, but he did not realize that he was creating dependent followers and frustrating the potential of other leaders. The worst aspects of clericalism surfaced in this lay leader.

Then a crisis hit that could have been a golden opportunity, but turned out to be his undoing. One elder confronted Wally with what he regarded as a "shady business deal." Because Wally refused to discuss it, the elder felt he had no option but to bring the matter to the other elders in Wally's presence. Pandemonium ensued. Wally was not willing to submit to his "peers" on any issue, and this stalemate continued to frustrate the elders, who remained motionless for almost a year. Ultimately, Wally left the church disgruntled and started another small congregation. The church lost his dynamic leadership and neither the new work nor the old one thrived. Why? Primarily because Wally did not change his leadership style to evoke the leadership of others as the church moved to a new level of system formation. He was also unwilling to use the challenge of being held accountable as a moment for growth in his own spiritual and moral life.

Making the Match

Remember our definition of leadership from chapter 1: "Leadership equals a function of the leader, the followers, and other situational variables": $L = (L, F, S)$. Leadership does not happen without a situation. A good leader learns to read the group's characteristics, determining whether it is mature, immature, or in process, responding to them with a style of leadership appropriate *to them*. Let's consider three dimensions of "reading the group."

First, the leader must learn to assess the group or congregation's readiness to take responsibility for the tasks it has.[18] Some groups are fully capable of carrying out their responsibilities on their own with little or no direction from the leader. Other groups, however, have not yet developed such capabilities and need much more direction from the leader. Of course, most groups fall somewhere between these two ends of the spectrum.

Second, the leader needs to become aware of the stage of growth of the congregation or group. Chris Argyris suggests that, as a group gradually matures through improved interpersonal skills, training, and experience, it moves from passivity to increased self-directed activity and from full dependence on the leader to relative independence as a group.[19] Groups mature over time, just as individuals do, in terms of self-directed activity and decision making. For example, a baby can make no decisions for itself; a child can make some; an adult can be more self-reliant. Just as a man does not relate to his wife as he would to his daughter, neither should a leader relate to an old, established, and capable congregation as he would to a new church in an early stage of formation.

Third, the leader needs to be willing to make quick and radical shifts in leadership behavior. Flexibility is the key. For example, a leader may need to shift from a passive involvement or person-oriented style to a task-oriented style to compensate for a radical regression in group maturity. Of course some leaders cannot, or will not, make the shift, and they are in trouble. But they could learn because leadership styles are learned.

Leadership style is one of the most controversial issues in North American churches. Because of poor matching of leadership styles, good churches split or wither on the vine. Gifted leaders resign in despair. Strong and talented lay leaders, frozen out of one church, move to another to look for a place to stand. The most common reason is not doctrinal differences or moral scandals, but mismatched leadership styles. If a leader wishes to work in a particular congregational system, he or she must know that system, join it, "read it" to see what leadership style is appropriate, and adjust to it. If the leader wishes to remain in the system, he or she must be willing to make adjustments as the group goes through various systemic changes. Is it worth it? Yes, if the congregational system grows to maturity, if lay leadership is liberated, if members become empowered to serve in the church and the world, and if the church itself becomes more mature. The purpose of pastoral leadership is to build the people of God. We close this chapter with a positive example of good and continuous matchmaking, again a composite of several people we have known, but here disguised.

Bernice is a church-planter and essentially task oriented. When she founded Hope Community Church, she went door to door in the suburb of a large Canadian city. She had the heart and energy of a pioneer. Some people say she is a workaholic, but, in the same breath, they admit that nothing good is ever started without sacrifice.

Knowing that baby-boomers like good sound and high-quality printing, she insisted on an expensive professional sound system in their first rented facility. And she had a professional advertising firm design the three-color church brochure that was distributed widely in the neighborhood. The church grew, partly by evangelism and partly by the recovery of lapsed Christians from other backgrounds, a combination we have come to accept as inevitable!

In time the church got large enough to build a facility, hire a second pastor, and offer a multitude of service ministries in the community:

counseling, day care, marriage resources, and a food bank. Bernice was directly involved in getting each one of these going, but you can imagine that she was getting more and more tired! At this point, many church-planters leave, considering that their calling is to get things going and not to bring them to maturity. But Bernice chose otherwise. She stayed, changed her leadership style, and invested heavily in equipping leadership, especially her staff and volunteer lay leaders.

The church has continued to grow and become a major influence in the city. After several years the church succeeded in planting two other churches by way of members moving to new communities. Bernice has become less and less visible, but she has not stopped leading. She has, however, found a way to adapt her preferred leadership style and adopt a back-up style. If she stays another decade, she will have to make changes once again. But she has already proven that she understands a systems approach to church leadership. She has a compatible relationship with the congregation, not because of her personality, but because she has matched her leadership style to the changing needs of the church.

CHAPTER V

Caring for the Subsystems

Greater is he that multiplies the workers than he who does the work.
John Raleigh Mott[1]

It's better to put ten men to work than to do the work of ten men.
D. L. Moody[2]

The role of the pastor is primarily to care for the subsystems that comprise the system of the church.
Mansell Pattison[3]

Criticism can be a good thing, but one does not usually feel good about it while it is being delivered! A good friend and colleague offered some helpful criticism of my (Stevens) first book, *Liberating the Laity*. He said, "You have simply made a new clericalism out of equipping. Instead of having a solo-minister, you will produce a solo-equipper." He was largely, though not totally, right. Davida Foy Crabtree, in the record of her efforts at Colchester Federated Church, came to a similar discovery. She said, "Ironically, here we were trying to strengthen the ministry of the laity, and the whole program was clergy dependent."[4]

Our single theme of this book is that the leader's role is to equip the saints *as a whole* so that the whole church equips itself. In the process the pastor liberates himself from being a pastor in the traditional sense and allows himself to be equipped by the people! Crabtree expresses this magnificently in these words: "It has come to be popular to describe the role of ordained ministers in the renewed church as 'equippers of the saints.' In recent months, I have come to question this model insofar as it implies equipping is a one-way street."[5]

The pastor is not the chief equipper of the saints, but rather is one of many who give leadership to the systemic life of the church so that the church as a whole lives consistently and congruently with its true biblical identity: the people of God invested in the world for Christ and his kingdom.

This gives the pastor a new job description. "I see the pastor," Mansell Pattison says, "as essentially a shepherd of systems. The pastor functions to nurture and guide the subsystems of the church." Pastoral care is "care of the church as a living system," not just the care of all the individual saints.[6]

We have been exploring this through several channels: the process of joining one's own church (and helping others to join), cultivating interdependence, discovering systemic giftedness, leading the process, cultivating the culture, facilitating systemic change, and matching our leadership styles. Each of these has dealt with the church as a whole. But in this chapter we will look into the body once again to see its subsystems, not just the individual members. Cultivating and caring for the subsystems is part of the pastoral task, especially in large churches.

Functional and Structural Subsystems

The church is composed of interdependent subsystems, each of which is important and needs the others—one more case of the Pauline principle "the eye cannot say to the hand, 'I have no need of you.' " Some subsystems are structural and others are functional.

Structural Subsystems

In the church structural subsystems are observable groups of people or organizationally defined groups of people that affect the whole and interact with other groups. One immediately thinks of couples' clubs, youth groups, choirs or music groups, seniors' groups, and singles' groups. These subsystems are important centers of influence and ministry within the body. One subsystem's interaction with another subsystem—as every seasoned pastor knows—is a crucial dynamic in the life of the church partly because they are often age-group or life-stage defined.

One of the most important structural subsystems today is the small group. Davida Crabtree has written helpfully about her use of "covenant groups" and "listening groups" to empower lay people for their ministry in the world Monday to Friday. We commend her work as a good example.[7] For a contemporary elaboration of how small groups can serve the corporate life of the institutional church, we suggest the chapter by Dan Williams in *The Equipper's Guide to Every Member Ministry*.[8] To the best of our knowledge it is the only truly systemic approach to small groups in print. Dan proposes that to develop small groups, pastoral leadership must work with the whole church and individual groups at the same time. Most authors deal only with the small groups. Further, Dan believes it is important to train groups to be groups at the same time that leaders are being equipped. Most authors put the emphasis exclusively on equipping small-group leaders. But Dan believes that the groups will raise up and equip leaders, and he is seeing this happen in his home church where he serves as small-group coordinator. It is a thoroughly systemic approach. Later we will explore one more structural subsystem in greater depth: the family.

Functional Subsystems

Functional subsystems are discernable *patterns of influence* and ministry within the body. These may not be institutionalized (in a board or program), but consistently affect the church systemically. For example, the educational/teaching subsystem provides a continuous learning environment, often unplanned, as well as programs of Christian education that are planned. The Christian education committee will be concerned about its own programs, but the subsystem is far more extensive in the congregation than the programs sponsored by the committee. These subsystems perform a *function*. They are not a definable group of people.[9] In this chapter we will explore two functional subsystems in more depth: the restorative-reparative subsystem and the lay leadership subsystem. But first, we will consider the family subsystem.

The Family Subsystem

The church is a family and, at the same time, a family of families—
composed of numerous subsystem families in which family potentials
and problems also surface. For the pastor there is often a third family of
importance—his or her own. Edwin Friedman makes these three families (church, families of the church, and the clergy family) his primary
concern in *Generation to Generation.*[10] He says that "unresolved issues
in any of the clergy's three families can produce symptoms in one of the
others, and . . . within that emotional interlock often lies the key to
knowledge or to further stress."[11] A marital problem spills over into a
bitter church meeting. A rejected husband attempts to triangle his pastor
"to get the church to force his runaway wife to come home." An addictive church makes such unrelenting demands on a workaholic pastor that
his spouse and children have a nonfunctioning husband and father.
Ideally, the congregation as system and the family as subsystem should
have a mutual synergy, and that is precisely what family ministry should
encourage.

The Church as Family

As a family—the family or household of God—the church is composed
of people joined together in God to be brothers and sisters (Mark 3:33-
35; Gal. 6:10). We have already seen that the congregation (as a family)
has many of the systemic potentials and problems of the family: fusion
and differentiation, "stuckness" and freedom, codependence and interdependence. As is the case with all families, unresolved problems in the
church family are passed on generation to generation. A church born of
a split may itself continue to split in each generation, never recovering
from what Friedman calls "the still active background radiation from the
big bang of that congregation's creation,"[12] until someone deals with the
systemic problem.

Dennis Guernsey, a family psychologist from Fuller Theological
Seminary, has adapted a family therapy chart to the interdependence of
members in the church. Graphically he brings together two factors—the
quality of relationships and the structure of those relationships—to help
us think about the church as a family.

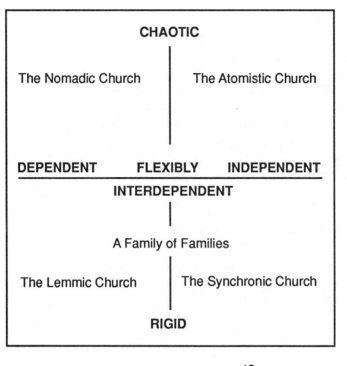

The Family of Families [13]

Figure 8

In Guernsey's terms, the nomadic church is one where families look to the church to meet their needs, but the real relationships within the congregation are tenuous. The church is filled with church-shoppers. This is probably the most common family-form of church in North America. The atomistic church has neither structure/order nor relationships. Corinth would be a good biblical example of this church. There are factions, and people are inclined to "do their own thing." Such churches have often had a scrape with an authoritarian high-control pastor, and the people are determined "never to let anyone control them again." The synchronic church is rigidly independent. There is an apparent harmony but no closeness. Many high-commitment evangelical churches and sects are synchronic. The lemmic church, named after the animals famous for mass migrations, blindly follow their leader. Disagreeing with the leader is perceived as treason against the cause. The classic example is the mass suicides in Jonestown.

The most desirable blend of structure and relationship is found at the intersection of the adaptiveness-cohesion scale: flexibly interdependent. Members are free to express their own dreams and ministry, *but they remain deeply connected.* They have enough liturgy, tradition, and structured ways of relating to be effective, but *are adaptable to change.* This kind of church could be healthy enough for many individuals to think of the church as their substitute family.

Should the Church Be a Substitute Family?

Early in my pastoral ministry I (Stevens) preached a sermon on the church as the family of God. I said that people should be able to find in the church what they missed at home. Afterward a young adult woman with a desperate family background came to me and said, "I do not believe you are able and willing to provide for me everything that was not given to me by my nuclear family!" She was at least partly right. We *could* not. And we should not.

As Kerr and Bowen say,

> Many people "escape" their families of origin determined to be different from them . . . They frequently develop "substitute families" through friends or organizations and invest emotionally much more in them than in their extended families.[14]

By declaring their independence from family and "joining" the church, they have not differentiated self. They did not leave home; they broke away. Nor have they resolved the emotional issues of their own past. Frequently they bring these unresolved problems from the past into the church, and pastors wonder, *where did that come from?* The church *cannot* substitute for the family. But one thing the church can do is help people reconnect with their families in helpful ways, differentiating themselves while remaining connected.

While the church should not be a substitute family, it can be an extended family. Family issues can be dealt with in the context of a church that is family. Mansell Pattison suggests that in the modern stripped-down nuclear family in the urban milieu, people in the church can become *functional relatives*.[15] This approach also provides a family model for including singles in the church.[16]

A Systems Approach to Family Ministry

The fundamental flaw in much that passes for family ministry is that churches treat families as a collection of individuals instead of a systemic whole. Family ministry in the church must empower families *as families*. We will illustrate this by expounding three principles of systems theory: working with the whole, discerning multigenerational issues, and systemic empowering.

1. Working with the whole family. Much of the church's program while intended "for the whole family" serves to compete with the family. The dissonance between stated theory and practice is deafening. James Dobson has discovered that thirty-nine percent of surveyed families believe that contemporary churches fragment the family by dividing up all activities according to age.[17]

As an early attempt to bring changes within families, my wife, Gail, and I (Stevens) ran a family Sunday school class for two years while serving West Point Grey Baptist Church in Vancouver. We invited four families at a time to withdraw from the regular Sunday school for eight weeks and become a family class. All ages were included. We chose eight scriptural passages that touched on family themes and designed a learning process that would include all ages. For example, the day we studied the passage in John 13 on mutual service, Gail, using a basin, washed everyone's hands and dried them with a towel as each person entered the room. It was remarkable how easily children welcomed this service and how reticent were the adults. This led to fruitful Bible study and sharing on mutual service in the home. Some of the parents made small steps toward being willing to be served. Some said it was their most fruitful Sunday school experience. Yet we struggled to recruit enough families for the sessions. Making multigenerational ministries happen and keeping them fruitful runs against the grain of the church program. Discerning multigenerational family issues in the families of the church, and dealing with them, is equally challenging.

2. Discerning multigenerational issues. A medical student in a secular university was once given a single question to answer in his three-hour psychiatry exam: " 'The sins of the fathers are visited unto the children to the third and fourth generation.' Comment!" While the examiner correctly referred to a biblical principle (Deut. 5:9; Exod. 20:5; Num. 14:18), he failed to note the accompanying promise: "but showing love to a thousand generations." Systems family therapist James R. Koch has written a paper detailing an in-depth study of the multigenerational pathology of the four generations of the family of promise, described in Genesis 12-50. He says, "In a narrative as shocking and insidious as today's most brazen soap operas, the Genesis account reveals a family pathology that spread like an unnoticed cancer."[18] The list of problems passed on from generation to generation is staggering.

Favoritism. Abraham loved Sarah and not Hagar (resulting in envy and jealousy). Isaac loved his son Esau; Rebekah loved her son Jacob. Jacob passes on the pathology to another generation by choosing a favorite child, Joseph (and his brothers almost eliminated him).

Triangles. Sarah and Hagar each triangled her children to get what she wanted. Both Isaac and Rebekah triangled a favorite child against a spouse. Each of Jacob's two wives, Rachel (the beloved) and Leah (the hated), triangled children to gain her husband's favor.

There were power struggles, failures to become properly differentiated (individuated), family secrets, exploitive relationships, marital disappointments that led to triangulation, favoritism-alliances, and sibling rivalries.

Koch says, "These strains of relational illness were passed on and added to, until by the third and fourth generations, they had mushroomed into a series of full-blown atrocities that few family lineages would ever want to claim."[19] There were attempted murders and rape and genocide. But the story also shows that God intervened, especially in the life of Joseph, partly by choosing *not* to remove the natural, long-term consequences of decisions and partly by inviting family members, through these painful experiences, to discover relationships based on grace and forgiveness. Some have found great inspiration in the phrase, "*the God* of Abraham, Isaac, and Jacob"; God's identification in love with this needy and sinful family contains the seed of the Gospel of Jesus and hope for learning from multigenerational problems.

3. Grappling with systemic power in the family. In his thesis for

Regent College, Ted Blenkhorne makes the following analysis of how power works in a family system.

> Power in a system is the ability one has to influence behavior, outcomes, or the environment of one's life. The Resource Theory of Power assumes that each family member or church member has some power based upon specific available resources. French and Raven identified six primary power bases.[20] *(1) Punishment: coercive power.* This involves corporal punishment or the power to withhold something desirable or necessary, as when a wife may punish her husband by withholding sexual relations. *(2) Positive reinforcement: reward power.* When one member believes another can provide something desirable, they may grant power to that individual. When a teenager, for example, wants to borrow the family car, he may cut and trim the lawn very dutifully. *(3) Expertise: knowledge power.* One member of the family may acquire specialized knowledge which is valuable to other family members, as when a computer buff helps her father learn a new program. *(4) Legitimacy: position power.* The role occupied by a member of the family may serve as a power base when other members recognize the legitimacy of the role as when a teenager may accept a curfew from his mother because he recognizes that she has the right to impose this restriction, even though she may not have the physical strength to enforce it. *(5) Identification: referent power.* When a family member sees himself as similar to another member, or would like to be identified with that member because he admires some of that person's traits, he may grant that member more influence, as when a boy, wishing to be like his father, may imitate his father's gestures. *(6) Persuasion: information power.* If a family member can marshal her arguments carefully and persuasively, other members may allow her to make decisions on their behalf.[21]

All these power bases are at work in the average home and the systemic pastor will equip families by explaining and expounding power in the home. Obviously some forms of power are more health giving than others. For example, Christians are not urged to use coercion power in the home. Fathers are urged not to exasperate their children (Eph. 6:4). Children are frustrated when parents coerce them into behavior patterns without explaining why they are appropriate or necessary. Husbands especially are exhorted to live considerately with their wives (1 Peter 3:7) because they are joint-heirs in life. But this raises the practical question of how power is managed in the Christian home, a question an equipping pastor cannot afford to ignore.

Jack and Judith Balswick have summarized the four basic approaches to the management of power in the family under the headings traditional patriarchal, democratic exchange, hedonistic self-interest, and empowerment.[22] As Ted Blenkorne's research shows, this last approach conforms most closely to the teaching of the New Testament.

> The term *empowerment* was coined by Julian Rappaport to express his conviction that social welfare and social workers should be guiding needy individuals and families to discover and use their own resources rather than become dependent upon governmental agencies.[23] *Empowerment* refers to action taken by those with power not merely on behalf of the less powerful, which often sets up a debilitating dependency, but treatment that gives power to the powerless.[24]

As the Balswicks' text shows, empowerment reflects several priorities instituted by Jesus Christ.

Many people, especially leaders and parents, fear that if they give power to others they will find themselves powerless. But the fear is founded on the mistaken assumption that power is a limited resource.[25] By way of contrast, the Bible says that power is available to all human beings. God has so arranged relationships that in everything we receive by giving. As the Balswicks observe ". . . increasing another person's power will not decrease one's own, but will instead multiply one's potential for further empowering."[26] Seen from this perspective, empowerment satisfies one of the fundamental principles of systemic thought. Because each element functions in an interdependent manner, each will benefit if each serves the whole. It also satisfies the requirements inherent in Paul's metaphor of the body in 1 Corinthians 12.

Applied to the church-and-family relationship, the equipping church consults families as families when decisions are being made that affect families, especially when one of the members is being asked to accept a major church assignment. This gives families *positional power* by prizing the legitimate place families have in the family of families. Churches that teach families in Sunday school classes or intergenerational small groups in homes are giving families *knowledge power*. Perhaps the enormous effort devoted over the years to maintaining the Sunday school would have been better spent empowering parents and children. Praying for families that undertake projects in their own neighborhoods gives families *referent power*. Other families can identify with them. By occasionally allowing families to lead services or to present something to a church meeting, the empowering church gives families *information power*—the power to persuade others. By praising and affirming a family that undertakes a project of receiving a refugee family in its home for short-term emergency housing, the church is giving the family *reward power*. Such positive reinforcement puts the family in the local church on the same level of significance as the family in third-world mission service.

Coercion power seems an inappropriate and counterproductive avenue for a church to express power in relationship to families. Indeed it seems to undermine all the other strategies of empowerment. Yet unconsciously we may be using a form of coercion in socializing families in a family-fragmenting church by maintaining structures designed exclusively for individual members rather than family subsystems.

The Restorative-Reparative Subsystem

Now we turn to two functional subsystems: the restorative- reparative subsystem and the lay leadership subsystem.

Sunday is the hardest and most exhausting day of the week for pastors, *and for many laypeople.* The more involved one is in church leadership and service in the world, the more necessary it is to find rest, restoration, and true sabbath. Not only do the members need it; the church as a whole needs it. The restorative-reparative subsystem is possibly the most neglected subsystem in the average North American church. Why? Because the church has been captured by the drivenness of our work-life and, simultaneously, our society's view of rest. Our society offers work and leisure. The Bible proposes work (or service) and sabbath. While leisure and sabbath overlap, they are not the same thing.[27]

Leisure and Pseudosabbath

Leisure and sabbath have much in common: They are both personally
restorative, enjoyable, nonutilitarian, and playful. Though sabbath and
leisure delightfully overlap, there are discernible differences. Leisure is
a matter of personal choice; sabbath is divinely mandated (Exod. 20:8-11).
Leisure is usually perceived as avocational—something we do alongside
our vocation; sabbath is vocational—part of the response of our entire
person to the call of God. Leisure is usually directed to self, while sabbath, which is also personally satisfying, is directed ultimately to the
pleasure of God. Both are aesthetic, but leisure tends toward hedonism
while sabbath invites contemplation. Sometimes we must admit that
leisure is more of a diversion from sabbath than an experience of it.

Reinventing Sabbath

In the deepest sense, we do not keep sabbath; the sabbath keeps us.
Sabbath was intended to be the leisured but intentional experience of
reflection on the source and goals of our life on earth. It keeps us turned
Godward and heaven-bound. The equipping pastor is concerned that
members of the church find a pattern of rest and sabbath that is restorative for them. Daily times of meditation, Bible study, and prayer are
part of this. So are personal guided retreats. But the systems pastor is
also concerned that the system finds rest and restoration. This happens
when the leadership of the church cultivates two dimensions of sabbath:
worship and play.

Worship is the most important thing we do in the gathered life of the
church. If sabbath means being liberated from the tyranny of productiv-
ity and performance to rediscover our identities through love, then worship is crucial to experiencing sabbath. Worship is deeply restorative.
Ironically, we experience restoration through worship when we do not
worship for what we get out of it. That would bring our utilitarian work
ethic into worship. Praise "works" precisely because it lifts us above our
compulsion to make everything useful. It is mere enjoyment of God,
nothing more, nothing less. The Latin American liberation theologian
Gustavo Gutierrez could hardly be charged with erring on the side of
contemplation. Yet he writes about the need for prayer in this way,

"Prayer is an experience of gratuity. This 'pointless' act, this 'squandered' time, reminds us that the Lord is beyond being categorized as useful or useless."[28] Sabbath seems to be a waste of time. In reality it is a way of experiencing the redemption of time.

The Playful Church

One other restorative-reparative dimension to be considered by the systems pastor is the role of play. It is commonly said that the church (or the family) that prays together will stay together. It is equally true, in our opinion, that the church that plays together will stay together. Play is not merely "the pause that refreshes"; Robert Johnston calls this the "Protestant viewpoint."[29] Play is good for its own sake. For adults, play and work have been tragically separated, whereas for children they are one experience. Children, according to Robert Johnston, have "un-adulterated" play![30]

Our use of language is significant. Athletes play their sports. Musicians play their instruments. They do not work at them. Why not play at ministry? God "played" when God made the world. Wisdom, which was from eternity before the world began (Prov. 8:23), played in the Father's presence when the world was created:

> Then I was the craftsman at his side.
> I was filled with delight day after day,
> rejoicing always in his presence,
> rejoicing in his whole world
> and delighting in mankind (Prov. 8:30-31).

As a feminine concept in the Bible, wisdom—*sophia*—deeply enriches our understanding and experience of God.

What would happen if every pastor regarded play as important as work? What if every pastor considered getting the people of the church to play as being part of her equipping task? At West Point Grey Baptist Church, the annual picnic was one of the highlights of the year. Many people invested dozens of hours inventing new games and creating a playful experience for everyone, from the youngest to the oldest. Over the years what had started as a "Sunday school" picnic had evolved into one great day of play. In one sense all those hours of preparation accomplished nothing. It was a "useless" day. In a broader sense it accomplished something vitally important. Pressured business executives, weary homemakers, and stressed professionals joined together in one great and glorious act of mutual enjoyment as the people of God. More was accomplished than by many committee meetings and perhaps than by many sermons. The soul of weary churches would be restored if this subsystem were nurtured.

The Lay Leadership Subsystem

Weary pastors, exhausted with the solo ministry syndrome, could be restored by cultivating the lay leadership subsystem.

Our thoughts about nurturing the lay leadership subsystem are equally valid in all three standard patterns of church polity: congregational, episcopal, and presbyterian. Each claims to find its structure in the New Testament. But no single church polity embodies the full New Testament view of leadership that includes the presbytery, episcopal overseers, deacons, pastor- teachers, elders, bishops (Acts 14:23; Titus 1:5), and even more. There is a rich diversity of leadership words in the New Testament. In Romans 12:8 the word for leadership is *proistemi* (the one who goes before); in 1 Corinthians 12:28, *kuberneseis* (those who lead and guide); in Philippians 1:1, *episcopoi* (overseers or bishops—also 1 Tim. 3:1 and Acts 20:17); in 1 Timothy 3:8, *diakonos* (minister, server, or deacon); in Titus 1:5, *presbuterous* (elders, council of elders, presbytery); in Ephesians 4:11, *poimenas* (pastors or shepherds).

Full Partnership with Lay Leaders

Leadership is a gift given by God to the church and not merely to the pastor. We are advocating full partnership in leadership between pastor and lay leadership, not merely a team of professional staff. In our experience this works best when the pastor functions within an eldership, board, vestry, session, or council composed of the pastor and lay leaders. Within that eldership the pastor will have to negotiate his or her role. It could range from being a secretary and implementer of the consensus (generally not a satisfactory role) to being a member of the team with more time and "the big view" (some personalities thrive on this) to being a leader among leaders (functioning as the primary influencer and equipper of fellow-leaders). But, in our opinion, the spirit of plural leadership is destroyed when the pastor puts him- or herself in the center of the group as the leader among advisers, the visionary goal-setter, and the solo helmsperson. To nurture this subsystem, a pastor-equipper must take lay leaders seriously and allow them to lead! As we have seen already, equipping is not delegating the pastor's ministry and leadership. Equipping involves releasing the ministry and leadership of the people.

There are practical reasons to commend this model.

It is sensible.[31] It leads to decisions that are more thoughtful, prayerful, and round. It discourages snap decisions or decisions based on insufficient counsel. As Proverbs 11:14 says, there is wisdom in a multitude of counselors.

It is spiritually sound. God works through the body and the leadership needs to be an experiential microcosm of the whole church. God may give vision to one person, but that vision needs to be tested, checked, complemented, and corrected by others.

It is strategic. The growth of the church will be strangled if the load of leadership is not shared.

Cultivating Lay Leaders

So the pastors who invest in cultivating and supporting lay leaders, who share the process of decision making with peers, who groom younger leaders, as Paul equipped Timothy, are doing the church a favor. They are also doing themselves a favor. They are liberating themselves from a job description that is humanly impossible.

A pioneer in the field of equipping, Elton Trueblood once said, "Lay persons are not assistants to the pastor, to help him do his work. Rather, the pastor is to be their assistant; he is to help equip them for the ministry to which God has called them." Trueblood wisely notes, "The difference is as revolutionary as it is total. Half measures are worse than nothing. Our hope lies in making big plans, in undertaking to produce a radical change, in aiming high."[32]

Developing lay leadership requires changes for the pastor in priorities,

ministry goals, and time allocation. It also requires adjustments in the
system as a whole. We have learned from systems theory that a person's
ministry and leadership emerge from within the system and are related to
his or her position in the system. They are also evoked by others who
recognize giftedness and see that people are positioned in the system
appropriately. Sometimes this means functioning in an informal but
highly influential position. For example, during a church retreat on
giftedness, we made a surprising discovery about one of the members of
my (Stevens) home church. At the time this man was the CEO of a
significant Christian institution. But everything we had learned about
him through his service within the local church and the inventories we
were using suggested that his leadership was expressed not primarily in
management and administration but in exercising wisdom in group processes. We concluded that the best way to release his ministry was to put
him on lots of committees (where he could exercise his gift of wisdom),
but *never as chairperson.*

As we said previously, many pastors are afraid to empower others
in leadership—as though leadership were a limited commodity. Just the
reverse; pastors who equip other leaders will be deepening their own
leadership. Their leadership will be based on an authentic spirituality
and not just on having a position or title. Such a ministry does not fear to
be associated with strong peers (whether lay or professional). One need
not fear to lose what one has only in God anyway. He is no fool who
gives away what cannot be kept for himself to receive what can only
come by giving. By liberating the laity, pastors liberate themselves. By
liberating pastors to equip all the saints, laypeople liberate themselves
into ministry and mission. What a gracious circle this is!

* * * * *

We have considered three examples of shepherding subsystems: the
family, the reparative-restorative subsystem, and the lay leadership subsystem. What is the job of a pastor-equipper? Davida Foy Crabtree expresses it well:

My job as ordained leader is not to do the equipping of the individuals (though in some cases I must) but to build up the community in

such a way that the community empowers itself by its living as the Body of Christ, by its explicit acts of training and teaching.[33]

Does this mean that the shepherd no longer cares for individual sheep? Not so. She cares so much that she must see individual members *in context.* Love demands no less.

CHAPTER VI

Discerning the Body

Sir, you wish to serve God and go to heaven? Remember that you
cannot serve him alone. You must therefore find companions or
make them; the Bible knows nothing of solitary religion.
                                        "Serious Man" to John Wesley[1]

The local church is organized in contradiction to its theological
purpose . . . . Harsh as it may sound, I would rather we lost people
than we lose the faith.
                                        Davida Foy Crabtree[2]

A hard-to-convince person at a point similar to the one we are reaching
in this book asked, "I can see it works in practice, but does it work in
theory?" It is a good question. Systems theory works. But now we must
ask whether is it true.

Until now we have been relying mainly on insights from the physical and human sciences to help us understand the process of joining a
church, leading the process, matching our leadership styles, and caring
for the subsystems. But it is important to ask whether there is biblical
warrant for a systems approach to pastoral leadership. In the last chapter
we considered the truth of the church as the family of God. In this chapter we will consider two more themes of biblical theology—the covenant
and the body of Christ—and compare them with the systems approach
we have been exploring. Our intent is to integrate truth in three realms:
science (general systems theory), psychology (family systems theory),

and biblical theology (the theology of the body of Christ, the family of God, and covenant). You may need to read this chapter a little more slowly. It is theological, but sound theology is the most practical and upbuilding thing on earth.

The Covenant People

The idea of covenant is central to biblical anthropology,[3] a biblical theology of the family,[4] and a theology of the people of God. A covenant is a binding personal agreement to belong together made between two parties. In the Old Testament Yahweh bound himself to his people. Even the land is taken up into this covenant as the prophet foresees the day when "[Israel's] land will be married" (Isa. 62:4), a stunning thought that finds its fulfilment in the new heaven *and the new earth* (Rev. 21:1). Similarly, in the New Testament Jesus makes a covenant with his bride, the church, "for better, for worse."

Covenant and Contract

The rich meaning of *covenant* in the Bible has often been eroded by defining it in contractual terms. A contract states an agreement in which two parties undertake to exchange goods or services on terms acceptable to both. Tragically, some people view their relationship with God contractually as an exchange of goods and services; God gives salvation in exchange for a lifetime of sacrificial service. This makes hired hands out of the people of God, and such contractual thinking was almost the undoing of the prodigal coming home from the far country (Luke 15:19). If either party breaks the contract, the other is released from obligation.

A covenant is not a performance contract that can be broken for noncompliance. The indicative of relationship *precedes* the imperative of performance. This is implied in the oft-repeated covenant formula: "I am your God; you are my people" (Exod. 19:5-8; Jer. 30:22, 31:33; Exek. 34:30-31). It is a statement of profound unity and irrevocable belonging. It starts with the initiative of God, but it evokes our full response. While God's covenant with God's people began as a *unilateral* covenant (Gen. 6:18; 17:2-8)—Noah and Abraham were given no

choice in the matter—it grew to become *bilateral*. Response and participation were expected, desired, and eventually were given as the people
say, "You are our God."

Unconditional Covenant

In the biblical covenant-community (Israel/church), the blessings of the
covenant are conditional upon obedience to the obligations of the covenant (the Law), but *the covenant itself is unconditional*. Although God
did not make the continuation of God's love conditional on the obedience of God's people to the obligations of the covenant, especially those
contained in the ten commandments, the blessings of the covenant were
conditional on obedience. Failure to keep the law—the lifestyle of the
covenant people—would bring curses, but not divorce (Hosea 2:19; 3:1;
11:8). In Exodus 19:4-5 it appears that being God's people is conditional
on keeping the law and worshipping God, that the covenant is a vicious
circle: God chooses me, but to be really God's I must perform my obligations. But, as Gordon Wenham so carefully shows in *Law, Morality,
and the Bible*, what looks like a vicious circle is really a gracious circle.
It brings the covenant partner to a fuller appreciation of the benefits of
her election and salvation. Wenham puts it this way: "Law both presup-
poses and is a means of grace."[5] That is how we are to understand the
blessings and the curses that go with the Law (Deut. 27:9-29:9). This
process can be shown graphically by the following diagram.

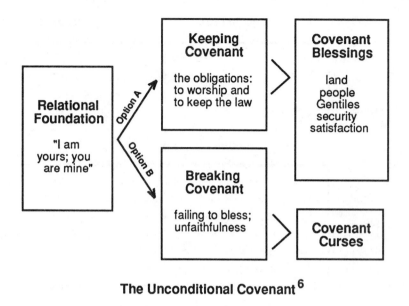

The Unconditional Covenant [6]

Figure 9

The Family Covenant

In a superb article on the theology of family life, Jack and Judy Balswick develop the covenant foundation of family life. They draw together several strands of analogy between God's covenant with God's people and the parent-child covenantal community. It starts with the parents making an unconditional commitment to love their children. This unilateral covenant is made before the children can reciprocate. As the child matures the parents struggle to love unconditionally. The Balswicks say,

> God's ideal for parent/child relationships is for the relationship which began as an initial (unilateral) covenant to develop into a mature (bilateral) relationship. The true reciprocity occurs when the parents themselves age and become socially, emotionally, and physically more dependent on their adult children. [7]

The Balswicks use the following drawing to show the various options people are exploring today including the "modern open" in which two people stay together as long as their mutual needs are being met.

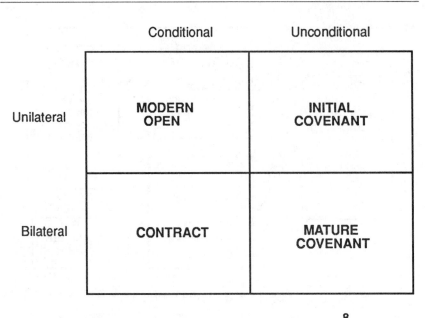

Types of Commitment in Family Relationships [8]

Figure 10

The implications of covenant for human marriage are significant. Our society enculturates us to think contractually about marriage as an exchange of services that if not continued can lead to the discontinuation of the contract. People recite the unconditional vows "for better, for worse" in church weddings, but they have an emotional loophole in their hearts. As I mention in *Married for Good*, a most dangerous trend today is that people are entering marriage with the thought that they can leave it. James Framo, observing the situation, says, "I have concluded that marriages that end in divorce are not greatly different from other marriages." [9] One significant difference between those who persist and those who do not is the covenant foundation. Of the two crucial dimensions by which we measure marriage health—stability and quality—the one most conspicuously missing today is stability.

The Covenant People and System

The marriage covenant is a profound illustration of God's covenant with Israel and Christ's covenant with his bride, the church. It also shows the deep correspondence in reality between the people of God and the ways systems operate. We will explore four dimensions of this.

First, the whole is more than the sum of the parts in both systems and covenant thinking. This is obviously the case in marriage. While one plus one normally equals two, in marriage, one plus one equals one (Gen. 2:24; Matt. 19:6) since "one flesh" points to the creation of a marital unit or system. The phrase *one flesh* points to much more than physical union through sexual intercourse. They are now kin. They are not simply two individuals who happen to live together, but a new social unity in which the unity is enriched by the diversity. Then again, marriage mathematics suggests that one plus one equals three: the husband, the wife, and the marital system. Where marriage is concerned, the Bible teaches us that the whole is greater than the sum of the parts.

Second, irrevocable belonging is experienced both in systems and covenant thinking. Remarkably, secular systems theorists use unconditional covenant thinking, without saying so, when they describe the effect of marriage break-up on the family system. As Galvin and Brommel argue:

> Divorce and death do not dissolve family systems; rather they alter them. These altered systems may become involved in a second marriage, necessitating the interweaving of three or more families into a remarried family system. The organizational complexity of such systems is often staggering as the systems and subsystems interweave to form a new whole.[10]

There are important differences between families and organizations that must be considered when applying systems theory to the church.[11] The church of Christ is both organism and organization. Members are free to leave one local church to join another while families can never ultimately annul the lifelong ties that bind them together. Nevertheless, a major component of Christian growth involves learning to love and relate to brothers and sisters in Christ *who were not personally chosen;* the church is a covenant community, not merely a collection of like-minded chosen friends. One is willy-nilly bound to others, and change in one brings change to another. Yet in the church we experience the great freedom of knowing we will never be divorced by Christ. And if other members try to divorce us, they can only alter the system.

Third, in both systems and covenant thinking, unity is enriched by diversity. The "two become one" (or two or three!) principle of the marriage covenant also helps us understand the systemic unity of the people of God. As a covenant people the church incorporates both Jews and Gentiles into a new humanity that is interracial, international, and cross-cultural (Eph. 2:11- 22).

Nothing thrilled Paul more than the mystery of God's dealings with Jews and Gentiles in Christ (Rom. 11:33-36) creating a new humanity that was more than the sum of the parts. Jews in Christ did not become Gentiles, and Gentiles did not become Jews. They were not merged, as some spouses are merged in sick, codependent relationships where they lose their identities in a marriage. Rather, Jews and Gentiles are incorporated into a transcendent unity in which each group is for the other and therefore more truly oneself. Paul gave himself to building this unity as a life-work and anticipated through this "systemic" leadership entering into "the full measure of the blessing of Christ" (Rom. 15:29). Similarly, pastors of covenant communities do not strive for mergers or dull uniformity, but for the rich unity within diversity that can be attained (Eph. 4:11-16) in Christ through leadership that equips the saints. Once more, systemic thinking is congruent with Scripture.

Finally, both systems and covenant thinking presuppose that health and growth come from members relating interdependently. In the church, growth takes place "as each part does its work" (Eph. 4:16) in the context of upbuilding the body in love. It is not only unkind but untrue (and unsystemic) for one Christian to say to another, "I don't need you!" (1 Cor. 12:21).

But this rich correspondence in reality between systems thinking and biblical theology becomes deeper when one considers the biblical witness about the body of Christ.

The Body of Christ

We will take one more look at the fundamental principle of systems theory—that *the whole is more than the sum of the parts*. In family systems theory as developed by Murray Bowen, the family is regarded as an emotional and relational entity.[12] The difference with general systems theory is significant. "Systems" describes what happens in relationships, but the "emotional system" accounts for what happens, what drives the process.[13]

People in families have less emotional autonomy than is commonly thought. There is reciprocal interacting, borrowing or lending strength from one another with cycles of distance and closeness. In describing the family as an emotional system, Kerr and Bowen show how members of a family operate reciprocally.

> A younger child shapes the behavior of an older sibling as much as the older one shapes the behavior of the younger one. An "over-functioning" person shapes the attitudes, feelings, and behavior of an "underfunctioning" person as much as the underfunctioning one shapes the attitudes, feelings, and behavior of the overfunctioning one.[14]

Kerr notes that the overfunctioning one may not feel this situation as a burden; in other words, the overfunctioning person *wants* it this way![15] As we mentioned earlier, Edwin Friedman uses this principle to ask hard questions about the clergyperson who is burning out trying to keep the church going.

The Body, Not the Bouquet

In the church there is a similar unifying reality by which every part finds its identity and is regulated in its functions. The church is a corporate *whole* that finds its life in the Head, Christ; it is not merely a bouquet of believers in social relationships with one another. Biblically, we must speak of the church as the body *of Christ* and not merely a body of Christians. "Thus," as L. S. Thornton says, "each partakes of a whole to which each contributes, and without which each would be poorer."[16]

While "the body" was first mentioned by Jesus himself in the gospels (John 2:21),[17] this concept finds its full theological development in the letters of Paul (Eph. 1:23; 2:16; 3:6; 4:4, 12, 16; 5:23, 28, 30). These are the primary texts that speak of the church as the body of Christ:

> The body is a unit, though it is made up of many parts; and though all its parts are many, they form one body. So it is with Christ (1 Cor. 12:12).

> Just as each of us has one body with many members, and these members do not all have the same function, so in Christ we who are many form one body, and each member belongs to all the others (Rom. 12:4-5).

> Because there is one loaf, we, who are many, are one body, for we all partake of the one loaf (1 Cor. 10:17).

> There is one body . . . (Eph. 4:4).

> From him [Christ] the whole body, joined together and held together by every supporting ligament, grows and builds itself up in love, as each part does its work (Eph. 4:16).

> He [Christ] is the head of the body, the church (Col. 1:18).

It is highly probable that Paul's experience of fellowship—especially the miraculous fellowship of Jews and Gentiles in Christ—and his own conversion experience formed the existential basis for his doctrine. Prior to being met by Christ, Paul had been persecuting individual Christians. But when confronted with the resurrected Christ, Paul heard Christ say, "Saul, Saul, why do you persecute *me*?" (Acts 9:4). Thus Paul must have encountered and *experienced* the identity and social intercourse of Jesus with his people. We agree with Ernest Best's verdict of "not proven" to the idea that Paul got the "body" metaphor from contemporary Greek thoughts of the body and its members (sometimes used to describe the state) or from contemporary Jewish parallels.[18] He got it from his experience of Jesus. Ernst Percy, a New Testament scholar, is surely correct in noting that "Pauline Ecclesiology is fundamentally nothing other than a Christology."[19] It is an organic systemic unity that finds its life in the Head, Jesus.

Ernest Best and J. A. T. Robinson have done some superb scholarship on the idea of the body as expressed in Pauline letters. They examine contextually such phrases as *in Christ, Christ in me, Christ in us,*[20] and *the body of Christ.* These pregnant phrases demonstrate that "in Christ" believers are not only related to Christ but also to one another. Further, who they are is more than the sum of all the members and the Head. Here are some of their discoveries.

The Impossibility of Being an Individual Christian

Consistent with the Old Testament, "the saints" in Paul's letters is really a unit. In the Old Testament it is not usual for an individual righteous person to be called "a saint" because Israel is the larger reality. In the New Testament "the saints" is the church, which is the body of Christ. As Ernest Best says, "it is this unit which is just as much in Christ as the individual believer."[21] Believers are held together in what can be conceived as a corporate, inclusive personality. It is biblically inconceivable for a person to be a believer in Christ and not a member of his or her community. And the body of Christ is not the local congregation but the whole church.[22]

Ernest Best aptly summarizes Paul's thoughts:

> For Paul there is no such thing as a solitary Christian; the faith that unites a man to Christ unites him also to other Christians; the Church is more than an aggregate of Christians; it is a fellowship . . . .[23]

He continues,

> It is impossible to conceive of a Christian who is not a member of the Church, which is related to Christ as in him and as his body . . . . Individual Christians consequently do not exist.[24]

This is remarkably close to the message given to John Wesley by a "serious man" as reported in the opening quotation. It was spoken to Wesley before he was converted to Christ.

For Paul the fundamental reality of the church is the organic unity
that finds expression in the diversity of its members. One cannot really
think of an individual disciple apart from that person's relatedness with
the body of Christ. The believer's identity is corporate as well as individual. In Christ we can say, "I am we!" Within the granular individualism of Western culture, the basic unit of the church is the individual
member. For Paul the basic unit of the church is the church! Systems
thinking is congruent with Paul's thought even more than the individualism of Western thinking.

Christians Are Not Christ

While Christians and Christ are united, they can and must be distinguished.[25] The unity of Christians and Christ makes the church more
than a mere human organization. As Thornton puts it, "Christ is filled
with God and the Church is filled with Christ."[26] And again, "Apart from
the Church God would be the heavenly Father without an earthly family.
His Beloved Son would still be the firstborn of the Father, but not,
'amongst many brethren.'"[27] But the church and Christ are not identical.[28] Christ is the Head. No member of the body (including the pastor-
teacher) can be the Head. To express the complex relationship of unity
and differentiation between Christ and Christians Paul uses the metaphor
of *body*. In speaking of metaphor we are not relegating the body to a
"mere metaphor" since ultimate mysteries that take us beyond normal
reasoning can be expressed only metaphorically.

More "Yourself" in Christ's Body

Christians become more themselves rather than less by being joined together in Christ's body.[29] As Best says, Christians

> do not lose their personalities "in Christ"; they are still fully respon-
> sible human beings; their personalities are not fused with Christ's.
> They rejoice, stand fast, and labour in Christ but it is still "they" who
> rejoice, stand fast, and labour. Their separate existence is not dimin-
> ished in the slightest; indeed they are given duties, responsibilities,
> and relationships one to another because they are "in Christ."[30]

The multiplicity of function is not only possible, it is necessary for the body to be the body of Christ. Where would the hearing be if the whole body were mouths? The body is only properly a body when every member is part of that whole, indispensably so. Eduard Schweizer, in his extensive article on soma (body) in Kittel's theological dictionary, notes that "for Paul man can never be understood as a self-contained individual who can be considered in himself. He is always man related to God and his fellow-men, authentic only in relation to them."[31]

So the biblical theology of body, on the one hand, calls for the repudiation of independence. By their cliquish independence the Corinthians were rejecting the implications of the body. Ananias and Sapphira experienced death because they functioned independently and treated the church as a human organization they could manipulate and deceive. They did not "discern the body" (1 Cor. 11:29 RSV).[32] On the other hand, codependence or fusion with the body is also rejected. The Christian is true to him- or herself neither in independence nor in dependence, but only in the experience of interdependence. There is a deep correspondence here between systems theory and biblical theology.

More Unity because of Diversity

The body is one because of the diversity and not in spite of it. The crucial passage on this, 1 Corinthians 12:12-27, shows how the unity and diversity fit together because the members are in Christ and not merely because they are human beings who need one another. Unity in Christ is not adequately realized if some of the members think they are superior or others regard themselves as unnecessary. Every person in Christ is part of that unity, and complexity is what makes the unity rich.[33] Paul himself relates the social unity of the body to the social unity within God (Eph. 4:4-6), showing that unity is not uniformity. For the sake of administrative efficiency, many church leaders long for uniform synchronization of their members, especially in the context of awkward church meetings or governmental boards. But church unity is a mystery of pluriformity or multiformity.[34]

A mystery takes us beyond normal human categories of thought to explore incomprehensible fact, transcendent truth, and realities that will be appreciated more through worship than simple cognition. The mystery of sexuality (Gen. 1:27),[35] the mystery of Christ and the church (Eph. 5:32), and the mystery of Jew and Gentile in a new humanity (Eph. 3:10; 2:11-22) are three mysteries that point us Godward to the transcendent unity within God (Eph. 4:4-6). This unity is a social complex. Father, Son, and Holy Spirit are diverse but gloriously one. Social Trinitarianism proclaims a unity in God deeper than the abstract unity of Islam or Unitarianism. Perhaps the ultimate irony in the history of religions is that, far from proclaiming tritheism, the Christian church humbly confesses the deepest truth of the Muslim creed: One God. And we do this by insisting that we have come to know God as Father, Son, and Holy Spirit. That is the mystery of the Holy Trinity and the focus of our social experience of Christ.

Dr. J. I. Packer's definition of *Trinitarianism* in *The New Dictionary of Theology* is succinct and helpful:

> Within the complex unity of his being, three personal centres of rational awareness eternally coinhere, interpenetrate, relate in mutual love, and cooperate in all divine actions. God is not only *he* but also *they*—Father, Son and Spirit, coequal and coeternal in power and glory though functioning in a set pattern whereby the Son obeys the Father and the Spirit subserves both. All statements about God in general or about the Father, the Son or the Holy Spirit in particular, should be "cashed" in the Trinitarian terms, if something of their meaning is not to be lost.[36]

The Orthodox church has probably best understood the awesome beauty of this. While the Western church, starting with Augustine, began with the philosophical notion of the unity of the Godhead and then attempted to explain the differences of the persons, the Eastern church started with the apostolic witness and the church's experience of three divine persons and then explored, as an act of worship, the marvelous unity within the Godhead. In Orthodox spirituality "the divine Trinity is the fundamental mystery of the Christian faith." The Orthodox theologian Tomas Spidlik notes that "only the Christian revelation teaches the highest and most intense union as embracing that which in the finite realm divides and is a principle of division: the personality."[37] In other words, God is more one because God is three.[38] The body of Christ is more one because it is composed of many members. An axiom of the spiritual life is that we become like the God we worship (Ps. 115:8). Idol worshippers become fixed and inexpressive like their gods. Trinity worshippers become celebrators of community and cohumanity. More to the point of this book, Trinity worshippers find their spiritual life in the body of Christ.

The Body Is a System for Being

Finally, the metaphor of the body looks primarily inward rather than outward. In Pauline thought, Christ does not use his body to get his work done on earth, as attractive as this idea might be. The metaphor is inward- rather than outward-looking. It is concerned with the structure and interrelationships within the church rather than how the church relates to the world.[39] In Paul's developed thinking on the subject in Ephesians, the members are called to edify one another by speaking the truth in love, each part contributing to the growth (4:16).

The body does serve God in the world. This truth is contained in Ephesians 1:22-23, 3:10, and 4:10 where the reconciliation of Jew and Gentile in Christ, the preaching of God's wisdom to all the "powers," and the "filling of the universe" with Christ are cosmic ministries of the body.[40] The body is a working model and a visual demonstration of the supremacy of Christ over all social, political, cultural, and spiritual contexts. In addition there are other metaphors, such as the royal priesthood, that more directly express the mission of the church in the world. But the primary emphasis of the body metaphor is inward. This is an important corrective for activist Christianity. Realizing unity is doing God's work. God is as concerned about being as God is with doing.

In a human marriage we express in vows the act of taking someone "to be my wedded wife," not to do domestic service. God's covenant with us is a covenant of being, not primarily a contract for doing. God invites us to be his people, not merely to share his enterprise on earth. Mansell Pattison says, "Church people have all but lost sight of the church as the social system for being."[41] The church takes its structure and its life from her Lord.[42] Father, Son, and Holy Spirit dwell together in a covenant of mutual othering, mutual glorying, and mutual love (John 17:3; 21; 24; 26).

"God is love" (1 John 4:8) is not a statement about one of the attributes of God. It is a sacred window on the interior social relationship within God. And we boldly affirm that the church exists, not as a tool to get God's work on earth done, but *for love*. Would that the world could say, "The church is love!" (see John 17:23).

Interdependence and the Body

Speaking to body-life in the local church, Paul said, "The eye cannot say to the hand, 'I don't need you!' " (1 Cor. 12:21); "If one part suffers, every part suffers with it; if one part is honored, every part rejoices with it" (12:26); and "Each member belongs to all the others" (Rom. 12:5). This means that each member has his or her part to play and each member is interdependently related to the other. As Best says, "If one member fails to exercise his gift, that hinders both the growth of the whole and the individual growth of each member (no member can grow apart from the whole)."[43]

Further—and this is the deepest mystery of all—Christ has made himself interdependently related to his own body. We humbly confess the limits of our understanding of how Christ influences and is influenced by the body. It is apparent that he influences the body both directly and indirectly through members who are joined to him (he in them and they in him). But he also influences the body in the way he has ordered and formed the body as a system. "God," Paul says, "has *combined* the members of the body" (1 Cor. 12:24). "The same God *works* all of them [differing gifts, services, and workings] in all men" (1 Cor. 12:6). "All of these [manifestations of the Spirit] are the *work* of one and the same Spirit, and he *gives* them to each" (1 Cor. 12:11). Systems thinking puts the emphasis on the *structure* of the system—how it is put together. Similarly, biblical theology emphasizes the divine structure of the body of Christ.

Chapter Summary

In considering both systems thinking and biblical theology, we have discovered a profound isomorphic correspondence in reality. In psychological and sociological terms, systems principles such as wholism, synergy, differentiation and fusion, and interdependence express at least some of the mystery of the family of God, the covenant community, and the body of Christ. In the epilogue of this book we will consider whether the presuppositions of systems theory warrant such a wholehearted endorsement. But for now we will affirm that, better than any other way of thinking about the church, systems thinking gives the equipping pastor a new and profoundly helpful church-view.

One fascinating line of inquiry was suggested by the pioneer in family systems, Murray Bowen, in the famous expose of his own struggle to bring health to his family of origin, an expose he presented to a conference of psychiatric professionals and subsequently published anonymously. He remarked that:

> The laws that govern man's emotional function are as orderly as those that govern other natural systems, and our difficulty in understanding the system is not so much the complexity of the system as in man's denial of the system.[44]

Research in family systems and church systems can be an attempt to sit down humbly as a child before creation, to understand and not to "overstand" arrogantly, with the purpose of discovering the way God made things work. It is then not only an acceptable practice, but it can also be an act of worship. Robert Capon insightfully says that the task of theology is to hold the world up for oohs and ahhs, not primarily to solve problems.[45]

Paul's letter to the Ephesians, perhaps more than his other letters, shows that all human relationships are significant of higher mysteries.[46] Every family is founded upon the fatherhood of God (3:14-15), and all family relationships are "in the Lord" (5:21ff; 6:1). Marriage is a metaphor of the mystery of Christ and the church (5:32). These human social realities are like a two-way lens through which both the divine and the human aspects of God's people may be viewed. Exploring the structure and character of the congregational system directs us to truths about the mystery of God and God's people. Exploring biblical revelation becomes a lens through which we can discover more deeply the systemic life of the congregation. We will better equip the saints for the work of the ministry if we look through the lens both ways.

CHAPTER VII

Becoming a Christian Leader

Every Christian has been set apart for Christ and his ministry. The ordained minister is set in the midst of those who have been set apart.

Davida Foy Crabtree[1]

The group is the womb of the leader.

Dietrich Bonhoeffer[2]

We once asked a group of church members a probing question: If Jesus is truly leading the church as Head, why do we need human beings in positions of leadership in the congregation? The following answers were given:

Without human leaders the worst of human nature will take over and the church will self-destruct. Leaders regulate the competing self-interest of members of the church. [This is the fallen human nature argument.]

Every human society needs an administrator. Things don't just happen. Somebody has to make the connections. [This is the pragmatic argument.]

Good leadership keeps bad leadership suppressed! If no one exercises authority on behalf of a group, someone who should not, will. [This is the argument from fear.]

Efficiency dictates that the buck must stop somewhere. If everyone
is responsible, no one is. [This is the expediency argument.]

Strong leadership produces growth. Every large growing church has
a strong leader. [This is the empirical argument.]

We need someone to represent God to us and us to God. [Richard
Foster describes this as the Old Testament priesthood argument:
"the desperate scramble to have a king, a mediator, a priest, a go-
between,"[3] rather than going directly to God for themselves, see
Exodus 20:19.]

Remarkably, no one mentioned that leadership is a gracious gift of
God to the church expressed usually in more than one member. We have
already explored the situational dimension of leadership in the formula.
Leadership equals the function of the leader, the followers, and the situation. Here we build on that definition to state that the purpose of this
gift in the congregation is to release ministry *in others. Christian leadership is the God-given ability to influence others so that believers will
trust and respond to the Head of the church for themselves, in order to
accomplish the Lord's purposes for God's people in the world.*
Several things are noteworthy about this definition. The concern is
more for *leadership* than leaders. In other words, we should work toward
the widest possible release of leadership rather than the equipment of a
few official leaders in positions of influence. The Bible is more concerned that the congregation have leadership than leaders.[4] Further,
leadership as defined in secular terms is marked by mere influence. In
contrast, the litmus test of Christian leadership is not whether the leaders
have followers, but whether the Lord is getting followers. Finally, the
goal of leadership should conform to the goal of the church: mission in
the world not ecclesiastical self-enrichment.
In this chapter we attempt a theology and spirituality of systemic
leadership. It is our conviction that the ministry of leadership emerges *in*
the systemic life of a congregation. As Bonhoeffer says, "The group is
the womb of the leader." But a matching synergy proves to be equally
important. The task and purpose of Christian leadership is to build a community of love and justice for the purposes of the kingdom of God. The
gift emerges in the context of the system; the gift serves the system by
enriching its corporate life. Christian leaders enrich the congregation by:

– representing God's interests,
– meeting needs,
– incarnating authentic spiritual authority,
– building community, and
– bringing justice.

But the systemic nature of Christian leadership has another dimension. The gift of leadership emerges in the context of the people's relationship with God. The group by itself is not the womb of the leader; it is the group in dynamic relationship with the Lord that evokes leadership. So leadership is not merely something done *for* God as an activity undertaken on behalf of an absent monarch; it is something done in God in the context of relationship with a present Lord. This leads to an important distinction.

Representing God's Interests—The *Shaliach*

Simply put, Christian leaders serve God and God's interests in the world first. Only secondarily do they serve people. The order is profoundly important. For a Christian leader, the need is not the call. The call originates in the initiative of God,[5] not the cry of humanity.[6] If it originated in the needs of people, the leader could easily be overwhelmed by needs that he or she cannot meet, and the leader would have no criterion for making the selection. Often such leaders exhaust themselves or become messianic. Some people, thinking they are servant-leaders, are actually functioning as doormats, thinking they are doing God's will by doing everyone else's will. In contrast, the Christian servant-leader is first of all a servant of God.

The Songs of the Servant

This profound insight is found in the Old Testament in the four servant songs of the prophet Isaiah that culminate in the well-known passion song of Isaiah 53. Each of the songs underscores the principle of being the Lord's servant and not merely the people's servant. And because the servant is dedicated to the Lord's interests, the deepest needs of the people will eventually be served. These songs have been compared to an hourglass, or two triangles, with the broadest part at the top (as represented in the first and second songs) involving the whole people of Israel as the servant. But as we progress through the songs, it is apparent that the whole people are not capable of serving in this way. There is a remnant of faithful people within the people of God, but even they cannot fully and finally represent God's interests in the world.

One solitary individual is envisioned as a servant, a person who can represent the service God's people should render to God, and the service God wishes to render to God's own people. George Adam Smith, the Old Testament scholar who first suggested this image, finds the Christ-Messiah at the narrowing of the hourglass in the passion song (Isa. 53) since he fulfills all that God meant for Israel, his servant, and is therefore rightly called the servant by the apostles (Acts 3:13).

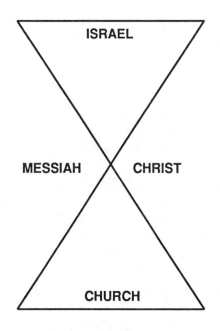

The Servant Community

Figure 11

Then, in Christ, all the people of God—both Jews and Gentiles—enter into the service of the Messiah (John 13:15) and so serve God, one another, and the hurting, needy world. Each song brings us nearer to this glorious crescendo.

The first song (Isa. 42:1-4) contains the servant's call. His service originates in the initiative of God: "Here is my servant, whom I uphold . . . I will put my Spirit on him" (42:1). The second song (49:1-7) is the servant's *vindication*. He finds his justification in God, not success in meeting people's needs:

> He said to me, "You are my servant,
>   Israel, in whom I will display my splendor."
> But I said, "I have labored to no purpose;
>   I have spent my strength in vain and for nothing.
> Yet what is due me is in the Lord's hand,
>   and my reward is with my God" (49:3-4).

In the third song (50:4-9) the servant goes through his *Gethsemane* of rejection by the people he came to serve but, he says,

> Because the Sovereign Lord helps me,
>   I will not be disgraced . . . .
> He who vindicates me is near.
>   Who then will bring charges against me? (50:7-8).

Finally, in the famous passion song (52:13-53:12), the servant bears *the cross*, but it is the cross laid on the servant by the Lord and for the Lord's saving purposes: "The Lord has laid on him the iniquity of us all" (53:6). In the ultimate irony of faith, when God could not find a suitable servant in his own people, God became his own servant! This is the background to the pregnant saying of Jesus about himself: "The Son of Man did not come to be served, but to serve, and to give his life as a ransom for many" (Matt. 20:28).

As followers of Jesus we enter into these songs and find our calling to serve God. We have Christian leadership neither in ourselves nor in our positions and offices. It is a systemic product of our real life in God. Only then can we fulfill the goal of the servant-leader so well stated by the Association of Theological Schools: a leader should "serve God, and people, without any thought of personal acclaim and/or public recognition."[7] There are profound theological reasons for this.

Trinitarian Leadership

The few inspired windows we have on the relationship of Father, Son, and Holy Spirit give us deep insights into the nature of ministry, and, consequently, into the nature of Christian leadership. The doctrine of the Trinity is not just a piece of systematic theology reserved for the professional theologian. It is the spiritual heartbeat for both the ordinary Christian and the Christian leader. Ministry is nothing more nor less than participation in the ministry within the Godhead. We may reverently suggest that Trinitarian ministry is systemic. Each one points to the Other. Each lives for the Other. Each finds identity in the whole. Each is for the Other; all are for the One. God is more one because God is three. The mystery of this relational interpenetration—a subject the Eastern church has understood better than the Western church—is the key to the life and service of the people who find their "home" (John 14:23) in the Trinity.

Father, Son, and Spirit dwell in a continuing relational covenant of mutual ministry. Jesus spoke of the love the Father had for him even before the creation of the world (John 17:24). There was ministry before there was a world, ministry before there were God-imaging creatures, ministry before there was sin. Ministry is not merely redemptive, patching up human and creational brokenness. It is also creative and unitive. The mystery of the Christian experience is that we are invited to participate in the life of God. As John said, "Our fellowship is with the Father and with his Son" (1 John 1:3). We are in him and he is in us—"just as you are in me and I am in you. May they also be in us" (John 17:21). The nature of the Christian experience is I-Thou-we—the mutual loving dialogue of people and God and of members with one another. The gift of leadership that arises from this splendid though mysterious fellowship is first of all directed, as was the leadership Jesus exercised on earth, to the pleasure of God rather than the approval of people. The Old Testament concept of *shaliach*[8] illuminates this.

The *Shaliach*

The *shaliach* was the "no-name" person who carried forward the stipulations of the suzerainty treaties with the vassal king on behalf of the "great king," the suzerain. In himself, the *shaliach* had no meaning. He often did not even have a name. His meaning was discovered in terms of the one who sent him on missions. His authority was not in himself, but in the one who sent him. The shaliach, though a slave or an ambassador, would be received by a vassal king in the same way the vassal king would have received his lord (the one who had conquered him in battle) if the lord had come in person. If honor was due to the great king in the eyes of the vassal king, then honor would be given to the *shaliach*. If the vassal king wished to rebel against the great king, then the *shaliach*, the king's messenger, would be dishonored. Perhaps he would be beaten and tortured, his head cut off. His head might be put on a plate and sent back to the great king along with the retinue of servants who had come with the *shaliach*. If the vassal wished to show honor to the great king, then the *shaliach* would be given beautiful clothes and rings, a banquet, and coins for his personal use.

The *shaliach's* well-being depended on the vassal's view of the great king to whom he was to bow within the suzerainty. The *shaliach's* safety also would be dependent on the vassal's view of the treaty. All would depend on whether the vassal would bow to the great king and the stipulations of the great king.

So it is for those who serve as Christ's ambassadors. They may be well-received or shafted. It does not really matter. They serve God. And their service is not dependent on the acceptance by those to whom they are sent.

I (Collins) accidentally met a *shaliach* in the Toronto General Hospital where I went to visit a Polish woman with three small children. She was dying of intestinal cancer.

I asked her, "Helen, would you like me to read a passage of scripture to you and have a prayer with you?"

"No thanks," she said, "I have my own religious faith."

I turned to leave, and the elderly woman in the next bed said, "Come here."

I do not remember her name. She might not have given it to me. She said, "Young man, I am just so glad that you have come here and that you want to serve the Lord and spread the Gospel of Jesus. I want you to know that I am a member of a Pentecostal Church and that I love the Lord Jesus as my Savior, and I want to praise him every day of my life. I want to pray for you."

I said, "Could I pray for you?"

She said, "No, you are not going to pray for me today. I am going to pray for you. Get down on your knees beside the bed here, bring your head over here so I can lay my hand on your head."

I did so. Then the woman prayed for me. I still remember some of the words she said.

I went away and came back two or three weeks later. I was looking for Helen. I didn't recognize the thin emaciated woman on the bed, but yes, it was she. She quickly interrupted me and said, "I want you to read the Bible to me and to pray for me. Pray for my safe journey to heaven."

"You do?" I said.

She said, "There has been a great change in my life since you came to see me."

"Really? Tell me how."

She said, "It had nothing to do with you. It was the lady who used to be in the bed next to me. You remember the lady who asked you to get on your knees and to pray? I was quite touched by that. That lady was the most selfless person I ever knew. She was always concerned about me and my children and my husband. But what really impressed me was that she was in great pain. She would often sit up in bed and scream with pain. Then she would say, 'Praise the Lord. Halleluja. Praise Jesus.' "

"I have come to believe. If that woman, dying in the midst of severe pain, could still praise God, there must be something about her religion. So I asked her about it, and she led me to Christ. I am going to heaven today or someday soon."

That Pentecostal woman was a *shaliach*, a no-name person, an ambassador for Jesus who thought not about herself, but only of others and what her Master wanted her to do. The *shaliach* illuminates one aspect of the servant-leader—a servant of God. But the Christian leader is also a servant of the people.

Meeting Needs—The Servant-Leader

The "servant-leader" idea, popularized by Robert Greenleaf, has now
become so commonplace that few people recognize the incongruity of
these two terms when they are brought together. In normal speech,
servants do what others tell them to. Leaders give direction to others.
How can *servant* and *leader* be brought into juxtaposition? Further,
some who have tried to bring together these two ideas have emphasized
one to the exclusion of the other. Take, for example, a pastor known to
us. He sought to be a servant without leading. He was always asking his
deacons and others what he could do to serve them. But they wanted
leadership! Others in the church finally took over and the pastor was
forced to move along to another opportunity. The tragedy is that he
could have learned to lead without denying servant theology. Pastor
Andrew, our case study in chapter 4, adopted a passive leadership style
because he thought he should be a "servant-leader"; he discovered the
hard way that his theology was poorly formed and his leadership style
mismatched to the congregation.

The Leader as Servant

Notwithstanding these difficulties, we affirm that Robert Greenleaf's
thesis is incontestable from the Christian perspective: those who are
leaders must serve those they lead, and only those who serve are fit for
leadership. He writes:

> The best test, and difficult to administer is: Do those served grow
> as persons? Do they, while being served, become healthier, wiser,
> freer, more autonomous, more likely themselves to become ser-
> vants?[9]

Greenleaf makes it clear that there is no real contradiction between the
words lead and serve, other than remarking that serving is first. But that
turns out to be the heart of it.

> The servant-leader *is* servant first . . . it begins with the natural
> feeling that one wants to serve, to serve *first*. Then conscious choice

brings one to aspire to lead. That person is sharply different from one who is *leader* first, perhaps because of the need to assuage an unusual power drive or to acquire material possessions.[10]

Greenleaf shows that genuine service and leadership (influencing and taking initiative) are thoroughly compatible. To underscore that the servant-leader is not a doormat, but a visionary leader, Greenleaf makes the point that servant-leadership is characterized by vision.[11] And vision is not an esoteric quality. It is a gift that can be developed in the Christian's personality through meditation on God's Word and serious consideration of the human situation. His example is Karl Barth, who exhibited unusual perception and creative leadership at the very time that the wave of nineteenth-century German liberal theology was cresting, by studying with equal seriousness the Bible in one hand and the daily newspaper in the other. Ray Anderson says something similar:

> I do not see that the development of leadership as an aspect of managing Christian organizations can take place *without acquiring the gift of discernment with regard to the signs of God's promises* in present events.[12]

So servant-leadership starts with service. It involves vision and discernment. It is not a procedure that can be taught in a classroom or seminar setting. If it were, seminaries could turn out graduates with certified competence in leadership, but they cannot. Leadership emerges in the corporate and spiritual life of the church when people serve God and serve one another. This raises the crucial question about the importance of the leader's position.

Leading from the End of the Line

When leadership is viewed in systemic terms, the official title or place does not matter as much as the influence a person has where he or she is placed in the system. In other words, one can lead wherever one is. An intriguing expression of this was proposed by P. T. Chandapilla, a leader of the Indian Inter-Varsity Christian Fellowship. He said we can "lead from the end of the line." In contrast to those who fight for first place in the line, line up three deep to get into the pulpit and seek positions of official influence, this Eastern brother has proposed that we simply follow Jesus and serve others where we are. In this we can become profoundly influential.

> Those committed in their vocation of servanthood . . . will voluntarily go to the end of the line. They will remain there to see the line move (the line is determined by the human factor in any situation). They . . . are happy to see others get ahead of them.

Then, commenting on the advantages of servanthood, Chandapilla says, "there is great freedom and plenty of time at the end of the line . . . for meditation and for reflection."[13]

Ironically, one can have a position, but little influence, or one may have extensive influence, but no recognized position. This begs the question of authority, and it is one with which our society is deeply confused.

Incarnating Authentic Spiritual Authority

Since the mass suicide of cult followers in Jonestown, anyone who aspires to leadership—or gets dragged into it kicking and screaming—has been caught between two antagonistic forces. On the one hand, this is the "day of the antileader," as Robert Greenleaf says.[14] Powerful forces of egalitarianism, equal rights, and parity make it hard for someone even to be "first among equals," as were the Hebrew kings in the Old Testament.

On the other hand, there is a deep hunger both in secular society and the church for strong leadership. In a permissive, hedonistic society that rejects any authority except the self, there are bound to be many who are beginning to feel the effects of every person doing what is right in his or her own eyes (Judg. 17:6). We reap in disorder what we sow in autonomy. The craving for an authority figure to clean up the mess is an understandable reaction to this. Neither Jonestown nor Hitler's rise happened in a vacuum.

Seeing the Leader from Behind

As Hitler rose to power, Bonhoeffer flayed the German public for its hankering after a leader who would become a misleader "so long as he did not clearly refuse to become the idol of the led."[15] In *No Rusty Swords,* Bonhoeffer put his finger on the essential comparison: "In the case of the *Leader*, the essential thing is the supremacy of his person . . . the focus of *leadership* is the person being led."[16] All too easily followers yield to the leader's ambition and hunger for power. Ray Anderson insightfully comments that when this happens, as it did with Hitler, the essence of the community is surrendered to the monolithic structure of the collective unit. "When this happens," Anderson suggests,

> the people no longer wish to see the face of the leader, in his human vulnerability and weakness, but only see him "from behind," as Bonhoeffer puts it, so that he becomes "larger than life," an object upon which they can project their own individualistic dreams for success and desire for power.[17]

Looking at leadership institutionally in secular society since Hitler's era, William Stringfellow believes that "the most poignant victim of the demonic in America today is the so-called leader."[18] Leadership is not merely the role performed by an individual on behalf of an organization. Complex principalities and powers (Eph. 6:12), which are simultaneously part of God's creation and tools of the evil one, victimize even the best intentions of leaders. "They are left with titles, but without effectual authority; with the trappings of power, but without control over the institutions they head; in nominal command, but bereft of dominion."[19] The pathology of leadership is structural and the church, which is both a divine and a human society, cannot escape it.

In the light of this, it is not surprising that so many church leaders choose the one-person-rule model. The "loneranger" leader easily builds a congregation around a personal vision. With a charismatic personality and task orientation, this person can build a large and growing church that will last for decades—provided that this leader does not give the leadership away. Robert Schuller, the founding and senior minister of Garden Grove Community Church in California, expresses this viewpoint: "Don't let laypeople get too involved in decision-making in the congregation."[20] Such an authority role is a lonely role. But was it intended?

Is There a Biblical Model?

Remarkably there is no biblical model for a leader, in the ordinary sense —no model for a person who occupies an office and is vested with authority by virtue of that office. Even Jesus is not a biblical "model" in that sense, as Ray Anderson says:

> . . . we do not find that he presents himself as a leader by virtue of position or office. He referred to himself as a shepherd and said that he did not come to be served, but to serve. He accepts the designation of Messiah, but defers in all matters to the One who has sent him. While he is called an apostle and high priest, he is recognized as having only the authority that is delegated to him by the Father.[21]

Jesus said that the "Gentile" rulers exemplified the leader-follower model (Matt. 20:25), with authority vested *in the leader* along with the power to carry out the leader's commands. On the other hand, those who are to provide leadership in the kingdom of God are to be followers and servants *of God*, as Jesus himself was! Anderson sheds light on this leader-model:

> The role of the leader as the Gentiles practiced it carried with it an assumption concerning the use of power to achieve the wishes of the leader. What is wrong with this model of the leader is that it tends to equate authority with power. Jesus, on the other hand, spoke as one having authority, (Mark 1:11; 2:10) *but not ultimate power*. Power belongs to God in heaven, and Jesus will sit on the "right hand of power" in the eschaton (Luke 22:69).[22]

A Systems Approach to Power and Authority

Now we must reflect on how the body of Christ submits to its persuasive leaders yet, at the same time, affirms their right to lead. Leaders cannot lead unless the people give them the right to do so. This is a systemic insight. Bonhoeffer makes this clear in *No Rusty Swords:*

... the group is the womb of the leader ... It gives him everything,
even his authority ... he is leader only as the one chosen by those
whom he leads ... he receives his authority only from his followers
... the authority of the leader ... is in the hands of the followers.[23]

But their leadership is also in the hands of God. Only as the Christian
leader serves what Bonhoeffer calls "the ultimate indescribable authority,
...the authority of God" will the leader find the people faithful to God.[24]
Thus Bonhoeffer integrates theory and theological thought and opens up
a new route for integrating secular and spiritual understandings.[25]

Spiritual Authority

Though we do not agree with all of Watchman Nee's thought, we affirm
that his *Spiritual Authority* is a classic with several deep insights.[26] He
provides some guidelines in understanding the quality of spiritual authority: It (1) is a part of the ethos of a God-anointed leader; (2) arises
from the clear evidence that God is speaking through the leader's life and
ministry; (3) relates to the influence the leader has on his or her followers
for *their* good; and (4) can be measured by the degree to which the followers are yielding and responsive to the leader's persuasive influence,
since the ultimate decision to obey from the heart rests with the follower.
In addition, such power brings about spiritual maturity in those who
come under the influence of the Christian leader.

Nee argues that God's power is "delegated"[27] and that it is received
through the obedience of the leader to God,[28] an obedience that is developed over a lifetime of Christian service. This authority, although delegated to the obedient leader, does not belong to this person, even though
she or he may be exercising it. It belongs to and remains with God. If it
is from God, it is never exercised for one's own personal benefit, but
rather for the sake of the believers (that is, the followers). According to
Nee, spiritual authority comes from a life and a ministry that demonstrates the presence of God. A life of prayer and practicing the presence
of God is crucial to this.

So the pastor who insists on obedience because "I am God's anointed
pastor" but is not followed may have lost authority in one or more of
the systemic dimensions that are crucial for leadership. Either he does
not have the anointing of God or he does not have "followership" from

the group. Possibly both. Today the problem of Christian leaders struggling with empty titles is not that power has been stripped from the titles or positions. All too often the problem is that we have empty leaders.

Christian leaders humbly admit that any authority that accrues to them, as Richard Niebuhr says, comes in being witnesses to divine authority that is neither under the leader's nor the Church's control.[29] As leaders grow in this authority they can risk being vulnerable. Leaders can allow their "faces" to be seen by their followers. They do not need to be "larger than life," because their authority does not derive from the force of their personality or the projection of people's individualistic dreams on them. The leader's authority is derived from outside as well as inside the leader through an authentic relationship with the God who works through the leader. This kind of authority does not need proof or defense. Its fruit, as Bonhoeffer so wisely suggests, will not be the surrender of the essence of the community to the monolithic structure of the collective unit—the "melting pot" church as we earlier named it—but rather the building up and equipping of the body, that rich interdependent community that God is forming out of God's people.

Building Community

Reflecting on the purpose of Christian leadership, Ray Anderson writes, ". . . leadership, from a biblical perspective, is not so much task oriented as it is community oriented . . . ."[30] A superb book written by Roman Catholic Stephen B. Clark takes this as the central leadership goal. "The goal of pastoral work is to build a people of God."[31] He offers this job description for the contemporary Christian leader:

> A leader in a Christian community has to do three things. First of all, he has to be able to present the ideal on which the community is based in such a way that people will understand it, accept it, and grow in commitment to it. Secondly, he has to be able to draw people together and to get them to relate to one another in a positive way. Finally, he has to be able to provide whatever organization is needed to see that everything which is needed for the people to live according to this ideal (or in the service of this ideal) is provided.[32]

Moses as Community Builder

Judged by Clark's standards, Moses was a good leader.[33] Or, to turn it around, judged by the model of Moses' leadership, Clark offers an important insight for those of us who would give leadership. Unfortunately, Moses is usually cited as a leadership model because of his use of delegation, albeit reluctantly and under pressure from his father-in-law (Exod. 18:17-26). Much more significant, in our view, is the fact that his leadership was primarily invested in building community. Indeed, his demise as a leader—and his being prevented from entering the Promised Land—appears to be directly related to his despising the very people he was called to build, as shown in his beating the rock in frustration (Num. 20:2-12).

He was given the task of leading the children of Israel out of the wilderness, away from slavery in Egypt, to freedom in the land of promise. As recorded in the four books of Exodus, Leviticus, Numbers, and Deuteronomy, the purpose of Moses' leadership was to establish a "community" that embodied the Word of God throughout every aspect of its social, civil, economic, and religious life. Moses was not only to provide the most expeditious method of moving more than one million people from one place to another, but also to develop a loosely knit conglomeration of tribal families into a "people of God."

He did not climb Mount Sinai to receive a strategic plan for moving the people of Israel across a trackless desert, but to receive the Word of God in order to translate Israel into a community that would embody the very character of God.[34] It took him forty years of wandering through the wilderness with his people, holding them together, through much disobedience, until he finally brought them as a "community" to the borders of the Promised Land.

Only a few months after they escaped from the Pharaoh, they were poised on the border of the land of promise. For all practical purposes, the goal was already at hand. They could have entered the Promised Land. But the majority of scouts sent to spy out the land exhibited a lack of faith. This led to the people "murmuring" against their leader, Moses. They turned their backs on the promise and determined to go back again to Egypt.[35] It became quite clear to Moses that the Israelites were not ready to enter the land. The primary task of developing them into an obedient and faithful community had not yet been completed.

What is remarkable about Moses? He did not take the shortest route to the Promised Land as a task to be completed; rather, he read the situation spiritually and judged they were not yet built into a community embodying the glory and praise of Jehovah. So he spent forty years with them, patiently wandering about the wilderness. Ultimately, he succeeded in holding them together as a people with whom God had made a covenant, and brought them again to the borders of the land of promise.[36]

The purpose of leadership is primarily to develop a community of people not merely to finish a job. All other tasks that occupy human purposes and demand the investment of human will and energies are qualified by this divinely given task. One further dimension of this leadership task is to see that the community is built on justice and brings justice into the world.

Bringing Justice

Greenleaf gives a very practical test for whether leaders are *servant-leaders:* "What is the effect on the least privileged in society: will they benefit, or at least not be further deprived?"[37] It is the question of justice.

The precedent for making justice a central purpose for leadership was set not only in Mosaic legislation, but also in the New Testament church. Significantly, the first sign of organization in the primitive church, the creation of the Seven, was instituted to solve a problem of justice between the Jews and the Hellenists and to free the apostles for prayer and the work of preaching (Acts 6:1-7).

Leadership can organize God's community for the distribution of justice, as an act of love, in two ways. One is through a careful study of the recorded incidents of the early church that required justice.[38] The other is to develop the spiritual character of the believers and the quality of their relationships so that love and justice thrive in all aspects of the congregation's life and mission in society.

If the church becomes a bulwark for party spirit, petty politics, or prefers the rich members over the poor, then justice has been turned into injustice. If justice is maximized, then *all* are free to concentrate on the witness of God's love to others and to bring justice into the world. A good illustration of this idea is provided by Robert K. Greenleaf:

Leaders work in wondrous ways. Some assume great institutional

burdens, others quietly deal with one person at a time. Such a man
was John Woolman, an American Quaker, who lived through the
middle years of the eighteenth century. He is known to the world of
scholarship for his journal, a literary classic. But in the area of our
interest, leadership, he is a man who almost singlehandedly rid the
Society of Friends (Quakers) of slaves.

It is difficult now to imagine the Quakers as slaveholders, as
indeed it is difficult now to imagine anyone being a slaveholder.
One wonders how the society of two hundred years hence will view
"what man has made of man" in our generation. It is a disturbing
thought.

But many of the eighteenth-century American Quakers were
affluent, conservative slaveholders, and John Woolman, as a young
man, set his goal to rid his beloved Society of this terrible practice.
Thirty of his adult years (he lived to the age of fifty-two) were
largely devoted to this. By 1770, nearly one hundred years before
the Civil War, no Quakers held slaves.

Greenleaf adds that what was remarkable about Woolman's leadership in
bringing justice is that he did not start a protest movement or hold an
office in a large organization. He exercised his influence through gentle,
clear, and persistent persuasion one to one.[39]

Being a Christian leader means recognizing, as Bonhoeffer said, that
"the group is the womb of the leader." More important, it means frankly
confessing that God is the ultimate leader and that the Christian leader
find his or her source and life in God. As Christians, all ministry and
leadership takes place in an "I-Thou-we" community with endless exchanges and interpenetration. We can never define ourselves as leaders
alone. And we can never define "our" leadership alone—because individually we do not have leadership! Perhaps this is why Jesus said,
"Do not let anyone call you leader! You have one leader, the Christ!"
(Matt. 23:8-12).

CHAPTER VIII

Liberating the Laity for Mission

There is no work better than another to please God; to pour water, to wash dishes, to be a souter [cobbler], or an apostle, all are one, as touching the deed, to please God.

William Tyndale[1]

The largest and deepest reference to the Gospel is not to the world and its social problems but to eternity and its social obligations.

P. T. Forsyth[2]

As the Father has sent me, I am sending you.

Jesus, John 20:21

The church is the one society on earth that exists for those outside her, yet the record of the average North American congregation does not seem to support this statement! Most churches are havens of refuge rather than dynamic centers for transformative mission in society. Celia Hahn cites an illuminating survey of twenty-nine urban congregations in which seventy percent of the members "defined ministry of the laity" as "doing things at church" only.[3] Thus defined, for most laypeople ministry would inevitably be restricted to the discretionary hours of the week. But in a church open to the world, ministry is related to all of life, 168 hours a week.

The church, like the circulation of the blood in the human body, is constantly on the move. It gathers for inspiration and instruction (*ecclesia*)—as the blood gathers in the heart and lungs for oxygenation and cleansing—to be pumped out into the world (*diaspora*)—as the blood carries nutrients, hormones, and enzymes to the most distant parts of the body. In the process the blood gets tired and dirty and must return once more. A still picture of the congregation—the building on the corner or the congregation seated in the sanctuary—can never capture the dynamic systemic life of the church. It requires a movie film or, better still, an angiogram, that marvelous videotape of the heart actually pumping. Almost all equipping books, programs, seminars, and materials concentrate on the gathered life of the church. This is a fatal oversight. As Elton Trueblood said years ago, "You cannot go to church; you are the church wherever you go."[4]

Constitutionally, the church is an outcropping of the kingdom of God that penetrates this present age like salt, light, fire, keys, and yeast. The church *is* mission. It does not "have" missions as one of its many optional activities. So in this chapter we will consider a systemic approach to empowering the laity for mission. First, we will summarize the entire book in ten systemic equipping principles. Then we will apply these ten principles to the greatest equipping challenge: the liberation of the laity in mission. Our approach will encompass both "how to" and "how come?"

Ten Principles for Systems Equippers

To blame the frozen state of the layperson on the clergy is far too simple and unkind. The nonclergy portion of the laity cannot be liberated or empowered simply by telling the clergy to move over and make room for the layperson. Nor will it happen simply by telling laypeople to move up and become one of the ministers of the church. We are dealing with complex historical forces that have impinged on the church's life over several centuries, forces that were only partially resisted by the Protestant Reformation. It is a systemic problem and it requires a systemic solution. So we now offer ten ways of thinking and acting to encourage systemic equipping. In the endnotes we will offer some biblical examples and insights on each of these principles.

1. Work with the Whole

The whole is more than the sum of the parts. Think of the church as more than the aggregate of all the members (a seed package, a melting pot, or a bouquet). The church is the body of Christ, the family of God, the covenant community God. Keep discerning the body (chapter VI).

Leaders cannot influence the whole until they have joined the system, and they will not continue to influence the system unless they continually renegotiate their place in the system (chapter I). To do this the leader (as a member of the system) must adjust his or her leadership style to the system and the stage of the system's formation (chapter IV). All leadership is systemically defined (chapter I).[5]

We take a paradoxical approach to equipping: The best way to equip individual saints is not to focus on the individual saints. Rather we should equip the church as a whole, and then the church (in its systemic life) will equip the members. Finally, equippers should embrace the goal of church growth using a deeper definition of church growth than the one normally used (chapter II).

2. Cultivate Healthy Interdependence among Members

Equipping is essentially a relational, rather than a programmatic, ministry; this involves building the people of God. Church membership should be understood systemically and the lost art of joining should be recovered (chapter I). Leaders have the challenge of building unity in the people without evoking compliance or autonomy; this involves encouraging people to remain connected and to define themselves and their own ministries rather than merely assisting the leaders in their ministry. Equippers must understand the twin needs "to be me" and "to be we" and understand how these affect the functioning of the community. The systems leader tries to avoid fostering the two ends of the relational spectrum: independence and dependence (or codependence). Healthy members are able to define themselves and still remain connected. There are synergistic benefits of such interdependence (chapter II).

Healthy interdependence starts with the leadership; this involves teaching and modeling interdependence and allowing people to minister to the leaders. Female pastors and leaders have frequently led the way in this. Further, equippers should exegete the community by recognizing giftedness; this involves helping people to "sound" their own dreams and visions, as well as helping others affirm the contributions of each and every member. Interdependence is crucial for the leader personally. The congregation is the womb of the system's leadership. The group's relationship with God is also the womb of its leadership. Finally, the leader's relationship with God is the womb of that leader's real authority (chapter VII).[6]

3. Lead the Process Not the People

The way in which the equipper engages the culture, makes decisions, and makes changes is more important than specific achievements accomplished. Leading the process involves envisioning, defining one's own convictions, and dreams. Changes must be made systemically and not merely organizationally. In one sense this *is* leading the people, but the ultimate leader of the people is Christ. Our job as equipping leaders is to facilitate the process of Head-body connection and help people find their source in Christ, not in the official leadership of the church (chapter III).[7]

4. Cultivate the Culture

Recognize culture as a systemic expression and a powerful influence in creating (or squelching) motivation and shaping behavior. Culture is composed of unspoken assumptions about relationships, beliefs, and purposes. These get expressed in values and symbols. Environmental influences will have greater impact than most programs. The body (in its cultural life) "speaks." The equipper functions as the guardian and cultivator of the culture (chapter III).[8]

5. Make Changes Slowly and Indirectly[9]

Remember that resistance, the tendency to return to the "tried and true" (homeostasis), is not necessarily resistance to the leader's ideas or personality but is the result of complex dynamics in the system (chapter III).

Systemic resistance may be related to the history of the system and to
dynamics at work in some of the subsystems, especially the family subsystem (chapter V). So equippers need to keep looking "into" the body
to see how the system functions. Instead of bringing change directly, an
equipper may accomplish much by reinforcing in the existing culture of
the church those very dimensions that best facilitate the release of the
members in ministry and mission. Change must be incremental and
usually takes a lot of time. Leaders must be willing to take the pain
themselves when others feel anxiety about the process of making positive change (morphogenesis, morphostasis).[10]

6. Sound Your Own Vision and Define Yourself

In doing this it is better to keep "oughts" and "shoulds" out of your language. Defining yourself is not an exercise in self-promotion. Nor is it
catering to autonomous individuality. It a systemic ministry. It is crucial
to remain connected while defining yourself. Your initiative will help
others define themselves (chapters I, II, III).[11]

7. Shepherd the System and the Subsystems

The pastor and other congregational leaders are shepherds of the congregational system. They care for individual members in context. They
also nurture and guide the interdependent systems that function in the
congregation. Both the functional subsystems (communication, environment, nurture/education, restoration) and the structural subsystems (small
groups, families, etc.) need to be nurtured. Equippers look *into* the body
to see correspondences (isomorphism) and not just "at" it to see individual members and activities.

Discover the way the congregation is put together and strengthen the
connections. Equip the subsystems that empower people for ministry.
Be aware of multigenerational problems that may surface (chapter V).[12]

8. Avoid Becoming Triangled

By siding with the relationship, the equipping pastor refuses to take sides when two others intend to triangle him or her into their problem. As relationship shepherds, equippers should be able to discern dysfunctional relationships. This involves taking appropriate actions to deal with over- and underfunctioning members, addictions, triangles, and the domination of the weak.

When individuals or groups attempt to draw you into counterproductive alliances, your "ministry" is to help people take responsibility for their own contribution to the congregation. Triangles are one of the most inhibitive factors in the systemic life of the congregation, and they prevent people from taking ownership of their own ministry and mission. In both families and churches some triangles are very old and may resurface generation after generation until someone detriangles him- or herself. Detriangling is not so much a technique as a way of thinking that leads to action, so that people get beyond scapegoating, side-taking, and guilt-inducing (chapter II).[13]

9. Maintain Open Boundaries with the World

Equip the church to be an open system interacting with systems outside of the congregation: neighborhood, society, media, and the principalities and powers (introduction, chapter V). To do this the church must maintain its own boundaries (knowing who belongs and what defines the community) while being "open" to the influence of outsiders. Further, an open system requires equipping the members to live, work, and minister authentically and consistently in the world (chapter VIII). Being an open church is a two-way street of influence; engaging in the mission of the church means the church does not go into the world merely as a benefactor.[14]

10. Relax: The Church Is in Good Hands

Yes, the church is in the good hands of Jesus, the Head of the church. That means the equipper can engage in leadership with a measure of playfulness (chapters III, V). You are not the only equipper. Let the Lord equip you through God's people (chapter I). Pastor and people, leaders and followers, are mutual equippers. Leaders cannot rescue the church or embody the entire ministry of the laos of God in their own persons. The deepest work of a Christian leader is to integrate spirituality and ministry, becoming a Christian leader whose authority is in God and not an office or role. The deepest equipping work involves getting the church to relate to the Head and to minister with liberating dependence on, and interdependence with, the Lord (chapter VII).[15]

Ten Ways to Empower the Laity for Mission

Now we will apply these to the liberation of the laity in mission. We start with a theology of mission that encompasses the whole church (and not merely those interested in "mission") and, as a matter of deep mystery, the church's systemic relationship with the Lord.

1. Work with the Whole: A Short Theology of Mission

The simplest and deepest statement of the mission of the church is found in the words of Jesus, in John 20:21 and 17:18: "As the Father has sent me, I am sending you."[16] Here Jesus defines the full incarnational style of the disciples' mission. They are to be in the world in all the ways he came to be with us: physically, aesthetically, culturally, politically, psychologically, and spiritually. But in this "greater commission" he is doing something more. Jesus defines the systemic nature and origin of the church's mission. As Jesus went into the world with the resources of the Trinity, being empowered by the relational life within God, so we are sent out with the resources of the Trinity and empowered by our access to the relational life within God.

The church's mission is God's continuing mission. It is not merely the sum of the church's activities in the dispersed, *diaspora*, phase of its life. Nor is mission merely something the church does as a human act, either in gratitude for salvation or in guilt for not living up to its mission mandate. It is God's mission in which we participate.

In this mission our "being sent" corresponds to Jesus' experience with the Father and the Spirit. It is much more than what we normally call "mission," more than saving souls. It is both creative and redemptive, both unitive and restorative. It embodies what God intended the first Adam to do (having communion with God, building community, and being cocreative in making God's world "work") *and* what the second Adam (Christ) began to do (restoring humankind to the creation mandate and inaugurating the kingdom of God on earth). The mission of the church includes making beautiful things (like needlepoint), empowering the poor, playing with children, and preaching the Gospel.

But the mission is more than any of these individual acts, more even than the sum of them, because it originates within God and is more than mere doing. It includes *being*. Sometimes it is expressed in healing the brokenhearted; sometimes in deepening the interdependence and unity of God's own people. The equipped community does good works, but it also works toward attaining unity (Eph. 4:11-12) and living in love (Eph. 4:15). The reason is simple: We are sent just as Jesus was sent from the Father.

So the body of Christ must never be merely "the body beautiful." It does not exist for itself, its own glory, its own self-improvement, or even its own mission. The body exists for God and God's purposes in the world. We must be willing to do with our own corporate life what Christ did with his body in love for the world—to interpose its life for the healing and salvation of others. But we can do and be this only because we find our meat and drink in doing the Lord's will and being "in" Christ.[17] Our life depends upon Christ, as his depends upon feeding on the Father's will. So, as L. S. Thornton says, "to feed upon him who was sent by the Father is to partake of the mission which was fulfilled on the Cross . . . [and to partake] of the living One in whom the fruits of his sacrificial death are ever present."[18]

A vivid example of this participation in the mission of Jesus is given by the late Tom Allen, a pastor and evangelist in the Church of Scotland. He and some members from his church, Saint George's Tron, would spend Saturday evening reaching out to prostitutes in downtown Glasgow. They would bring some back to the church basement where they were running a coffee house. One evening Tom spent two hours, late into the night, listening deeply and compassionately to the sordid life story of one woman. About 2:00 a.m. he arranged to have her taken home while he went home himself. He felt dirty all over. When he went into his home he washed his hands and showered, but he still felt dirty, as he did when he woke up the next morning. Yet, on her way home, the prostitute turned to the man who was taking her home and said, "Talking to that man made me feel clean." This story leads to the next principle: doing and being God's mission together.

2. Cultivate Healthy Interdependence among Members

Davida Foy Crabtree tells how she used a listening team to get people to talk about their work. A team composed of a machinist, an executive, a data base analyst, and a pastor invited various occupational groups to spend an evening discussing the joys, struggles, and faith-issues that were experienced in the course of their daily work.[19] The pastor agreed to accept the discipline of silence! Without saying so, she was cultivating interdependence as a *precondition* of empowering members for the workplace. We had the privilege of doing something similar during an experimental theological education program in Africa.

The leaders of an indigenous African denomination, with which we are working in a contextualized theological education project,[20] expressed their concern in words that have a global application: "The laity [in the usual sense of the word] are on the receiving end of ministry; the pastors are on the giving end. Nothing important can be done until the pastor arrives, or unless the pastor does it. What," they asked, "can be done to communicate that a Christian leader *needs* the ministry of the laity?" The problem boils down to a one-way priesthood and truncated unity of pastor and people. Paul's concern in Ephesians 4:1-16, the key "equipping" passage, is not with equipping, but with unity (4:12, 15-16). And there will never be visible, demonstrated, and powerful unity in the people of God until pastor and people, clergy and laity, are truly mutual and interdependent priests. So we tried to turn the thing around.

Why not let the laypeople teach the pastors, the reverse of the usual way? The most precious resource we had in this group of leaders in a rapidly growing denomination in Africa (about 25 percent per year) was the people who were there to be equipped as "lay pastors." We had a class of twenty-four clergy and six laypeople including a forestry official, an inspector for the government pension fund, a school teacher, a manager of a small restaurant, two homemakers, a school bursar, and a businessperson who manufactured tables and caskets. We divided the class into small groups with a layperson in each group acting as the resource person. Each group had to discuss three questions with its lay leader.

First, what are the issues you face in your daily work? Second, what difference does your faith make to how you handle these issues? Third, what can the church do to help equip you for your full-time ministry as a servant of Christ on the job? The effect was electric.

In our class of thirty an amazing unity grew among those who were ordained and those whose primary ministry was in society. *They became one people.* We were reaffirmed in the conviction that theological education must be for the whole people of God, not just pastors. Further, we became convinced that laypeople are crucial to the theological education of pastors. We returned to Canada asking why pastors in North America are not inviting their laypeople to become their priests and equippers. This, however, is also an example of the next principle.

3. Lead the Process, Not the People: Evoking Gifts for Mission

By listening, teaching, consulting, and clarifying, the pastor will work with all parts of the church as the spokesperson for a mission that the whole body can embrace. There are some inadequate ways of doing this. One is sheer persuasion: "You should do what I say." Another is by using personal charisma: "Wouldn't you like to follow me?" Finally, the pastor can rely on the consensus achieved in one brief long-range planning retreat: "You should do what you agreed to." But, in each of these, systemic growth and/or the pastor's leadership can be lost. There are important theological and sociological reasons for this. The whole church will accomplish only a mission that the whole church has embraced. The people will do what the people have had a part in planning. The pastor's goal is the equipping of *all* the saints, not just the ones most friendly to the pastor's personal vision.

One practical way of discovering gifts for mission in a congregation is for a pastor, in the context of appropriate teaching and worship, to pass out cards for members to write their names and the answer to a simple question: If time, talent, and training were not obstacles (these three can all be found!), what would you really like to do for God in the church or the world? The answers will be a pleasant and challenging surprise. But the systemic pastor knows that discovering spiritual gifts is not something a person does alone. Gifts and ministry emerge at the "joints" or "ligaments" (Eph. 4:16) of the body, the places of real connection. So working with individual response is just the beginning. The equipping leader must cultivate a culture that reinforces that ministry is not just what a person does with "discretionary time" but with all of life.

4. Cultivate the Culture:
Empowering Symbols for Diaspora Mission

The average North American person spends some 88,000 hours on the job from the first day of full-time employment until retirement. Work occupies about 40 percent of one's waking life. In contrast, a dedicated Christian is estimated to spend as few as 4,000 hours in a lifetime in church meetings and church-related activities.[21] Concentrating on the latter, the church has made spirituality into a leisure-time, discretionary-time involvement that provides a welcome relief from the boredom of much work or a challenge to the idolatrous demands of the marketplace. But true spirituality is more subversive than that.[22] It sneaks into the center of our lives rather than the circumference, compelling us to find God in the down-to-earth rather than the up-in-heaven.

If ministry is reduced to a discretionary-time activity, people will think of mission and ministry as edification, evangelism, and good works. The professional ordained minister who does this "full time" will remain the epitome of ministry just as the professional overseas missionary will remain the defining model of a person engaging in mission. But the church's cultural message is out of sync with the Bible. Richard Broholm clearly analyzes this situation:

> In spite of sermons on the "priesthood of all believers" and admonitions to "live your faith in your daily work," the organizational and liturgical practices of the church continue to reinforce the assumption that there is no valid ministry outside the organizational church.[23]

Most liturgical churches miss the weekly opportunity they have to endorse the *diaspora* life of the church in the celebration of the Eucharist. Because the bread and wine communicate our participation in the present victory of Christ's kingdom and the certainty of its complete coming, we should view the Eucharist as a public demonstration of a change of government from the revolutionary—as evidenced by the arrogant claim of the rebellious "powers" to control us (Eph. 6:10-18)—to the constitutional—as evidenced by the visible tokens in the bread and wine that express Christ's legitimate and victorious reign. The Eucharist has been called "the weekly meeting of rebels, a society of rebels against a Mammon-worshipping world-order" and "the feast of National Emancipation."[24] Customarily in city churches the bread has gone through the industrial process. For want of bread, millions starve. The wine is real wine, the same wine that leads to drunkenness. But this sacrament must be expounded for the *diaspora* life and not just for *ecclesia.* This feast has empowering symbolism for the people of God as they move into society for six more days!

Davida Foy Crabtree correctly concludes that until the culture of the church reinforces long-term proven ministries of laypersons in society, the systemic message of the church will remain focused on the pastor as the model minister. She says,

> In the churches' traditions, we have liturgies for many passages of life: baptism, confirmation, marriage, death. Yet when an adult comes to a new awareness (or wants to affirm a life-long awareness) of God's will for his or her use of the life that God has given, we have nothing to offer.[25]

Several authors have proposed simple services of dedication for people recognized for the ministry of everyday life. One such service is included in the Appendices of *The Equipper's Guide to Every Member Ministry.* But it would be folly for an equipping leader to move in a few short months from zero recognition of societal-ministers, to ordaining everyone!

5. Make Changes Slowly and Indirectly:
Linear and Incremental Steps for the Recognition of Lay Mission

One simple "first step" is to interview church members during the Sunday service, one per week. Usually recognition is given to visiting missionaries, Sunday school teachers, and lay elders. But an equipping leader could strategically draw into visibility the hidden people in the church and recognize their mission in the world. A sample interview could include three questions: (1) What do you do for a living? (2) What are the issues that you face in your faith in the context of your daily work? (3) How would you like us to pray for you as a church, in your ministry from Monday to Friday? A church could make a substantial shift in priorities in the course of one year if such three-minute interviews were consistently practiced every week.

Crabtree also suggests offering prayers for various people in the workplace and gives some samples of prayers for electricians and hairdressers.[26] Further she carefully evaluates the *way* she encouraged change in her own church[27] in the light of Jackson W. Carroll's statement of factors facilitating acceptance of proposed changes.[28]

6. Sound Your Own Vision and Define Yourself: Proclaiming the *Diaspora* Mission

As we indicated in chapter III, the pastor has a magnificent opportunity to sound the biblical vision of the people of God in *ecclesia* and *diaspora* from the pulpit. In the New Testament we are introduced to a church that is a ministerium engaged in continuous mission. But we will not succeed in planting this vision without understanding how far the church has departed from the empowering vision of the New Testament church.

In the New Testament the usual singular word for *layperson (laikoi)* is never used to describe a Christian. But the Greek plural word *laos*, a word that once meant "crowd," is invested with incredible dignity, referring to the people of God (1 Peter 2:9-10). There is one people. While in the contemporary church we find the clergy and "the people," in the New Testament we find people (*laos*) with leaders among them. An ordained pastor can rise to no higher dignity than being a member of God's laity! But the Greek word for *clergy (kleros)* is used to express the inheritance and the ordination (or being chosen by lot) of all the laity (Col. 1:12; Eph. 1:11; Gal. 3:29). So, ironically, in the church described in the New Testament, *everyone is a clergyperson* (in the biblical sense of that term) *and no one is a layperson* (in the usual sense of that term). It took three centuries for the word *layperson*, as commonly understood, to be used in the church to distinguish the clergy from the less educated, less responsible, and less prepared.[29] Until then, the laity was not distinguished from clergy.

From the third century onward there was a growing institutionaliza-
tion of the clergy-lay distinction. This has had profound ramifications
for the ministry and mission of the ordinary Christian. Alexandre Faivre
says:

> From this time onward, the layman's function was to release the
> priest and levite from all his material concerns, thus enabling him to
> devote himself exclusively to the service of the altar, a task that was
> necessary for everyone's salvation.[30]

So from the fourth to the sixteenth centuries the laity was at the
bottom of the ladder for the clerical career. The clergy dressed differently and were prepared for ministry in an enculturating seminary. Ordination became an absolute act that left an indelible imprint on the person.
In sum, the clergy ministered and the laity received the ministry of the
clergy. Sounding a countercultural vision in contrast to this would be
costly, as William Tyndale discovered. He was burned at the stake for
saying, among other things: "To pour water, to wash dishes, to be a
souter [cobbler], or an apostle, all are one, as touching the deed, to please
God."[31] The reason is systemic: It is a multigenerational problem.
Clericalism is passed on generation to generation. Consequently, as
Oscar Feucht said, "The priesthood of all believers can be lost in a single
generation."[32] And with the loss of every-member ministry goes every-
member mission. It is our task to find out why and to address the multigenerational dimension of the problem.

7. Shepherd the System and the Subsystems: Addressing the Multigenerational Bondage of the Laity

One way of trying to get into the depth of the problem is to ask why the
Protestant Reformation failed to bring about the permanent release of the
laity in ministry and mission. The Protestant Reformation spawned
denominations that took seriously the ministry of all believers: Quakers
(with no clergy); Moravians (with lay missionaries); Puritans (primarily
lay-centered); Baptists and Anabaptists (whose preachers were usually
laypersons); Disciples of Christ and Methodists (all lay oriented). But
each of these has substantially lost the original vision.[33] The mainline

Protestant denominations, all nurtured by the vision of the priesthood of all believers, have yielded to the clerical captivity of the church.[34] Why?

We here offer some directions for the equipping leader to explore. These all indicate the multigenerational nature of the problem.

1. The preacher replaces the priest. The replacement of the Mass with the sermon as the central act of Protestant worship (the Protestant "Christ-event") may have set the church up to give the preacher-expositor the same clerical standing as the Catholic officiant at the Mass. The scholarship implicit in such a ministry easily led to taking the Bible out of the hands of the layperson once again and putting it into the hands of the biblical scholar. Using our understanding of church culture (chapter III), we could say the symbols were exchanged (pulpit replaced the altar as the center), but the underlying assumptions were left untouched.

2. Inadequate structures for renewal. The Reformation did not provide an ecclesiology appropriate to its rediscovered soteriology. Even denominations stemming from the so-called "radical reformation" now have gravitated to the old clergy-lay distinction. One reason for this is that few government, ministry, and mission structures reinforce and express belief in every-member ministry and mission.

3. The Catholic seminary system was eventually adopted. While important exceptions existed (and still do),[35] the seminary system became the universal model for equipping a generation of pastors, guaranteeing the indoctrination of almost all pastors into the clerical culture. Theological education remains, by and large, the exclusive preoccupation of those intending a career in the clergy.[36]

4. Neither a theology of the laity nor by the laity was written. The story of ministry and theology itself has almost always been written by the clergy for the clergy. Kraemer's first attempt at such a theology and William Rademacher's recent work in the Catholic context, building on the seminal work by Yves Congar and Vatican II, are but clouds the size of a man's hand. William Diehl's *Thank God, It's Monday* has the distinct advantage of being written by a person who is not a pastor.

5. Kingdom ministry has been almost totally eclipsed by church ministry. The resulting preoccupation with *ecclesia* has helped define ministry as what is done in the gathered life of the church (or in its expansion through evangelism) rather than the totality of life under the rule of God. Ministry is viewed as advancing the church rather than the kingdom. The New Testament letters are the primary guide; the gospels have been eclipsed.

6. Ordination is still retained almost universally for the full-time supported church worker; no adequate recognition of lay ministries in society exists. Most denominations still regard ordination as conferring a priestly character rather than recognizing Christian character and call. No denomination known to us ordains people to societal careers and missions.[37]

7. Calvin's "secret call" to the ministry of the Word perpetuates a two-level call to the ministry: a general call to all and a special call to the few. Even denominations claiming to proceed from the radical reformation still require in their ordination councils a testimony of the secret call to *the* ministry different from the call that comes to all the laity.

8. An adequate lay spirituality has hardly ever been taught and promoted. While the Reformation rejected the two-level spirituality of the monastery, most Protestant spirituality has focused on either charismatic and "mystical" experience or the deeper life of outstanding Christian leaders, rather than exploring the holiness of the ordinary Christian in the totality of life. In the West the church has never become free of Greek dualism, which relegates bodily life to a lower level.

9. Because of an inadequate understanding of the relationship of the Old and New Testaments, Old Testament priesthood and leadership concepts have been applied to the Christian clergy rather than to Jesus, their true fulfillment. Cyprian, bishop of Carthage (249 A.D.), made it clear that a member of the clergy *is not a member of the laity.* Using the analogy of the Levites, he argued that while all Christians should avoid becoming overly involved in the world, clergy must not become so involved, in order properly to attend to the ministry of the altar.[38] Things have not changed much since Cyprian.

10. The same cultural and social forces at work in the first sixteen centuries are still at work today: secular management models; professional-lay analogies; the tendency to deal with outside threats by increasing central government. The church must continuously fight the "fleshly" predisposition to divide into two peoples—clergy and laity. The concept of the priesthood of all believers can be lost in a single generation.[39] Keeping the church oriented to lay ministry and mission is like keeping an airplane in the air. It can happen only if the engines thrust it forward all the time, not resting for a moment! Otherwise gravity will take over.

Liberating the laity for mission in the world is a multigenerational problem. To deal with this we must deal with underlying assumptions and beliefs and recover the New Testament vision of the church. Theological education must be provided for all the people of God. We need to learn from churches in the Third World, churches that have bypassed some of our problems. Ministry and mission must be redefined to include the layperson's nondiscretionary time. A spirituality that is both contemplative and active must be developed for the laity. Accomplishing this may take us well into the twenty-first century. Meanwhile, the equipping leader must deal not only with the past, but with the present.

8. Avoid Becoming Triangled:
Get People to Take Responsibility for Their Own Ministry

The possibility of triangles forming in the context of the church's mission is almost limitless. The church board wants the pastor to concentrate exclusively on the nurture of church families. Meanwhile a radical and lively group within the church, reacting to the in-grown board, wants the pastor to support and equip them for a mission to single parents. Each group wants to forge an alliance with the pastor. Here is another possiblity: A youth minister is caught between the triangling efforts of parents in the congregation, who want their own children cared for, even though these children want nothing to do with the church, and the senior pastor (representing those parents whose children have already left home), who wants the youth minister to reach unchurched youth in the neighborhood. This is even more complicated by the fact that the youth pastor's salary is paid partly by the parents through the budget, while his supervisor is the senior pastor.

A typical illustration of the victim-persecutor-rescuer triangle involves the church as a whole. A minority group in the neighborhood is being victimized by rich and powerful people in the city who have invested in the housing of the area. The victims cry "poor me." The wealthy investors justify themselves and continue their financial exploitation through which they make exorbitant profits. The church plays the role of rescuer by providing alternative housing, but fails to address the other two points of the triangle. Years later the former "victims" complain that now the church is victimizing them! Only then does the church discover that the "victim" is often the most powerful in the triangle, though not in a healthy sense. Systemic mission involves getting all three parties off the triangle and helping them take responsibility for their own lives.

9. Maintain Open Boundaries with the World: Equipping the Church with Permeable Boundaries

This true story will suggest another dimension of systemic equipping.

A prominent lawyer in a Canadian city owns a cluster of small stores in a upper-middle-class district. He has knowingly rented one store to a triple-X-rated porn video shop. This is one of several such shops being established like "convenience stores." However, this video store is located at the corner where all the elementary and secondary school students cross a main thoroughfare.

Many of the parents are outraged and try to gain public support for closing down the store by going door-to-door with a petition. But they are greeted by other parents and home owners who feel that in a pluralistic society people must be free to make such choices. "But," says the mother with petition in hand, "do you want to live in a society in which a man who has been programmed by hard-core porn will be free to rape or abuse your daughter?" Local residents take their case to the city council, but find that the issue is not simple. Councilors are divided among the competing political pressures in this issue: the fact that no law is being broken, the commercial interests of some outstanding citizens, influential friends of the landlord lawyer, women's action groups, and church groups who are condemning hard-core porn outlets everywhere.

The person involved in this neighborhood ministry is trying to understand what is happening to her neighborhood. Is it the war between the flesh—human nature as it has become through sin—and the Spirit? Is the problem one of fallen social structures and societal mores, such as

the growing acceptance of amoral sexual expression? Was she dealing
with complex economic and political structures that are more than the
sum of all the people involved in this little drama? Was this an outright
attack by a powerful evil personage, invisible to the eye but effective in
the world, Satan himself?[40] Further, she must ask whether the church can
support her in this ministry and whether others will join her so that it is
more than an individual mission. At least she, and her friends from
church, were "out there" and not just huddled together in the church
building.

The church is, by God's design, an open system.[41] It has boundaries, but they are permeable. Celia Hahn in *Lay Voices in an Open
Church* compares the "closed system" view of the church—rigid, static,
and with the world out of sight—with the "open system" concept—
ministry moving through the laity into the world.[42] Such mission requires dealing with the social, political, and spiritual structures that
frustrate and complicate our life in society. Individual people—the poor,
strangers, outsiders—must always be the *center* of the church's neighbor-
love, but the *circumference* must encompass the principalities and the
powers that make up the invisible backdrop of our neighbors' lives.

This hidden world makes our neighbors—and us ourselves—feel
powerless, controlled by forces, structures, and powers over which they
—we—have no control. Mission requires gaining a biblical worldview,
one that includes dominions, powers, angelic beings, demons, authori-
ties, rulers, social structures, patterns, and traditions of behavior both
social and religious. Some of these are visible and easily discerned.
Others are complex and ambiguous. The problem is systemic, and dealing with such problems involves asking questions some Christians would
rather ignore. Archbishop Romero once remarked, "When I feed the
poor, they call me a saint. When I ask why the poor are poor, they call
be a communist!"

Let's look at three effective strategies against the false claims of the
powers.

1. The power of the Gospel. The first and most effective strategy is
preaching the Gospel. Berkhof says, "The Powers are still present; but
whenever Christ is preached and believed in, a limit has been set to their
working."[43] Our duty is not to bring the powers to our knees; this is
Christ's task. Our duty is to arm ourselves with Christ (Eph. 6:10-18)

and to preach his cross. However much we attempt to "Christianize" the powers, we must not bypass preaching the Gospel and calling people to embrace the reign of Christ through repentance and faith.[44]

   2. The power of public discipleship. Christ's complete victory over the principalities and powers, over Satan, sin, and death (Col. 2:13-15) assures us that no place in the universe is so demonized that a Christian might not be called to serve there.[45] Since we fight a war that is already won, as far as now possible Christians should Christianize the powers by bringing Christian values and perspectives to the public domains where these powers reign. As part of our creational task, we should seek to "peace" the powers through involvement in education, government, and social action, all the while knowing that the task of subjugating the powers is reserved for Christ alone (Eph. 1:10; Phil. 2:10-11). Men and women in Christ work on the problems of pollution, food distribution, injustice, genetic engineering, and the proliferation of violence and weaponry, knowing that this work is ministry and holy. In the short run this work may seem unsuccessful, but in the long run it will be gloriously successful because the believer cooperates with what Christ wants to do in renewing all creation.

   3. The power of intercessory prayer. Karl Barth once said, "To clasp the hands in prayer is the beginning of an uprising against the disorder of the world."[46] The last book of the Bible provides an empowering picture of the crucial role of the prayers of the saints. The purpose of this last visionary book in the Bible is not to exhort us to pray, but rather to present the reality of the One to whom we pray so that prayer will be evoked. Revelation is an appeal to the faith of beleaguered saints in all centuries by means of the imagination.
   The vision of the Lamb on the throne, of incense and smoke together with the prayers of the saints going up before God from the hands of a mighty angel, and of a heaven that responds with thunder, rumblings, flashes of lightning, and an earthquake (Rev. 8:4-5) and all this preceded, even more eloquently, by a half hour of silence (8:1), is enough to empower the weakest intercessor to pray. Pascal said that "prayer is God's way of providing man with the dignity of causality."[47] P. T. Forsyth takes a systemic approach to the church's intercession:

The real power of prayer in history is not a fusillade of praying units of whom Christ is the chief, but it is the corporate action of a Saviour-Intercessor and His community, a volume and energy of prayer organized in a Holy Spirit and in the Church the Spirit creates.[48]

Forsyth's words direct us to have faith in a God who is joined (systemically) with God's own people.

10. Relax: The Church Is in Good Hands

Jesus is the Head of the church, so you can trust God with the results of your equipping ministry.

Christian action, Gospel proclamation, and intercession are ways of dealing with the powers. But faith is needed whether one is fighting the porn battle or attempting to contribute helpfully to society as a Christian artist working for a secular advertising agency. Faith means simply trusting God. Such trust means not being dependent on *seeing* the results of one's work and ministry.

Summary

Ten ways to liberate the laity for mission. As the church penetrates society in its dispersed life, the church must not conform to the world and so become indistinguishable (Rom. 12:1-2). Rather the church is sent as Jesus was sent, to be a transforming influence (John 20:21). But it is not entirely a one-way street, as is commonly thought. The transforming community is also being transformed. In the process of engaging in mission, we ourselves become missionized. So Christians enter the world not only to speak but to listen, not only to serve but to be served, not only to give but to receive. Elizabeth O'Connor aptly summarizes this:

As the artist discovers that there is a direct relationship between the inner and outer forms of material, so we discover that creativity in our inner lives has a direct relationship to creativity in the world. *We can never be in the world only as its benefactors.* This does not make for authentic relationship. All that we genuinely do is very personal and calls into being our own personality. The covenant of the Church to call forth gifts is extended to the whole of mankind. I say to the world, "I will be an instrument of God in the continuing act of creation," and the world fulfils in me its side of the covenant. It brings forth in me the new creation.[49]

Thinking Systemically

Fall on your knees and weep, for God is dead!

Frederick Nietzsche

Science too is dead!

Jean Paul Sartre[1]

In writing this book we have immersed ourselves in five kinds of literature: general systems theory, family systems theory, leadership theory, theological texts, and the Bible. The reason is found in our journeys. We have found that the Bible and theology take us into life-issues (such as those issues considered by systems theory), and life invites us to reflect theologically with our Bible in hand. Integration is required by the Bible itself. Neither of us wants to be a professor of unapplied theology! We believe that *theoria,* i.e., reasoning and theoretical reflection, leads us to praxis, i.e., the practice of ministry. We also believe that *praxis* should lead us back to *theoria* in what should become a cycle of reflection-action-reflection-action. It is actually a spiral of learning in which we keep entering theoria or praxis at a deeper level.

Why Systems Theory?

In this context we have commended systems theory as a way to get a handle on congregational leadership for equipping the saints. We have several good reasons for doing so.

1. It is a theory and not merely a method, and therefore it provides
a mental framework for looking at reality and not merely a *modus
operandi.* The failure to release the laity into full ministry is largely a
theological and theoretical failure, not a failure in technique. In family
therapy, as Kerr and Bowen indicate, "the clinician's therapeutic approach is guided by his conceptual framework."[2] In the absence of an
integrative theory that "would provide a systematic way of collecting,
organizing and integrating information from all levels of observation . . .
there is a strong tendency in all clinicians to compartmentalize knowledge and to focus treatment on a particular compartment."[3]

The same holds for church leadership. By refusing to reduce potential influence in a human society to one single programmatic intervention, systems theory provides a more comprehensive way of working
with the congregation. So the systems approach provides *a way of
thinking,* a worldview (or a "church-view") that proves to be more essential than a pocketful of programs to release the ministry of every
member. One who knows "how come?" is more likely to come up with
an appropriate "how to."

2. It provides a way of relating to the church as a whole. This
wholistic approach is often neglected because each leader has a special
area of interest and therefore looks at the church through tinted glasses.
The word *system* comes from a Greek word that means "standing together."[4] Systems thinking permits a person to see members of the
church *together.*

3. It helps us deal with the complexities of church life better than
any single organizational or management principle. Matters such as
multigenerational problems, triangles, and homeostasis expound some of
the negative experiences of leaders, while synergy, isomorphism, and
holism prove to be important principles for maximizing the ministry and
life of the people. Within the framework of systems theory, one can
more easily predict the results of pastoral interventions.

*4. It gives us a fresh approach to discovering spiritual giftedness
and ministry in congregational interactions,* thereby counteracting the
granular individualism that Western society has imposed on all discussions of giftedness and ministry.

5. It encourages a humbler, more playful approach to church leadership. It invites the leader to regard her- or himself as an influential member who can give leadership to the process, but who is not the absolute leader of the people.

6. The concept of "open system" helps church leaders reconceptualize the mission of the church by putting the church system in relationship to other systems in its environment.[5]

7. The systems approach most approximates the view of reality revealed in the Bible. It is substantially consistent with the biblical witness about the way things work and the way things exist in both the new humanity and the old and especially in the mixed reality of the Christian church.

Exploring the Assumptions

We do not feel competent to evaluate family systems theory as a therapeutic tool and a therapeutic way of thinking. However, we offer in the endnotes some reflections on the assumptions of systems theory, on systems family theory in particular, and on the new generation of post-systems theories as they apply to the task of leading the church and equipping the saints for the work of the ministry.[6]

The bottom line, so to speak, is that secular systems theory lacks a revelational base and is therefore subject to conflicting philosophical trends and fashions. Paul F. Dell speaks wistfully about the wilderness wanderings of contemporary systems thinkers:

> The efforts to provide a solid foundation for the social and behavioral sciences have been notoriously unsuccessful. As Bateson[7] has noted, the social sciences are composed of (a) a maze of "imperfectly defined" concepts, (b) which are poorly related to one another, and (c) which have no common foundation such as that which is possessed by the concepts which are found in chemistry and physics. Theorists in the behavioral sciences have vacillated, on the one hand, between (unsuccessful) attempts to emulate the hard sciences and, on the other hand, insistent declarations that the social sciences

are radically different from physics and chemistry. Through the years, various explanatory metaphors (e.g., Newtonian mechanics, electricity, hydraulics, thermodynamics, information processing, etc.) have been used to generate theories of social phenomenon. Each of these metaphors has proved to be interesting, and ultimately, unsatisfactory.[8]

The latest generation of systems thinkers, sometimes called eco-systemic or second-order cybernetic, argue that reality is not discovered through objective means, but agreed upon through social interaction, through conversation. Objectivity is a myth.[9] As Terry Real says, "Things 'are' what we agree to call them."[10] The therapist cannot be a "change agent." He refers to Archimedes' boast that he could move the whole earth if he had a lever large enough and a place to stand. The therapist, Real argues, pretends to be like Archimedes acting upon the system in the same way a doctor acts upon a patient. But in the framework of second-order cybernetics, "Archimedes could never make this claim because, first, there is no place outside the system upon which to rest, and second, being on earth and not apart from it, one could never wield such a lever."[11]

While not entirely disagreeing, we beg to differ on the fundamental issue of whether there is a place "outside the system." This is surely what the Christian means by the kingdom of God; it penetrates the here and now from outside, though it is not yet consummated—now and not yet, here and not yet fully here. Further, there is a reality that speaks *both* from within the system and *to* the system. The Christian humbly confesses the reality of an infinitely personal, immanent, yet paradoxically transcendent God. The Christian makes the audacious claim that the lever that can move the world is a wooden cross because its fulcrum is outside the systems of this world.

Paul continuously struggled with the awkwardness of this wisdom, which appears to the world as mere foolishness. But he delighted, as we in hindsight delight, in the power and presence of the Spirit in the primitive church to accomplish what systems theorists call morphogenesis—systemic change. The system was influenced from the *inside* (through human equippers) and from the *Outside* (through God's work as the ultimate equipper). And it can be so today.

There are also practical reasons to hold systems theory lightly and

tentatively. Research evidence suggests that various therapy methods
work equally well and *equally poorly*.[12] Jay Efran and Michael D.
Lukens further note that "paraprofessionals appear to do as well as the
most expensively trained,[13] and placebo methods produce successes right
alongside treatments that are more thoughtfully-devised."[14] This leads
Efran and Lukens to turn to Humberto Maturana, the Chilean therapist,
to explain what they secretly believe: that therapists are *not* change
agents; that the therapist does not have direct control over anyone; that
communication does not exist, and that neither systems nor individuals
have built-in purposes to be discovered.[15]

While earlier therapists questioned the simple linear causality (the
billiard-ball approach that assumes a therapeutic or pastoral intervention
results in some change), second-order, poststructural therapists are skep-
tical about circular causality (that the daughter who shoplifts to get
attention will stop shoplifting when the parents go to therapy with her,
but will start shoplifting again when they stop attending to her because
her behavior has improved, and so on).[16] What they (and particularly
Maturana) propose is therapist and family members getting caught up
with one another and "codrifting" until the "coupling" breaks down.[17]
While this appears to be a rather pessimistic and passive approach, they
illustrate that carefully tuned environments like Disney World and
Alcoholics Anonymous are very effective precisely because they do not
force people to change.[18]

Toward Systemic Integration

Christians in the field have a further challenge. Most attempts by
Christians to integrate biblical revelation with social science have been
halfhearted. The most common approach is to accept uncritically the
conclusions of social science in psychology and then authenticate this
by appealing to proof texts or "principles" found in the Bible. Equally
inadequate is the attempt to make biblical truth palatable by finding
correspondences in some contemporary psychological theory. Some will
claim that we have done just this with systems theory. Hardly anyone
known to us has attempted a thoroughly consistent and genuine integration, although there are some illuminating examples of "first steps."
Perhaps this dearth exists because each attempt at integration appears to

be a solo effort, usually from the side of science or the side of theology. This book is an invitation to explore a systemic approach to the integration of systems theory and biblical theology. It must be done *together*. And even this book, written by two applied theologians, contains this fatal "systemic" flaw.

Full Christian integration will be a social effort including both theologians and social scientists. Perhaps this book will evoke such a dialogue, but such integration must be done with "no holds barred." Far too frequently what keeps pastors and theologians from such a genuinely systemic encounter with truth outside their own camp is fear, fear that they will find out that their revealed truth is "revealed" partly in nature and not exclusively in the Bible. But Spurgeon once answered the question of how to defend the Bible by saying, "You defend it the same way you defend a lion—by letting it out." In this case the pastor and theologian, confident that they can do nothing against the truth and being truly in love with the truth, can let themselves out of their own cages!

There is always a measure of tentativeness in this enterprise. For the biblical Christian this involves holding in tension views that stand in contradiction to revealed truth in the Bible. The Bible will offer a perspective that cannot be offered by social science. As L. S. Thornton puts it:

> in the disintegration of western thought the Church has been treated as [only] a sociological entity; its human, visible aspects have become separated in idea from its mystical and divine aspects . . . .
> Thus the conception of a single divine-human organism reaching from heaven to earth tends to be broken up into compartments between which a great gulf is fixed.[19]

On the other hand, social science will offer perspectives that, though not against it, are not included in the Scripture.

Systemic integration does not mean simply buying in to the latest version of systems theory or buying in to the latest theological expression of the reality of the church. Integration, to be truly systemic, involves engaging in patient and continuing dialogue and then returning to one's discipline to look with opened eyes yet once more. On many questions about subjects that are deep mysteries, biblical Christians must accept ambiguity and transcend normal categories of speech and explanation. Truth on this matter of dialogue and systemic interdependence of theologians and social scientists will be a rich and complex social unity, like the unity of God, the Father, Son, and Holy Spirit, after which all church unity is derived (Eph. 4:3-6).

To say truth that is one, as we are advocating here, does not eliminate the need for revelation, a word "from the other side." The layperson with the Bible in hand may know more than the most sophisticated social scientist or theologian. That layperson (and his or her pastor) may conclude that there is a universe (and not a multiverse), that information does exist (even if we are never free of subjectivity in knowing and communicating truth), that God is not only immanent in creation, but above it, and that Christians can make a difference in the world and the church (in other words, that some change can be made not only in oneself, but in the system one embraces). But the Christian must engage in this dialogue with epistemological humility, for that Christian may not be reading the Bible correctly, and the truth may be more ambiguous than expected.

There is much to be gained by this conversation. Certain of the revealed, transcendent dignity and nature of the people of God, the equipping pastor can gain from systems theory in its multitudinous forms something more valuable that another fistful of how-to's. The pastor and Christian leader can gain some deep insights about "why" and "Who." It is our contention that, having done that, we will be sent back to biblical theology with freshly opened eyes to see in the Bible what we never saw before. It is our prayer that the church will be the richer for the systemic dialogue, and that the saints (corporately) will be liberated. Certainly church leaders can hope for liberation because they need it perhaps more than the rest of the laity!

APPENDIX 1

PATTISON'S STAGES OF SYSTEM DEVELOPMENT

Stage 1. Storming
Amorphous, unstructured. Individually autonomous behavior.
Systemic behavior generated only by the leader.

individuals   leader

Stage 2. Forming
Development of a common identity and unity. Individual autonomy sub-
verted in the cause of group cohesion and group identity, the development of a "group mind" and "group will." The leader is separate from the
system but allowed to relate to it.

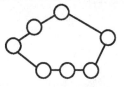

system   leader

Stage 3. Norming
Members experiencing anxiety over threatened loss of individual identity
and autonomy. Individuals distancing themselves from the group. The
leader is caught in the same tension between identification with the system
and assertion of one's unique leadership role.

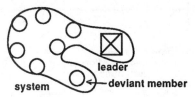

leader
system   deviant member

Stage 4. Performing
Dialectical tension between individual identity and system identity, between commitment to self and to the system. The leader role is found to
be only one example of the general tension shared by all.

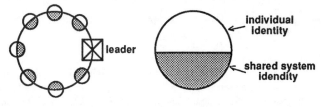

leader   individual
identity

shared system
idendity

Mansell Pattison, *Pastor and Parish: A Systems Approach* (Philadelphia: Fortress Press,
1977), 57-63.

APPENDIX 2

TWO-DIMENSIONAL VIEW OF LEADERSHIP STYLE

A graphic protrayal of a dwo-dimensional view of leadership style has been developed by Blake and Mouton.

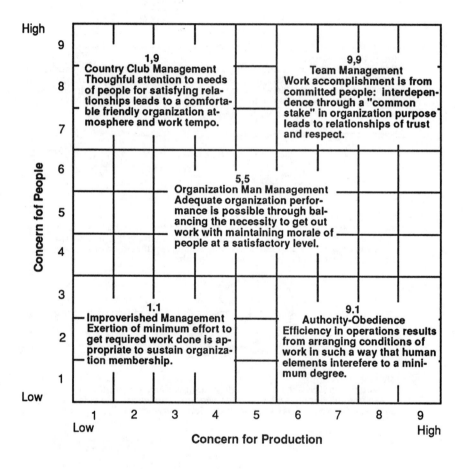

Robert B. Blake and Jane S. Mouton, *The Managerial Grid* (Houston: Gulf Publishing Co., 1964). An update may be found in *The Managerial Grid, III* (same publishers, 1985), p. 12. Original grid may be found in Robert R. Blake, Jane S. Mouton, Louis B. Barnes, and Larry E. Geiner, "Break-through in Organization Development, " *Harvard Business Review* (November/December, 1964), p. 136.

APPENDIX 3

IMMATURITY-MATURITY CHART FOR GROUPS

IMMATURITY-MATURITY CHART FOR GROUPS

ABOVE AVERAGE MATURITY	AVERAGE MATURITY	BELOW AVERAGE MATURITY
Independent —————————————		———————— Dependent
Active ————————————————		————————— Passive
Flexible Behavior ———————————		———————— Rigid Behavior
Concern for Others ———————————		———————— Concern for Self
Long Time Perspective —————————		———————— Short Time Perspective
Deeper & Stonger Interests —————————		———————— Erratic Shallow Interests

Chris Argyris, "Immaturity-Maturity Theory," from Paul Hersey and Kenneth Blanchard, *Management of Organizational Behaviour, Utilizing Human Resources* (Englewood Cliffs, NJ: Prentice-Hall, Inc., 4th ed., 1982), pp.. 53-56.

APPENDIX 4

GROUP MATURITY AND LEADERSHIP STYLE

This diagram illustrates that as a group's maturity level increases, leadership behavior, to remain appropriate, requires less and less structure (task), accompanied by increased person oriented and relationship support. As the group eventually moves toward above average maturity, the leader responds by decreasing socio-emotional (relationship) support. This reality carries great implications regarding a leader's effectiveness as he, or she, moves from one task situation to another.

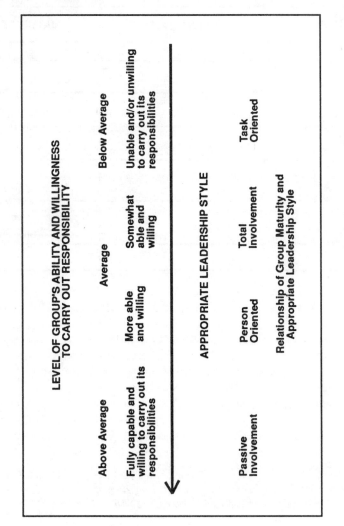

NOTES

Introduction

1. Davida Foy Crabtree, "Empowering the Ministry of the Laity in Work-place, Home, and Community: A Programmatic and Systemic Approach in the Local Church" (D.Min. thesis, Hartford Seminary, 1989), 35.

2. Key turning points for us were the publication of Elton Trueblood, *Your Other Vocation* (New York: Harper & Row, 1952); Yves M. J. Congar, *Lay People in the Church: A Study for a Theology of the Laity*, trans. D. Attwater (Westminster, Md.: Newman Press); Hendrik Kraemer, *A Theology of the Laity* (Philadelphia: Westminster Press, 1958); Elton Trueblood, *The Company of the Committed* (San Francisco: Harper & Row, 1961); Mark Gibbs and T. Ralph Morton, *God's Frozen People* (London: Fontana, 1964); Ray Stedman, *Body Life* (Glendale, Calif.: Regal Books, 1972); Richard Mouw, *Called to Holy Worldliness* (Philadelphia: Fortress Press, 1980); Lawrence O. Richards and Gib Martin, *A Theology of Personal Ministry: Spiritual Giftedness in the Local Church* (Grand Rapids: Zondervan, 1981); William Diehl, *Thank God, It's Monday* (Philadelphia: Fortress Press, 1982); Frank Tillapaugh, *The Church Unleashed* (Ventura, Calif.: Regal Books, 1982); Anne Rowthorn, *The Liberation of the Laity* (Wilton, Conn.: Morehouse-Barlow, 1985); Robert Banks, *All the Business of Life: Bringing Theology Down to Earth* (Sutherland, Australia: Albatross, 1987). A comprehensive bibliography on the theology of the laity and equipping is available through Regent College Bookstore. Gerry Schoberg and R. Paul Stevens, *An Annotated Bibliography on the Laity and Equipping* (Regent College, 5800 University Blvd., Vancouver, BC V6T2E4 Canada).

3. These four reasons are developed in R. Paul Stevens, *Liberating the Laity* (Downers Grove, Ill.: InterVarsity Press, 1985).

4. Edwin Friedman, *Generation to Generation: Family Process in Church and Synagogue* (New York: Guilford Press, 1985), 217-19.

5. We are aware that the term *stuck* in systems thinking has a specific

meaning: fused, undifferentiated. The term is customarily used to describe a person who has not emotionally separated from his or her family of origin and who makes decisions nonrationally on the basis of emotional bonding. But we use the term here to describe the complex, systemic dimensions of church problems that are resistant to simplistic and rational solutions.

6. Crabtree, "Empowering the Ministry," 49.

7. Source of the statistics: The Alban Institute (Washington, D.C.).

8. "Ministry Profile Instrument" (Vandalia, Ohio: The Association of Theological Schools, 1980). Note the cluster groupings.

9. *Survey of Evangelistic Programs* (Calgary: The Evangelism Committee, The Baptist Union of Western Canada), 1981.

10. Michael E. Kerr and Murray Bowen, *Family Evaluation* (New York: W. W. Norton, 1988), 75.

11. Some of these concepts were first introduced to us by Mansell Pattison, *Pastor and Parish: A Systems Approach* (Philadelphia: Fortress Press, 1977), 6-8. Pattison himself gained some of his insights from Frederick K. Berrien, *General and Social Systems* (New Brunswick, N.J.: Rutgers University Press, 1968); Charles W. Churchman, *The Systems Approach* (New York: Delacorte, 1968); Kenneth de Greene, *Systems Psychology* (New York: McGraw Hill, 1970); Marvin D. Mesaronic, *Views on General Systems Theory* (New York: George Braziller, 1968); John M. Yinger, *Toward a Field Theory of Behavior* (New York: McGraw Hill, 1965). Our own sources will be identified later.

12. Ludwig von Bertalanffy, *Perspectives on General Systems Theory: Scientific-Philosophical Studies* (New York: George Braziller, 1968), 12.

13. George J. Klir, *Trends in General Systems Theory* (New York: Wiley Interscience, 1972), 1.

14. von Bertalanffy, *Perspectives on General Systems Theory,* 31.

15. Ibid., 68-69.

16. Ibid., 54-88.

17. Ibid., vii.

18. "Japan's Stock Woes Batter Other Markets," *Time,* 3 August 1992, 15.

19. Friedman, *Generation to Generation.* Pattison, *Pastor and Parish.* Pattison refers to two earlier attempts to use systems thinking to guide pastoral care: Mansell Pattison, "Systems Pastoral Care," *Journal of Pastoral Care* 26, no. 1 (1972): 2-14, and Patrick T. Walsh, "Role of Chaplain as a Catalyst: In a System Theory Approach to the Delivery of Community Health Services," *Association of Mental Health Chaplains Forum* 26, no. 1 (1973): 42-48; Leith Anderson, *Dying for Change* (Minneapolis: Bethany House, 1990). More recently Davida Foy Crabtree has published her D.Min. project recounting her experience of using the systems management process for releasing lay ministry in the world: Davida Foy Crabtree, *The Empowering Church: How One*

Congregation Supports Lay People's Ministries in the World (Washington, D.C.: The Alban Institute, 1989). In R. Paul Stevens, *The Equipper's Guide to Every Member Ministry* (Downers Grove, Ill.: InterVarsity Press, 1992), chap-ters 7 and 8 give a preliminary exploration of a systems approach to equipping.

20. Douglas A. Anderson, "Spirituality and Systems Theory: Partners in Clinical Practice," *Journal of Pastoral Psychotherapy* 1, no. 1 (Fall 1987): 19-32.

21. Kerr and Bowen, *Family Evaluation*, 16. von Bertalanffy, *Perspectives on General Systems Theory*, 11.

22. The rich literature on this subject includes such authors as Kerr and Bowen, Napier and Whitaker, Satir, Reiss, Gurman and Kniskern, Wynne, McDaniel and Weber, and Brommel and Galvin. These authors represent a wide spectrum of approaches, not all of them bearing a clear relationship to general systems theory. Murray Bowen, for example, carefully distinguishes family systems theory from general systems theory. Although there are some fundamental points of contact, and each represents a paradigm shift in thinking, family systems theory involves a new set of assumptions that are not part of general systems theory, namely that differentiation and chronic anxiety are the key variables that allow us to explain how people function in family relationships. There is great diversity in the theoretical structures of these therapies, so much so that some argue that Bowen, on which Edwin Friedman is heavily dependent, does not promote family systems theory, but Bowen Theory. In our epilogue we will reflect on some of the theoretical assumptions that are brought to this multifaceted field.

23. Kerr and Bowen, *Family Evaluation*, ix, 346. Murray Bowen developed simple terms and concepts to describe crucial elements in his own theory, including (1) the family diagram (called by others the genogram); (2) the emotional system (as a way of understanding the solidarity of a family in feeling); (3) the differentiation of self (to denote the ways in which a person is basically different from others); (4) triangles (to describe the way three people relate in family contexts to form the basic emotional building block, to be distinguished from diads and triads); (5) fusion (to describe the ways people borrow or lend self to others); (6) cut offs (to denote the immature separation of people from one another); (7) the nuclear family emotional system (to describe the complex ways that parents handle the emotional process in a single generation); (8) the nuclear family projection process (to describe the automatic transmission of problems into future generations); (9) the extended family emotional system (to denote the unseen involvement of the extended families); (10) the multigenerational transmission process (to denote the patterns of emotional process through the generations); (11) the therapists' involvement of self (to describe the process by which the therapist can be involved in the family emotional process or separate from it; (12) that all of the above are systems components of the large emotional system that is the family; and (13) the meshing of the family system

with the environment (to describe the ways the family is part of the total society).

24. Jack O. Balswick and Judith K. Balswick, *The Family: A Christian Perspective on the Contemporary Home* (Grand Rapids: Baker Book House, 1989).

25. John D. Friesen, Darryl N. Grigg, Jennifer A. Newman, "Experiential Systemic Therapy: An Overview (March 1991)" (Vancouver: Department of Counselling Psychology, University of British Columbia). Other articles are listed in the bibliography.

26. This is sometimes called an ecological approach. See John D. Friesen, "An Ecological Systems Approach to Family Counselling," *Canadian Counsellor/Conseiller Canadien* 17, no. 3 (1983): 98-104. Friesen is dependent on U. Brontenbrenner, *The Ecology of Human Development: Experiments by Nature and Design* (Cambridge, Mass.: Harvard University Press, 1979).

27. In place of the Haley Model of systems family therapy, Friesen (and others) propose "Experiential Systemic Therapy," which they describe as a "second order, post structural" therapy consistent with our most-modern world and the new science. Experiential Systemic Therapy (ExST) is primarily concerned with relationships and consists of three interlocking dimensions: *the experiential* (on the assumption that what clients need to engage in relational novelty is not an explanation, but an experience), *the symbolic* (through the use of symbols—such as a beer bottle to an alcoholic family—in the therapeutic process to permit the client to externalize parts of the client's inner world in ways that would not be accessed by rational explanation), and *the systemic* (which goes far beyond conventional systems theory to include progressively larger and more complex systems, even to the universe). Friesen, Grigg, and Newman, "Experiential Systemic Therapy," 1-7.

28. Ibid., 12.

29. Pattison, *Pastor and Parish*, 64.

Chapter 1

1. Mansell Pattison, *Pastor and Parish: A Systems Approach* (Philadelphia: Fortress Press, 1977), 21.

2. Ibid., 62.

3. John, as with all other examples in this book, is a fictitious character based on numerous true stories all disguised to render identification impossible. In a few cases the authors tell their own stories, and this will be obvious.

4. Edwin Friedman, *Generation to Generation: Family Process in Church and Synagogue* (New York: Guilford Press, 1985), 250-73. This chapter on "Leaving and Entering a Congregational Family" is a brilliant exposition of the

systemic dimensions of the process. Friedman exposes what he calls the "lame duck myth" for the period between resignation and leaving. His four strategies for leaving that minimize pathological residue are (1) regulating one's own emotional reactivity to others; (2) permitting emotional reactivity in others; (3) nonanxiously being part of the transition process; and (4) staying in touch after one has left, but continuing to detriangle. Similarly he offers a threefold strategy for entering an established relationship system: (1) avoid interfering with or rearranging the triangles in the established relationship system; (2) be wary of efforts by members of the congregation to triangle you with the "departed" or with other members of the system; (3) work at creating as many direct one-to-one relationships as possible with key members of the "family." He recommends that a playful and paradoxical approach be taken by successors to popular pastors. For example, John's successor at First United might quote John in every sermon and personally sell John's tapes. Eventually the people will let go!

5. See Elton Trueblood, *The Company of the Committed* (San Francisco: Harper & Row, 1961). This is the central message of R. Paul Stevens, *Liberating the Laity* (Downers Grove, Ill.: InterVarsity Press, 1985).

6. The church is a system in such a way that the behavior of a member in one relationship is different from the behavior in another. On a larger scale, any church member will function differently in another church body. See Ludwig von Bertalanffy, *Perspectives on General Systems Theory: Scientific-Philosophical Studies* (New York: George Braziller, 1968), 55-56.

7. Biblical covenants have stipulations and obligations, but the essence of the covenant God made with Israel (and Christ with his bride) is the fact of unconditional belonging. While the *blessings* of the covenant are conditional upon obedience, the covenant itself is unconditional. Biblical covenant theology is expounded by Walther Eichrodt, *Theology of the Old Testament,* vol. 1, trans. J. A. Baker (Philadelphia: Westminster Press, 1961), and R. K. Harrison, *Introduction to the Old Testament* (Grand Rapids: Eerdmans, 1975). Jack O. and Judith K. Balswick use the covenant theme to expound a theology of family in "A Theological Basis for Family Relationships," *Journal of Psychology and Christianity* 6, no. 3: 37-49; the covenant theme is also the fundamental theological basis for the view of marriage expressed in R. Paul Stevens, *Married for Good: The Lost Art of Staying Happily Married* (Downers Grove, Ill.: InterVarsity Press, 1986).

8. Jay Efran and Michael D. Lukens, "The World according to Humberto Maturana," *Networker*, May-June 1985, 28.

9. Quoted by Harold Mitton, "The Crisis of Leadership" (Paper delivered at J. Willox Duncan Lectureship, Carey Hall, University of British Columbia, Vancouver, November 16, 1984).

10. Robert K. Greenleaf, *Servant Leadership: A Journey into the Nature of Legitimate Power and Greatness* (New York: Paulist Press, 1977), 4.

11. Paul Hersey and Kenneth H. Blanchard, *Management of Organizational Behavior* (Englewood Cliffs, N.J.: Prentice-Hall, 1977), 84.

12. Jerry Robinson and Roy Clifford, *Leadership Roles in Community Groups* (Urbana: College of Agriculture, University of Illinois, 1975), 2.

13. George R. Terry, *Principles of Management*, 3rd ed. (Homewood, Ill.: Richard D. Irwin, 1960), 493.

14. Robert Tannenbaum, Irving R. Weschler, and Fred Massarik, *Leadership and Organization: A Behavioral Science Approach* (New York: McGraw-Hill, 1959). Quoted in Hersey and Blanchard, *Management of Organizational Behavior*, 84-85.

15. Norman Shawchuk, *How to Be a More Effective Church Leader* (Glendale Heights, Ill.: Organizational Resources Press, Spiritual Growth Resources, 1981), 6.

16. Pattison, *Pastor and Parish*, 57-63.

17. Ibid., 50, 60.

18. H. Newton Malony, "Conflict Management in the Local Church" (Class notes, Seminar PM713, Fuller Theological Seminary, Pasadena, Calif., August 1983).

19. Davida Foy Crabtree, *The Empowering Church: How One Congregation Supports Lay People's Ministries in the World* (Washington, D.C.: The Alban Institute, 1989), 12.

20. Ibid., 13-14.

21. Michael E. Kerr and Murray Bowen, *Family Evaluation* (New York, W. W. Norton, 1988), 77-78.

22. Ibid., 107.

23. F. Kefa Sempangi, "Walking in the Light," *Sojourners*, February 1978, 27.

Chapter 2

1. Stephen B. Clark, *Building Christian Communities: Strategy for Renewing the Church* (Notre Dame, Ind.: Ave Maria Press, 1972), 22.

2. Virginia Satir, *Peoplemaking* (Palo Alto, Calif.: Science and Behavior Books, 1972), 119.

3. Other family therapists work with the family through the individual they are counseling.

4. Virginia Satir, *Conjoint Family Therapy*, rev. ed. (Palo Alto, Calif.: Science and Behavior Books, 1983), 228.

5. Michael Kerr and Murray Bowen comment that Newton's cause-and-effect theory was not only a scientific breakthrough, but a systemic one. Newton postulated that bodies, such as the planets, consist of corpuscles that act

instantaneously upon each other from a distance. Kerr and Bowen suggest that Newton's development of a theory of universal gravitation, a *process* rather than content discovery, was worthy of being considered, in a limited way, as systems thinking. Each planet does not have a mind of its own but contributes to a gravitational "field" that regulates the velocity and path of each planet. *Family Evaluation* (New York: W. W. Norton, 1988), 16-17.

6. L. Segal, "The Myth of Objectivity," in *The Dream of Reality: Heinz Von Foerster's Constructivism* (New York: W. W. Norton, 1986), 13.

7. Edwin Friedman, *Generation to Generation: Family Process in Church and Synagogue* (New York: Guilford Press, 1985), 16.

8. We acknowledge indebtedness for this phrase to Edwin Friedman, "Body and Soul in Family Process" (Lectures at the Pastoral Institute of British Columbia, Vancouver, May 1991).

9. Quoted by Edward O. Wilson, *Sociobiology: The New Synthesis* (Cambridge, Mass.: Harvard University Press/The Belknap Press, 1975), 257, cited in Kerr and Bowen, *Family Evaluation*, 52.

10. John D. Friesen, "An Ecological Systems Approach to Family Counselling," *Canadian Counsellor/Conseiller Canadien* 17, no. 3 (1983): 102.

11. Kerr and Bowen, *Family Evaluation*, 64. Emphasis added.

12. Ibid., 68. Kerr offers a useful diagram to show the continuum between fused relationships and the theoretically totally individual relationship. Bowen developed a sophisticated measuring scale from 0-100 on pages 100-107 in which he explains each level of differentiation.

13. Ibid., 69.

14. Ibid., 70, 97. Kerr and Bowen developed a scale of differentiation based on the degree to which people are able to distinguish thinking and feeling and to take action on the basis of thought or feeling.

15. Ibid., 69-70.

16. For example, Mansell Pattison, *Pastor and Parish: A Systems Approach* (Philadelphia: Fortress Press, 1977), 69. Pattison describes seven leadership functions in the system: symbolizing, being, sharing, intentionality, modeling and risk taking, limit setting, and "the catalytic and enabling" function. It is clear from the text that Pattison means what we call "equipping" where he uses the term *enabling*.

17. We acknowledge our indebtedness to family counselor Kerry Montgomery for these expanded definitions in notes from a lecture she gave at John Knox Presbyterian Church, Seattle, Wash. She has used thoughts from H. G. Lerner, *Dance of Anger: A Woman's Guide to Changing the Patterns of Intimate Relations* (New York: Perennial Library, 1989).

18. Friedman, *Generation to Generation*, 211.

19. Ibid., 240.

20. Anne Wilson Schaef, "Is the Church an Addictive Organization?" *The*

Christian Century, 3-10 January 1990, 18-21.

21. Ibid., 18.

22. Ibid.

23. See also Anne Wilson Schaef and Diane Fassel, *The Addictive Organiation* (San Francisco: Harper & Row, 1988).

24. Kerr and Bowen, *Family Evaluation*, 134-62. They devote a whole chapter to triangles. Their view is that the triangle is the basic molecule of the family's emotional system and that triangles outlive the people who participate in them—thus appearing in a later generation with new characters. They believe that triangles are the product of the undifferentiation in the human process. Friedman, *Generation to Generation*, 212, applies the concept of triangles to the congregational task.

25. This specific elaboration of the triangle theory has been developed by Paddy Ducklow, founder and former director of The Burnaby Christian Counselling Group, Burnaby, B.C.

26. Kerr and Bowen, *Family Evaluation*, 290.

27. This appears to be an emphasis in Ephesians 4:11-12 where the apostle does not categorize gifts—such as "prophecy"—but describes people functioning in ministry—prophets and pastor teachers. We believe that "spiritual gifts" are not simply what people are through birth—there is anointing, infilling, transformation—but we insist that the gift is related to the person as he or she was created by God to be. The dichotomy of talents and gifts is therefore unfortunate.

28. This principle that the gift emerges in the context of actual relational ministry seems to be suggested by Romans 12:8: ". . . if it is showing mercy, let him do it cheerfully." The "extra"—which some would call the special gifting of God—is the cheerfulness with which one shows mercy. But the gift emerges in the act and in relationships.

29. We view the three gift-lists as flexible and exemplary.

30. Kerr and Bowen are, we think, right in saying that systemic work is not a method but a theory, and the appropriate action is not a single method to be universally applied in every situation, but one that arises from applying the theoretical framework to the system.

Chapter 3

1. Eric Fromm, *Escape from Freedom* (New York: Holt, Rinehart and Winston, 1963), 74ff., quoted in Mansell Pattison, *Pastor and Parish: A Systems Approach* (Philadelphia: Fortress Press, 1977), 41.

2. Jay Efran and Michael Lukens, "The World according to Humberto Maturana," *Networker*, May-June 1985, 23.

3. Michael Kerr helpfully defines process as "a continuous series of actions or changes that result in a given set of circumstances or phenomena." Content "refers to the circumstances or phenomena out of the context of those actions and changes . . . ." He compares this with a movie where the individual frame is the "content" and the movie itself is the "process." Michael Kerr and Murray Bowen, *Family Evaluation* (New York: W. W. Norton, 1988), 14.

4. It is argued by some that Virginia Satir is not truly a systems therapist, in the von Bertalanffy sense, but a blend of psychology, humanism, and MRI-style cybernetics/communication. However, we include her in our consideration of systems theory because she treated families wholistically and understood the interdependence of members.

5. Virginia Satir, *Conjoint Family Therapy*, rev. ed. (Palo Alto, Calif.: Science and Behavior Books, 1983), 251-52.

6. Some of these thoughts were first published in R. Paul Stevens, "Systemic Equipping: Beyond the Packaged Program," *Pastoral Sciences: Interdisciplinary Issues in Psychology and Theology* 10 (1991): 61-75.

7. Markus Barth, *The Broken Wall* (Chicago: Judson Press, 1959), 45. "When no tensions are confronted and overcome, because insiders and outsiders of a certain class or group meet happily among themselves, then the one new thing, peace, and the one new man created by Christ, are missing; then no faith, no church, no Christ is found or confessed."

8. We recognize that environment and culture are not used interchangeably in leadership literature; we will later distinguish them.

9. Kenneth van Wyk, *A Model for Equipping Church Laity for Ministry* (Garden Grove, Calif.: Crystal Cathedral, 1981), 8.

10. Kerr and Bowen explore a parallel reality in family life under the rubric of "emotional field." They show that once there is movement in one element, a reaction is triggered that attempts to restore that element to its original place. *Family Evaluation*, 263.

11. Edgar H. Schein, *Organizational Culture and Leadership: A Dynamic View* (San Francisco: Jossey-Bass Publishers, 1991), xi.

12. Ibid., 6. Schein offers a useful chart on page 14 showing how basic assumptions (which are taken for granted) give rise to values (which are testable in the physical environment) and finally to artifacts and creations (which are visible expressions of the culture).

13. Schein proposes analyzing the culture to discover whether or not a consensus exists on these underlying assumptions, thereby indicating a "strong" or a "weak" culture; he cautions against trivializing culture by defining a culture too quickly on the basis of observed values or norms of behavior. Ibid., 111.

14. Ibid., 191.

15. Ibid., 241.

16. Ibid., 270ff.

17. Ibid., 300-301.

18. Ibid., 297-327.

19. Edwin Friedman, "Body and Soul in Family Process" (Lectures given at the Pastoral Institute of British Columbia, Vancouver, May 1991).

20. Friedman, *Generation to Generation: Family Process in Church and Synagogue* (New York: Guilford Press, 1985), 22.

Chapter 4

1. Sheldon Harnick (lyrics) and Jerry Bock (music), "Matchmaker," from the motion picture, *Fidder on the Roof,* The Time Square Music Company, Winona, Minn., 1964 (Released by United Artists Corporation, 1971), Magnetic Video Corporation, Industrial Park, Farmington Hills, Mo., 1981.

2. Friedman, *Generation to Generation: Family Process in Church and Synagogue* (New York: Guilford Press, 1985), 67. Friedman mentions that in another version the rabbi tells the woman, "Go try it!" She tries but returns after a total failure; in her "matchmaking," the partners had afflicted one another in various ways.

3. Robert Tannenbuam and Warren Schmidt, "How to Choose a Leadership Pattern," *Harvard Business Review* 51, no. 3 (March-April 1956): 162-180.

4. In our experience seventy-five percent of people who choose professional pastoral ministry are person-oriented leaders. Many of the task-oriented leaders who pursue professional ministry end up in denominational leadership or parachurch societies.

5. My doctor of ministry thesis was dedicated to discovering better patterns of making pastoral matches in the Baptist Union of Western Canada and has many resources that can be used by denominational officials in discerning better matches in the process of pastoral placements. Philip Collins, "Chosen to Lead: An Intentional Application of Situational Leadership Styles to the Placement of Professional Ministry in the Baptist Union of Western Canada" (D.Min. dissertation, School of Theology, Fuller Theological Seminary, 1986). Available through Carey Theological College, 5920 Iona Dr., Vancouver, B.C. V6T1J6 Canada.

6. Elsewhere Stevens has written on the importance of covenant as the missing ingredient in the modern contractual marriage, but here we are considering the question of incompatibility itself.

7. Friedman, *Generation to Generation,* 68.

8. Robert R. Blake and Jane S. Mouton, *The Managerial Grid III* (Houston: Gulf Publishing, 1964/1985), 12.

9. This graph is commonly used. See Norman Shawchuk, *How to Be a More Effective Church Leader* (Glendale Heights, Ill.: Organization Resources

Press, Spiritual Growth Resources, 1981), 30; Paul Hersey and Kenneth Blanchard, *Management of Organizational Behavior,* 4th ed. (Englewood Cliffs, N.J.: Pentice-Hall, 1969/1982), 82.

10. Friedman, *Generation to Generation,* 219.

11. The descriptions of the four basic styles of leadership are a combination of the writer's (Collins) reflections on personal experience and a distillation of the material presented by the following writers and theorists: Shawchuk, *How to Be a More Effective Church Leader,* 19-27; Jerry Robinson and Roy Clifford, *Leadership Roles in Community Groups* (Urbana: College of Agriculture, University of Illinois at Urbana-Champaign, 1975), 3f.; Robert C. Worley, *Change in the Church: A Source of Hope* (Philadelphia: Westminster Press, 1971).

There is a fifth leadership-style category that this writer is consciously leaving out, known variously as "5,5," "Compromise," and "Organization Man Management." This style has an intermediate concern for completing the task, while maintaining a moderate concern for people. If a stress situation develops between people and task, this style leads off with a trade off—giving up half of one to keep half of the other. He or she is trying to get a balance going. Steady progress comes from compromise and a willingness to yield some advantages to gain others. If introduced into our discussion, this category is apt to confuse readers and diminish their ability to grasp the four basic styles of leadership. At least this has been the experience of this writer in field-testing the material.

12. The graph is adapted from Robert B. Blake and Jane S. Mouton, *The Managerial Grid* (Houston: Gulf Publishing Co., 1964). See Appendix 2.

13. See Appendix 4, "Group Maturity and Leadership Style."

14. H. Newton Malony, a professor in organizational management at Fuller Theological Seminary, has a theory that conflict cannot actually be *resolved.* It can only be *reduced* to a problem. The problem can be resolved, but always with the recognition that the conflict can rise again. This theory is called conflict reduction. Class notes, "Conflict Management in the Local Church," Seminar PM713, Fuller Theological Seminary, Pasadena, Calif., August 1983.

15. Norman Shawchuk, "Are You a Flexible Leader?" *Leadership,* Spring 1981, 89-93.

16. We recommend Jay Hall, Jerry B. Harvey, and Martha Williams, *Styles of Leadership Survey,* Telemetrics International, 1755 Woodstead Ct., The Woodlands, TX 77380 (713-367-0060), and Norman Shawchuk, *How to Be a More Effective Church Leader,* Spiritual Growth Resources, A Division of Organization Resources Press, P.O. Box 5276, Glendale Heights, Ill. 60132, (800) 359-7363.

17. Shawchuk, *How to Be a More Effective Church Leader.* Supported by Robinson and Clifford, *Leadership Roles in Community Groups,* 3; and

Hersey and Blanchard, "Tri-dimensional Model on Leader Effectiveness," in *Management of Organizational Behavior*, 95f.

18. The terminology *group task relevant maturity* used for this is suggested by Chris Argyris and is found in Hersey and Blanchard, *Management of Organizational Behavior*, 61-62, 308-310.

19. Ibid., 53-56. See our Appendices 3 and 4 for charts on relevant leadership styles for groups at various levels of maturity.

Chapter 5

1. Quoted in Oscar Feucht, *Everyone a Minister* (St. Louis: Concordia, 1979), 146.

2. Quoted in ibid., 146. The danger of these two opening quotations is that it suggests that the equipper is a delegator. As we have seen over and again, the equipping leader is concerned that members be released for their own ministry.

3. E. Mansell Pattison, *Pastor and Parish: A Systems Approach* (Philadelphia: Fortress Press, 1977), 50.

4. Davida Foy Crabtree, "Empowering the Ministry of the Laity in Workplace, Home, and Community: A Programmatic and Systemic Approach in the Local Church" (D.Min. thesis, Hartford Seminary, 1989), 11.

5. Ibid., 62.

6. Pattison, *Pastor and Parish*, 50.

7. Davida Foy Crabtree, *The Empowering Church* (Washington, D.C.: The Alban Institute, 1989), 1-7.

8. Dan Williams, "Small Group Leaders," in R. Paul Stevens, *The Equipper's Guide to Every Member Ministry* (Downers Grove, Ill.: InterVarsity Press, 1992), 37-53.

9. See Pattison, *Pastor and Parish*, 28-47. When I (Stevens) first read Pattison's list of subsystems—proclaiming, symbolizing, moralizing, learning-growth, sustaining-maintaining, and the reparative subsystem—I found them remarkably similar to the four subsystems I have been expounding for years, now published in *The Equipper's Guide to Every Member Ministry*, chap. 7, though each of us came to his list independently. The four analogies I develop are (1) the nervous system—communication between members and between the body and the Head; 2) the digestive system—teaching learning patterns; (3) the circulatory system—the environment and culture; (4) the bone-muscle system—the structures that give stability and movement to the body. There are no revealed or normative subsystems. What Pattison and I have attempted to do is to offer examples of systemic thinking and acting.

10. While this book will not deal with clergy families, we heartily recommend Friedman's thoughts. Edwin Friedman, *Generation to Generation:*

Family Process in Church and Synagogue (New York: Guilford Press, 1985), 277ff.

11. Ibid., 195.

12. Ibid., 196.

13. Dennis Guernsey, *A New Design for Family Ministry* (Elgin, Ill.: David C. Cook, 1982), 103.

14. Michael Kerr and Murray Bowen, *Family Evaluation* (New York: W. W. Norton, 1988), 272.

15. Pattison, *Pastor and Parish,* 14-16. He offers some helpful guidelines for evaluating the "health-growth" potential of a system, especially a healthy church.

16. Henrika Vande Camp and G. Peter Schrenk, "The Church's Ministry to Singles: A Family Model," *Journal of Religion and Health 20* (1981): 141-55.

17. Clarence Hibbs, "A Systems Theory View of the Church," *Journal of Psychology and Christianity 2,* no. 2: 27.

18. James R. Koch, M.A., "From 'The Sins of the Fathers (and Mothers)' to 'All My Children' " (1983), 1.

19. Ibid.

20. These terms are derived from Ronald E. Cromwell and David H. Olsen, eds. *Power in Families* (New York: John Wiley & Sons, 1975), 218-19.

21. Ted Blenkhorne, "A Systemic Approach to Christian Family Education" (M.Th. thesis, Regent College, 1990), 47-49.

22. Jack Balswick and Judith Balswick, *The Family: A Christian Perspective on the Contemporary Home* (Grand Rapids: Baker Book House, 1989), 234-38.

23. Julian Rappaport, "In Praise of Paradox: A Social Policy of Empowerment over Prevention," *American Journal of Community Psychology 9,* no. 1 (1981): 1025.

24. Blenkhorne, "A Systemic Approach to Christian Family Education," 74.

25. Jack Balswick and Judith Balswick, "A Theological Basis for Family Relationships," *Journal of Psychology and Christianity 6,* no. 3: 46. Balswick and Balswick show that, in a family, relationships, authority, and power should be distinguishable. Parental authority is an ascribed power. Parents have authority (*exousia*) over their children because of the parental position in relationship to them. "The process of empowering [children] does not mean 'giving up' this position of authority nor does it mean that parent becomes depleted or drained of power" (*dynomic*). They say "successful parenting will result in children gaining as much personal power as their parents."

26. Balswick and Balswick, The Family, 240.

27. Some of these thoughts are more fully developed in Paul Stevens,

The Disciplines of the Hungry Heart: Christian Living Seven Days a Week
(Wheaton, Ill.: Harold Shaw, 1993).

28. Gustavo Gutierrez, *A Theology of Liberation* (Maryknoll, N.Y.: Orbis
Books, 1973), 206, quoted in Jon Sobrino, "Christian Prayer and New Testament Theology: A Basis for Social Justice and Spirituality" in *Western Spirituality*, ed. Matthew Fox (Sante Fe: Bear and Co., 1981), 79.

29. Robert K. Johnston, *The Christian at Play* (Grand Rapids: Eerdmans,
1983), 85. Remarkably, however, there is even in Puritan writings a strong
sense of the importance of the balanced life. Richard Baxter in *Christian Ethics*
advised, "If it be possible, choose a calling which so exerciseth the body, as not
to overwhelm you with cares and labour, and deprive you of all leisure for the
holy and noble employments of the mind; and which so exerciseth your mind, as
to allow you some exercise for the body also." *The Practical Works of Richard
Baxter* (Ligonier, Pa.: Soli Deo Gloria Publications, 1990), vol. 1, 377.

30. Johnston, *The Christian at Play*, 43.

31. We acknowledge indebtedness for this outline to John Finney, a
British equipper-evangelist whom we heard teach at Fuller Theological Seminary. He is a priest in the Church of England.

32. Elton Trueblood, quoted in Richard Foster, "Elton Trueblood: A Life
of Broad Strokes and Brilliant Hues," *Christianity Today*, 23 May 1980, 22.

33. Crabtree, *The Empowering Church*, 34.

Chapter 6

1. Quoted in Howard A. Snyder, *The Radical Wesley and Patterns for
Church Renewal* (Downers Grove, Ill.: InterVarsity Press, 1980), 148.

2. Davida Foy Crabtree, "Empowering the Ministry of the Laity in Workplace, Home, and Community: A Programmatic and Systemic Approach in the
Local Church" (D.Min. thesis, Hartford Seminary, 1989), 46.

3. Ray Anderson, *On Being Human: Essays in Theological Anthropology*
(Grand Rapids: Eerdmans, 1982), 37.

4. Jack Balswick and Judith Balswick, "A Theological Basis for Family
Relationships," *Journal of Psychology and Christianity* 6, no. 3: 22-26.

5. Gordon Wenham, "Grace and Law in the Old Testament," in *Law,
Morality, and the Bible* ed. Kaye Wenham and Gordon Wenham (Downers
Grove, Ill.: InterVarsity Press, 1978), 17.

6. This diagram was first published in R. Paul Stevens, *Married for Good*
(Downers Grove, Ill.: InterVarsity Press, 1986), 85.

7. Balswick and Balswick, "A Theological Basis for Family Relationships," 41-42.

8. Ibid., 42.

9. James Framo, "Breaking the Ties That Bind," *Networker* (September-October 1985), 51.

10. Kathleen Galvin and Bernard J. Brommel, *Family Communication: Cohesion and Change* (Glenview, Ill.: Scott, Foresman and Co., 1986), 39.

11. William T. Merkel and Linda B. Carpenter, "A Cautionary Note on the Application of Family Therapy Principles to Organizational Consultation," *Journal of the American Orthopsychiatric Association* 57, no. 1 (1986): 111-15.

12. Michael Kerr and Murray Bowen, *Family Evaluation* (New York: W. W. Norton, 1988), 7.

13. Ibid., 11.

14. Ibid., 55.

15. Ibid., 56.

16. L. S. Thornton, *The Common Life in the Body of Christ*, 2nd ed. (Westminster: Dacre Press, 1944), 159.

17. John A. T. Robinson repudiates that this cryptic reference has any connection with the church. *The Body: A Study in Pauline Theology* (London: SCM Press, 1977), 48. However, L. S. Thornton argues that "the evangelist must have known that for St. Paul the Church as the Body of Christ, is the temple of God . . . . The evangelist wishes us to understand that the enigmatic form of our Lord's saying about the temple (2:19) indicates simultaneously two aspects of his 'body.' When Christ's body was raised from the tomb, we too were raised. For we, Christ's members, are included in that body, 'made without hands,' which was nailed to the Cross and raised 'in three days.'" *The Common Life*, 318-19.

18. Ernest Best, *One Body in Christ: A Study in the Relationship of the Church to Christ in the Epistles of the Apostle Paul* (London: S.P.C.K., 1955), 84, 215. See Eduard Schweizer. "Soma," in G. Kittel, ed. *The Theological Dictionary of the New Testament*, trans. and ed. Geoffrey W. Bromiley (Grand Rapids: Eerdmans, 1971), 7: 1024-94.

19. Ernst Percy, *Der Leib Christi*, 45, quoted in Best, *One Body in Christ*, x.

20. Ernest Best shows conclusively that Adolf Diessmann's *Paul: A Study in Social and Religious History*, trans. William E. Wilson (London: Hodder and Stoughton, 1926) fails to give a satisfactory explanation of the social nature of being in Christ. *One Body in Christ*, 12.

21. Ibid., 25.

22. Ibid., 113.

23. Ibid., 193.

24. Ibid., 190.

25. This distinction is almost lost in Dietrich Bonhoeffer who said, "Christ exists as the Church." From *The Communion of Saints* (1960) as quoted in G. C. Berkouwer, *The Church* (Grand Rapids: Eerdmans, 1976), 85.

26. Thornton, *The Common Life*, 306.

27. Ibid., 310.

28. This is the problem of viewing the church as "the extension of the incarnation." See Best, *One Body in Christ,* 195.

29. Best critiques the application of corporate personality and racial solidarity too easily to the conception of the body. Ibid., 21.

30. Ibid., 23.

31. Schweizer, *"Soma,"* 1081.

32. It is our view that the primary reference in 1 Corinthians 11:29, "without recognizing the body of the Lord," is a failure in fellowship.

33. J. A. T. Robinson thinks that Paul's statement of the unity of the church in the main clauses ("we who are many form one body" Rom. 12:5) is an argument that the fundamental reality of the church is the organic unity that finds its expression in the members. The singularity of Christ's resurrection body is taken for granted; it is the multiplicity that must be explained. *The Common Life,* 60. However, Ernest Best disagrees with Robinson's reading of the context of these statements. Best believes that Paul is showing that unity and diversity go together, and that Paul's readers, who already understood the multiplicity, needed to be reminded of the unity. *One Body in Christ,* 96.

34. See Berkouwer, *The Church,* 51ff. Berkouwer applies the idea of pluriformity to the various forms that the concrete visible church now takes; he uses this thought to express that while a plurality of church is antithetical to being one church, pluriformity is a way of celebrating the diversity in the unity. In this book we are using the idea on the local church level in which the same multiformity/pluriformity of diverse members is seen to enrich the unity rather than threaten it. As Berkouwer says, "God loves multiformity" (52). However, we disagree with his thought that the doctrine of the pluriformity of the church does not arise from biblical unity, but from the development of the church in history. As we show in the text, it is implicit in the God whose people we are.

35. Some of the following thoughts were first expressed in R. Paul Stevens, "Breaking the Gender Impasse," *Christianity Today,* 22 January 1992, 28-31. They are further developed in R. Paul Stevens, "The Mystery of Male and Female: Biblical and Trinitarian Models," *Themelios* 17, no. 3 (April-May 1992): 20-24.

36. J. I. Packer, "God" in *The New Dictionary of Theology* ed. Sinclair B. Ferguson, David F. Wright, and J. I. Packer (Downers Grove, Ill.: InterVarsity Press, 1988) 274-77.

37. Tomas Spidlik, *The Spirituality of the Christian East: A Systematic Handbook* (Kalamazoo: Cistercian Publications, 1986), 45.

38. Ibid., 44. Expounding this, Spidlik maintains that "the texts of the Greek Fathers . . . remained faithful to the terminology of the New Testament: the expression *ho theos* is reserved for the father of Christ (Rom. 5:6, 2 Cor. 11:31, Eph. 1:3). The Father Almighty is the creator of heaven and earth, and

hence the principle of cosmic unity in the extra-divine universe. This Father, however, is also the source of intra-divine unity. The Son and the Spirit are one in the Father. And since the function of the divine Persons corresponds to the place each occupies in the bosom of the Trinity, the salvic value of the mystery of the trinity is manifested."

Commenting on this in an unpublished paper, Dr. James Houston argues that "to all intents and purposes, Augustine states that the relations within the godhead are irrelevant to their being God...It is as if God is God, in spite of the Trinity!" In contrast to this the Greek Fathers insisted that God's relations with humanity are internal to God's own character. In harmony with this, Dr. Houston traces the fact that in Western spirituality there has been a renewed mysticism (a direct personal experience of the presence of God) whenever there was contact with the trinitarian insights of the Greek Fathers. Trinitarian faith invites and evokes relationship. James Houston, "Trinitarian Spirituality" (Paper for coursework at Regent College, Vancouver B.C., 1989).

39. Best, *One Body in Christ,* 113.

40. Schweizer, "*Soma*," 1076, 1078.

41. Mansell Pattison, *Pastor and Parish: A Systems Approach* (Philadelphia: Fortress Press, 1977), 11.

42. See Berkouwer, *The Church,* 48.

43. Best, *One Body in Christ,* 187.

44. Anonymous, "On the Differentiation of Self," in *Family Interaction: A Dialogue Between Family Researchers and Family Therapists,* ed. J. Framo (New York: Springer, 1972), 168.

45. Robert F. Capon, *An Offering of Uncles: The Priesthood of Adam and the Shape of the World* (New York: Crossroad, 1982), 163-64.

46. Thornton, *The Common Life,* 221.

Chapter 7

1. Davida Foy Crabtree, *The Empowering Church* (Washington, D.C.: The Alban Institute, 1989), 44.

2. Dietrich Bonhoeffer, *No Rusty Swords: Letters, Lectures, and Notes 1928-1936, in The Collected Works of Dietrich Bonhoeffer,* ed. Edwin H. Robinson and John Boweden (New York: Harper & Row, 1965), 1:190-204.

3. Richard Foster, *The Celebration of Discipline: The Path to Spiritual Growth* (San Francisco: Harper & Row, 1978), 18-19.

4. The word *leader* does occur six times in the Bible, three times in the singular and three times in the plural. However, these references do not indicate that "power" rests with a leader because of his or her office. It is always exegeted as *servant.* See Paul S. Rees, "The Community Clue," *Life of Faith,*

26 September 1976, 3.

5. Biblical examples of this principle are: Isaiah, who "overheard God's call" and then dealt with the needs of the people (Isa. 6:1- 13), and Paul, who was motivated primarily not by the needs of the Gentile world, but by his vision of the resurrected Christ as Lord of both Jews and Gentiles (Acts 26:19; Gal. 1:16).

6. We also affirm that God hears the cry of God's people (Exod. 2:23- 25) and the needs of people become the testing ground of the call of God for God's servants (Jer. 8:20-9:2). The parable of the Good Samaritan is a good example of how neither the New nor the Old Testament will allow us to say in face of obvious need, "This is not my problem" (Luke 10:25-37). The point we are making is this: The source of the ministry is a divine empowerment and an initiating call, a call that comes to all the people of God (Eph. 4:1), rather than our own capacity to respond to the human condition.

7. This is our restatement of the first characteristic that both congregations and pastors felt should be in first place for the clergy, according to research used to develop the instruments for providing field education interns in seminary with a personal ministry profile, by the Association of Theological Schools, Vandalia, Ohio. See Cluster No. 34, Professional, Readiness for Ministry Program, 1979.

8. Collins is indebted to Meredith G. Kline, a former professor, for the idea of the *shaliach*. Two small but excellent books written by Dr. Kline are recommended: *The Treaty of the Great King* (Grand Rapids: Eerdmans, 1966) and *By Oath Consigned* (Grand Rapids: Eerdmans, 1968).

9. Robert K. Greenleaf, *Servant Leadership: A Journey into the Nature of Legitimate Power and Greatness* (New York: Paulist Press, 1977), 13.

10. Ibid., 13.

11. This is also made in Robert K. Greenleaf, *The Servant as Religious Leader* (Peterborough, N.H.: Windy Row Press, 1982).

12. Ray S. Anderson, *Minding God's Business* (Grand Rapids: Eerdmans, 1986), 66-67. Emphasis added.

13. Rev. P. T. Chandapilla (Paper delivered at the Bible and Medical Missionary Fellowship International Consultation on Personnel).

14. Greenleaf, *Servant Leadership*, 4.

15. Dietrich Bonhoeffer, *Life Together* (New York: Harper & Row, 1954), 10.

16. Bonhoeffer, *No Rusty Swords*, 188. Emphasis added.

17. Anderson, *Minding God's Business*, 79.

18. Quoted in William Diehl, *Thank God, It's Monday!* (Philadelphia: Fortress Press, 1982), 15.

19. Ibid.

20. William Bockelman, "The Pros and Cons of Robert Schuller," *The*

Christian Century, 20-27 August 1975, 732.

21. Anderson, *Minding God's Business*, 63. Emphasis added. Of course, the word *leader* does occur six times in the Bible; three times in the singular, three times in the plural. However, these references do not indicate that power rests in a leader because of the office. It is always exegeted as "servant." For further elaboration, read Rees, "The Community Clue," 3. Anderson's statement is supported by Matthew 20:25-28; Mark 10:35-45; John 10:11, 35-45; Hebrews 3:1-2.

22. Ibid., 64. Emphasis added. We recognize that there is considerable discussion about the difference between power and authority. Power is the capacity to exert influence, while authority is the leader's *right* to exert influence. However, the Christian idea is that, while authority is earned, it is also a gift from God. Power, or the capacity to exercise direction on others, is also granted by God, but only as the leader practices the presence of God.

23. Bonhoeffer, *No Rusty Swords*, 196, 201.

24. Ibid., 203.

25. A secular author worth reviewing is James MacGregor Burns, *Leadership* (New York: Harper & Row, 1978). His thesis is that the needs and wants (including self-esteem) of people determine who will and who will not lead. Relying heavily on Maslow's hierarchy of needs, Burns specifies two types of leadership: transactional (bargaining and exchanging) and transforming (recognizing and exploiting a need or demands so that others are uplifted).

26. Watchman Nee, *Spiritual Authority* (New York: Christian Fellowship Publishers, 1972).

27. This is a dangerous idea for New Covenant leaders, but it contains the truth that leaders who touch people for God have an authority that arises from an authentic life of obedience.

28. Ibid., 58.

29. H. Richard Niebuhr, *The Purpose of the Church and Its Ministry* (New York: Harper & Row, 1956), 67.

30. Anderson, *Minding God's Business,* 69. The idea of community is supported by other theologians such as Barth, Torrance, Thielicke, T. W. Manson, and Schillebeeckx.

31. Stephen B. Clark, *Building Christian Communities: Strategy for Renewing the Church* (Notre Dame, Ind.: Ave Maria Press, 1972), 22.

32. Ibid., 134-35.

33. We are indebted for the illustration of Moses to Anderson, *Minding God's Business*, 69-71. We have summarized his work.

34. Exodus 19-40.

35. Numbers 13:25-14:10.

36. Writers' synopsis of Anderson ends.

37. Greenleaf, *Servant Leadership*, 13.

38. Scriptures suitable for such a study: the relief mission to the dispossessed and hungry saints in Jerusalem during the famine (Acts 11:27-30); Paul's love-gift from the Gentile churches for the Jewish believers, each contributing from personal wealth to the other's poverty so there could be equality (Rom. 15:25-29; 2 Cor. 9:13-15); Paul's concern that the disciplined sinner in Corinth be truly forgiven and restored (2 Cor. 2:5-11); the concern of James about preference for the rich in the church and neglect of the poor (James 2:1-13); Mary's song (Luke 1:46-55); the announced mission of Jesus (Luke 4:18-19); and the blessings and woes of Jesus (Luke 6:20-26).

39. Greenleaf, *Servant Leadership*, 29.

Chapter 8

1. William Tyndale, "A Parable of the Wicked Mammon" (1527), in *Treatises and Portions of Holy Scripture* (Cambridge: Parker Society, 1848), 98, 104.

2. P. T. Forsyth, *The Church and the Sacraments* (London: Independent Press, 1917), 29.

3. *OSCM Yearbook*, quoted in *Action Information* 7, no. 1.

4. Elton Trueblood (Lecture given at McMaster Divinity College, Hamilton, Ont., 1959).

5. For biblical examples refer to the teaching of Paul on the body of Christ (1 Cor. 12:12-20) and his practice of disciplining and instructing churches (1 Cor.; 2 Cor.). See also the biblical teaching about covenant and the family of God (Matt. 12:50).

6. For example, consider the "together" descriptions of Christians in Ephesians 2:19-22, the "interdependence" statements in 1 Corinthians 12:14-26, and the systemic emergence of Paul's ministry after his conversion largely through the equipping intervention of Barnabas (Acts 9:27; 11:25-30). In his own community-building ministry, Jesus transformed competitive relationships in the disciple group into mutual service (John 13:14) and interdependence (Mark 9:33-37).

7. For example, consider the theological teaching of Paul on the headship of Jesus (1 Cor. 11:3; Eph. 1:23; 4:15; Col. 1:18). An Old Testament example is the equipping ministry of Eli who taught Samuel to respond to the Lord for him-self (1 Sam. 3:8-9). In the gospels we discover that most of Jesus' ministry took place during interruptions in his planned activities (Luke 8:40-44).

8. For example, Paul's circumcision of Timothy (Acts 16:3) was done out of cultural sensitivity, while Paul's righteous indignation at the practice of circumcision in the Galatian church (Gal. 1:6; 6:12-16) arose because of a fundamental incongruity between the culture of salvation by works and a culture

of grace. Paul considered Peter's hypocritical withdrawal from table fellowship with Gentiles (Gal. 2:11-13) to be an event that symbolized prechristian assumptions and would have a powerful influence on the church. Jesus spoke with the Samaritan woman in public (John 4:9) because he had assumptions about Samaritans and women that were different from contemporary Jews and even his disciples (John 4:27). The last book of the Bible (Revelation) is an empowering vision of the culture of the Christian's final home.

9. In ten points Paddy Ducklow, previously quoted, interprets Murray Bowen's approach to making changes in a family: (1) Play the role of the sideline coach, questioning, challenging, interrupting, being more "crazy" than the family. (2) Model immediacy by making "I" statements. (3) Refuse to take sides by siding with the relationship. (4) Adopt the goal of further differentiation from the family of origin. (It's never too late to grow up!) (5) Affirm the supremacy of reality and decision making over emotionality and catharsis (fusion). (6) Consider who should change: the identified patient or the identified resource? Always work with the strongest in the family. (7) Accept the power of benevolent disinterest in handling urgencies. ("The only crises I recognize are my own.") (8) Adopt an attitude of gratefulness, enjoyment of the humorous in the midst of the muck, which detoxifies an emotional situation. (9) Focus on the need to belong (security) and the need for separateness (significance). (10) Do family therapy and not family counseling. (The latter supports the belief that the identified patient is the sick one in the family.) The Burnaby Christian Counselling Group, Burnaby, B.C., 1992.

10. For example, Paul's passion to inculcate and incarnate Jew-Gentile mutual dependence in Christ involved a lifetime of cultural and spiritual change making, including (1) the relief mission to the poor Jews (Acts 11:27-30); (2) facilitating the Jerusalem Council decision (Acts 15:1-35); (3) raising among the Gentile churches the great offering for the poor Jewish believers in Palestine (2 Cor. 8-9); (4) personally delivering the love gift (Rom. 15:25-29; Acts 20:16; 21:1-16); (5) but taking a Jewish vow when he got to Jerusalem to present the gift (Acts 21:17-26).

11. For example, Paul recounts the revelation of his Gentile mission to the apostles in such a way that the other apostles were freed to work with the Jews while affirming Paul's vision (Gal. 2:1-10). Jesus defined his own mission to differentiate himself from contemporary views of the Messiah (Matt. 16:13-38). Further, he deliberately healed on the Sabbath as a vision statement to the Jews (John 5:16-18).

12. For example, Paul encouraged "household churches" (Rom. 16:5; 1 Cor. 16:19) and nurtured a mobile mission and training structure called "Paul and his companions" (Acts 13:2; 13:13; 15:40; 16:1-3, 6; 18:1-3; 20:4-6). In the context of his ministry to the crowd and the Seventy, Jesus nurtured the Twelve (John 6:3) and instituted the Eucharist (Matt. 26:17-30) as a symbolizing and

sacramental subsystem of the church's life. (Paul continued to shepherd this subsystem.) In dealing with the family subsystem, Jesus challenged family idolatries (Matt. 12:46-50), but provided for his own mother from the cross (John 19:25-27).

13. For example, Jesus refused to be triangled by Martha against Mary (Luke 10:40-42) or by the mother of James and John to prefer her sons over the rest (Matt. 20:20-28). Jesus also refused to be triangled by two brothers, each wanting him to take sides to settle their estate conflict (Luke 12:13-15). On one occasion Paul appears to allow himself to be triangled into the Pharisee-Sadducee conflict, but actually he was forcing them to address their own differences instead of being obsessed with Paul's belief in Jesus. In the process Paul saved his own skin (Acts 23:6-10).

14. For example, the apostles call the church to guard the integrity of its own life (Heb. 13:9) thus defining itself as a transformed community (Rom. 12:1-2). But the apostles also call the church to welcome strangers (Heb. 13:2). For the church to function as a corporate priesthood in the world (1 Peter 2:9-11) the church must be an open rather than a closed system. Jesus defined the boundaries of the disciple community in statements that communicate a deep truth about permeable boundaries and the exclusive/inclusive nature of his own claim: "He who is not with me is against me" (Matt. 12:30) and "whoever is not against us is for us" (Mark 9:39).

15. For example, Jesus breathed the Spirit on the disciples to empower them for their continuing ministry (John 20:21-23) and trusted them to do what the Spirit wanted to do through them (Acts 1:4-8). Paul directed the Ephesian elders to God rather than to himself (Acts 20:32-35) and trusted God for his own future in spite of the attempts of his friends to dissuade him from going to Jerusalem (Acts 21:4; 21:10-14). Paul's "last will and testament" to Timothy was an equipping message to be strong in the Lord (2 Tim. 2:1-3).

16. Commonly, evangelicals take Matthew 28:18-20—the so-called Great Commission—as their total definition of the mission of the church, while many mainline Protestants look to the so-called "Creation" or "Cultural Mandate" (Gen. 1:28) as their primary definition of the church's mission. Biblically, keeping the Great Commission should result in renewed human beings fulfilling the original intention God had for humankind. The separation of these two mandates has led to the tragic separation of social action and evangelism, a separation that is now institutionalized in denominations that hold to one or other of these mandates. It is our conviction that John 20:21 encompasses both the Great Commission and the Creation Mandate, and makes a deeper statement of the source and systemic character of that mission. An illuminating discussion of this is found in Lesslie Newbigin, "Cross-Currents in Ecumenical and Evangelical Understandings of Mission," *International Bulletin of Missionary Research* 6, no. 4 (October 1982): 146-55.

17. Reflecting on John 4:34, Thornton draws out the connection between the mission of the Son of God and the nourishment of the disciples by their participation in the Lord. L. S. Thornton, *The Common Life in the Body of Christ*, 2nd ed. (Westminster: Dacre Press, 1944), 428, see also 369-70.

Thornton puts the relation of the church to the Lord's life in the Father this way: "Our Lord's communion with his Father was the basis of his whole incarnate life on earth. The life of human response to 'my God' was sustained by the Son's eternal interchanges of love with 'my Father'. . . . So the circuit of the Son's response to the Father includes us within its orbit. In this, too, redemption corresponds to creation. Our created affinity to the eternal Son means that our filial response to the heavenly Father belongs to the plan of creation. Redemption restores this plan and brings it to fulfilment through the sacrificial response of the incarnate Son. The organism of that sacrificial response is the Body of Christ. By inclusion in his Body we are included in his sacrifice, the true worship which the Father seeks in his worshippers and finds only in his Son," 425.

18. Ibid., 429.

19. Davida Foy Crabtree, *The Empowering Church* (Washington, D.C.: The Alban Institute, 1989), 1-2.

20. Our first four-year project in the Certificate in Ministry from Carey Theological College in Vancouver, B.C., is described in "Equipping Equippers Cross-Culturally: An Experiment in the Globalization of Theological Education," *Missiology*, forthcoming.

21. John Redekop, "Christian Labour—A Place for Christians?" *Faith Today* (September-October 1989), 18-23.

22. See Kenneth Leech, *True Prayer: An Invitation to Christian Spirituality* (San Francisco: Harper & Row, 1980), 79.

23. Richard R. Broholm, "Toward Claiming and Identifying Our Ministry in the Workplace," in *The Laity in Ministry: The Whole People of God for the Whole World*, ed. George Peck and John S. Hoffman (Valley Forge: Judson Press, 1984), 150.

24. Quoted in Kenneth Leech, *True Prayer: An Invitation to Christian Spirituality* (San Francisco: Harper & Row, 1980), 91.

25. Davida Foy Crabtree, "Empowering the Ministry of the Laity in Workplace, Home, and Community: A Programmatic and Systemic Approach in the Local Church" (D.Min. thesis, Hartford Seminary, 1989), 28.

26. Crabtree, *The Empowering Church*, 6.

27. Ibid., 24.

28. Ibid., 64-68.

29. Alexandre Faivre, *The Emergence of the Laity in the Early Church* (New York: Paulist Press, 1990), 15-40.

30. Ibid., 69.

31. Tyndale, "A Parable," 98, 104.

32. Oscar E. Feucht, *Everyone a Minister: A Guide to Churchmanship for Laity and Clergy* (St. Louis: Concordia, 1974), 36.

33. The response of the Catholic Church to the Reformation is documented in William Rademacher, *Lay Ministry: A Theological, Spiritual, and Pastoral Handbook* (New York: Crossroad, 1991), 73, 79.

34. This phrase was coined by Anne Rowthorn in *The Liberation of the Laity* (Wilton, Conn.: Morehouse-Barlow, 1986), a book printed at the same time as my (Stevens) *Liberating the Laity*. Her chapter "The Clerical Captivity of the Church" surveys this material with great clarity.

35. See R. Paul Stevens, "Marketing the Faith: A Reflection on the Importing and Exporting of Western Theological Education," *Crux* 28, no. 2 (June 1992): 6-18.

36. Examples of colleges that are dedicated to theological education for all the people of God are Regent College, Vancouver, B.C.; New College, Berkeley; London Institute, U.K., now called Christian Impact, and others. In addition, several traditional seminaries have adopted very exciting lay theological educational programs that are not peripheral to their purpose. In most seminaries lay programs are definitely second class and not part of the central mission of the school.

37. See Greg Ogden, *The New Reformation* (Grand Rapids: Zondervan, 1990), 188-215.

38. Faivre, *The Emergence of the Laity*, 106-107.

39. Hendrik Kraemer offers some comments on the subject of why the Reformation did not go far enough. In addition to some we have named above, Kraemer points out that Luther's insistence of the power of the baptized Christian did not take seriously that not all "baptized" were truly believing Christians and that the laity could not suddenly function as mature spiritual adults. *A Theology of the Laity* (London: Lutterworth Press, 1958), 63-69.

40. In *The Equipper's Guide to Every Member Ministry* (Downers Grove, Ill.: InterVarsity Press, 1992), I (Stevens) spend a whole chapter (8) on equipping for justice ministry in light of biblical teaching on the principalities and powers. I take a comprehensive view of the complexity of social evil and structural sin encompassing structures, at one end, and the demonic, at the other.

41. Ludwig von Bertalanffy devotes a whole chapter to the "open system" in *Perspectives on General Systems Theory* (New York: George Braziller, 1975), 139-154. "An open system is defined as a system in exchange of matter with its environment, presenting import and export, building up and breaking down of its material components," 141.

42. Celia A. Hahn, *Lay Voices in an Open Church* (Washington, D.C.: The Alban Institute, 1985), 41.

43. Hendrik Berkhof, *Christ and the Powers* (Scottdale, Penn.: Herald

Press, 1962), 43.

44. Commenting on Christ's dominion over the principalities and powers, Markus Barth says, "far from being an indigestible burden to 'modern' man's credulity or faith, the references [to principalities and powers] show that the immense problems facing modern man are still within the scope of the gospel." *Ephesians 1-3: The Anchor Bible* (Garden City, N.Y.: Doubleday, 1974), 176.

45. Broholm, "Toward Claiming and Identifying Our Ministry," 150.

46. Quoted in Leech, *True Prayer*, 68.

47. Quoted in Eugene H. Peterson, *Reversed Thunder: The Revelation of John and the Praying Imagination* (Cambridge: Harper & Row, 1988), 95.

48. Quoted in ibid., 87.

49. Elizabeth O'Connor, *The Eighth Day of Creation: Gifts and Creativity* (Waco, Tex.: Word, 1971), 10. Emphasis added.

Epilogue

1. Mansell Pattison, *Pastor and Parish: A Systems Approach* (Philadelphia: Fortress Press, 1977), 31-32. Pattison describes the connection of these two sayings in these words: "Nietzsche is said to have run in the streets crying, 'Fall on your knees and weep, for God is dead!' And following him, the preeminent philosopher of our times, Jean Paul Sartre, looked out on the streets of science and saw that science too was dead!" As we shall see, systems thinking—a solidly scientific approach to human relationships—has been replaced by a postscientific approach as represented in such thinkers as Gregory Bateson and Humberto R. Maturana.

2. Michael Kerr and Murray Bowen, *Family Evaluation* (New York: W. W. Norton, 1988), vii.

3. Ibid., viii.

4. Harris W. Lee, *Theology of Administration: A Biblical Basis for Organizing the Congregation* (Minneapolis: Augsburg, 1981), 29.

5. Alvin J. Lindgren and Norman L. Shawchuk, *Management for Your Church: How to Realize Your Church Potential through Systems Approach* (Nashville: Abingdon, 1977), 26-27.

6. Essentially our critique follows three lines: (1) The issue of *anthropology*, that is, the implicit view of humankind assumed. Bowen theory is based on an evolutionary assumption. While Darwin claims to have discovered the physical link between humankind and lower species, Bowen claims to have discovered the behavioral link. While there is a service to be rendered in this viewpoint, it can hardly do complete justice to mixed reality of the people of God, partly human nature in its raw, though corporate expression and partly redeemed by the infusion of the Holy Spirit, a "being- redeemed" humanity.

(2) The issue of *soteriology or redemption.* Bowen theory assumes that two fundamental variables control all family processes: chronic anxiety and differentiation of self. A biblical perspective would view these as "symptoms" of a more fundamental disharmony with our Creator, just as the "sins" listed in Romans 1:22-32 are really symptoms of the fundamental sin of irreverence and ingratitude (Rom. 1:21).

(3) The issue of *epistemology* or how and what we know. Some of the systems thinkers we considered in the "Beyond Systems Theory" section of the introduction, thinkers like Bateson and Maturana, argue that we can never know a thing in itself. For the pastor this means that one can never claim to know the church, or even the members of the church, but only one's experience of being in the church. Information is impossible and the therapist cannot bring changes to the system (in other words, the part cannot change the whole). Important philosophical presuppositions lie behind these statements: that reality is monistic (of one and the same substance) and that we live in a multiverse rather than a universe. For Bateson, God (which he calls "the mind") is the sum of all the parts of the multiverse and does not exist over and above as well as immanently within God's own creation. The biblical leader cannot accept the conclusions of these thinkers uncritically without examining their presuppositions. From the point of view of biblical revelation, their presuppositions are not entirely adequate.

7. Gregory Bateson, *Steps to an Ecology of Mind* (New York: Ballantine, 1972), xviii.

8. Paul F. Dell, "Understanding Bateson and Maturana: Toward a Biological Foundation for the Social Sciences," *Journal of Marital and Family Therapy,* January 1985, 15.

9. L. Segal, "The Myth of Objectivity," in *The Dream of Reality: Heinz Von Foerster's Constructivism* (New York: W. W. Norton, 1986), 7-30.

10. Terry Real, "The Therapeutic Use of Self in Constructionist/Systemic Therapy," *Family Process* 29 (September 1990): 258.

11. Ibid.

12. Jay Efran and Michael Lukens, "The World according to Humberto Maturana," *Networker*, May-June 1985, 24, cite the following studies: R. C. Miller and J. S. Berman, "The Efficacy of Cognitive Behavior Therapies: A Quantitative Review of the Research Evidence," *Psychological Bulletin* 94 (1983): 39-53; D. A. Shapiro and D. Shapiro, "Meta-Analysis of Comparative Therapy Outcome Studies: A Replication and Refinement," *Psychological Bulletin* 92 (1982): 581-604; M. L. Smith, "What Research Says about the Effectiveness of Psychotherapy," *Hospital and Community Psychiatry* 33 (1982): 457-61; M. L. Smith and G. V. Glass, "Meta-Analysis of Psychotherapy Outcome Studies," *American Psychologist* 32 (1977): 752-60.

13. J. A. Hattie, C. R. Sharpley, and H. J. Rogers, "Comparative

Effectiveness of Professional and Paraprofessional Helpers," *Psychological Bulletin* 95 (1984): 534-41, cited by Efran and Lukens, "The World according to Humberto," 24.

14. L. Prioleau, M. Murdock, and N. Brody, "An Analysis of Psychotherapy versus Placebo Studies," *The Behavioral and Brain Sciences* 6 (1983): 275-310, cited by Efran and Lukens, "The World according to Humberto," 24.

15. Efran and Lukens, "The World according to Humberto," 24.

16. Ibid., 25.

17. Ibid., 27.

18. Ibid., 73.

19. L. S. Thornton, *The Common Life in the Body of Christ*, 2nd ed. (Westminster: Dacre Press, 1944), 2.

BIBLIOGRAPHY

Anderson, Douglas A. "Spirituality and Systems Theory: Partners in Clinical Practice." *Journal of Pastoral Psychotherapy* 1 (Fall 1987): 19-32.

Anderson, Ray. *On Being Human: Essays in Theological Anthropology.* Grand Rapids: Eerdmans, 1982.

_____. *Minding God's Business.* Grand Rapids: Eerdmans, 1986.

Anonymous. "On the Differentiation of Self." In *Family Interaction: A Dialogue Between Family Researchers and Family Therapists,* edited by J. Framo. New York: Springer, 1972.

Auerswald, Edgar H. "Thinking about Thinking in Family Therapy." *The Family Process* 24 (March 1985): 1-12.

Balswick, Jack O., and Judith K. Balswick. *The Family: A Christian Perspective on the Contemporary Home.* Grand Rapids: Baker Book House, 1989.

_____. "A Theological Basis for Family Relationships." *Journal of Psychology and Christianity* 6(3): 37-49.

Barth, Markus. *Ephesians: The Anchor Bible.* 2 vols. Garden City, N.Y.: Doubleday, 1974.

Bateson, G. *Steps to an Ecology of Mind.* New York: Ballantine, 1972.

Berger, Brigitte, and Peter L. Berger. *The War over the Family: Capturing the Middle Ground.* Garden City, N.Y.: Anchor Books, 1983.

Berkhof, Hendrik. *Christ and the Powers.* Scottdale, PA.: Herald Press, 1962.

Berkouwer, G. C. *The Church: Studies in Dogmatics.* Translated by James E. Davison. Grand Rapids: Eerdmans, 1976.

Best, Ernest. *One Body in Christ: A Study in the Relationship of the Church to Christ in the Epistles of the Apostle Paul.* London: S.P.C.K., 1955.

Blake, Robert R., and Jane S. Mouton. *The Managerial Grid III.* Houston, Tex.: Gulf Publishing, 1964/1985.

Bockelman, William. "The Pros and Cons of Robert Schuller." *Christian Century.* (20-27 August 1975): 732.

Bonhoeffer, Dietrich. *The Communion of Saints.* New York: Harper & Row, 1963.

_____. *Life Together.* New York: Harper & Row, 1954.

_____. *No Rusty Swords: Letters, Lectures, and Notes 1928-1936. In The Collected Words of Dietrich Bonhoeffer,* vol. 1. Edited by Edwin H. Robinson and John Boweden. New York: Harper & Row, 1965.

Bowler, T. Downing. *General Systems Thinking: Its Scope and Applicability.* New York: North Holland, 1981.

Broholm, Richard R. *Identifying Gifts and Arenas.* Newton Centre, Mass.: Center for the Ministry of the Laity, n.d.

_____. "Toward Claiming and Identifying Our Ministry in the Workplace." In *The Laity in Ministry: The Whole People of God for the Whole World,* edited by George Peck and John S. Hoffman. Valley Forge, PA: Judson Press, 1984.

Brommel, Bernard J., and Galvin, Kathleen M. *Family Communication: Cohesion and Change.* Glenview, Ill.: Scott, Foresman and Co., 1986.

Carroll, Jackson W. "Some Notes on Planned Social Change."

Clark, Stephen B. *Building Christian Communities: Strategy for Renewing the Church.* Notre Dame, IN: Ave Maria Press, 1972.

Collins, Philip. "Chosen to Lead: An Intentional Application of Situational Leadership Styles to the Placement of Professional Ministry in the Baptist Union of Western Canada." D.Min. dissertation, School of Theology, Fuller Theological Seminary, 1986.

Cosby, Gordon. *Handbook for Mission Groups.* Washington, D.C.: The Church of the Saviour, n.d.

Crabtree, Davida Foy. *The Empowering Church: How One Congregation Supports Lay People's Ministries in the World.* Washington, DC: The Alban Institute, 1989.

_____. "Empowering the Ministry of the Laity in Workplace, Home, and Community: A Programmatic and Systemic Approach in the Local Church." D. Min. thesis, Hartford Seminary, 1989. Substantially reproduced in *The Empowering Church.*

Cromwell, Ronald E., and David H. Olsen, eds. *Power in Families.* New York: John Wiley & Sons, 1975.

Dell, Paul F. "Understanding Bateson and Maturana: Toward a Biological Foundation for the Social Sciences." *Journal of Marital and Family Therapy,* January 1985, 15.

Diehl, William. *Thank God, It's Monday.* Philadelphia: Fortress Press, 1982.

Diessmann, Adolf. *Paul: A Study in Social and Religious History.*
Translated by William E. Wilson. London: Hodder and Stoughton,
1926.

Efran, Jay, and Michael D. Lukens. "The World according to Humberto
Maturana." *Networker* (May-June 1985): 23-75.

Faivre, Alexandre. *The Emergence of the Laity in the Early Church.*
New York: Paulist Press, 1990.

Feucht, Oscar E. *Everyone a Minister: A Guide to Churchmanship for
Laity and Clergy.* St. Louis: Concordia, 1974.

Foster, Richard. "Elton Trueblood: A Life of Broad Strokes and Brilliant Hues." *Christianity Today (*23 May 1980): 22.

_____. *Celebration of Discipline: The Path to Spiritual Growth.* San
Francisco: Harper & Row, 1978.

Framo, James. "Breaking the Ties That Bind." *Networker* (September-
October 1985): 51-56.

Friedman, Edwin H. *Generation to Generation: Family Process in
Church and Synagogue.* New York: Guilford Press, 1985.

_____. "Body and Soul in Family Process." Lectures given at the
Pastoral Institute of British Columbia, May 1991.

Friesen, John D. "An Ecological Systems Approach to Counselling."
Canadian Counsellor/Conseiller Canadien 17(3) (1983): 98-104.

Galvin, Kathleen, and Brommel, Bernard J. *Family Communication:
Cohesion and Change.* Glenview, Ill.: Scott, Foresman and Co.,
1986.

Greenleaf, Robert K. *Servant Leadership: A Journey into the Nature of
Legitimate Power and Greatness.* New York: Paulist Press, 1977.

_____. *The Servant as Religious Leader.* Peterborough, N.H.: Windy Row Press, 1982.

Guernsey, Dennis B. *A New Design for Family Ministry.* Elgin, Ill.: David C. Cook, 1982.

Gurman, Alan S., and David P. Kniskern, eds. *Handbook of Family Therapy.* New York: Brunner/Mazel, 1981.

Hahn, Celia A. *Lay Voices in an Open Church.* Washington, D.C.: The Alban Institute, 1985.

Hersey, Paul, and Kenneth H. Blanchard. *Management of Organizational Behavior.* Englewood Cliffs, N.J.: Prentice-Hall, 1977.

Hibbs, Clarence. "A Systems Theory View of the Church." *Journal of Psychology and Christianity* 2(2): 168.

Johnston, Robert K. *The Christian at Play.* Grand Rapids: Eerdmans, 1983.

Joy, Donald M. *Re-Bonding.* Waco, TX: Word, 1986.

Kerr, Michael E., and Murray Bowen. *Family Evaluation.* New York: W. W. Norton, 1988.

Kline, Meredith G. *The Treaty of the Great King.* Grand Rapids: Eerdmans, 1966.

_____. *By Oath Consigned.* Grand Rapids: Eerdmans, 1968.

Klir, George J. *Trends in General Systems Theory.* New York: Wiley-Interscience, 1972.

Koch, James R. "From 'The Sins of the Fathers (and Mothers)' to 'All My Children,'" 1983.

Kraemer, Hendrik. *A Theology of the Laity.* London: Lutterworth Press, 1958.

Krone, Lynne C. "Justice as a Relational and Theological Cornerstone." *Journal of Psychology and Christianity* 2(2): 36-46.

Lawson, David. "Differentiation in Premarital Preparation." *Journal of Psychology and Christianity* 4(3): 56-63.

Lee, Harris W. *Theology of Administration.* Minneapolis: Augsburg, 1981.

Leech, Kenneth. *True Prayer: An Invitation to Christian Spirituality.* San Francisco: Harper & Row, 1980.

Lindgren, Alvin J., and Norman L. Shawchuck. *Management for Your Church: How to Realize Your Church Potential through Systems Approach.* Nashville: Abingdon, 1977.

Merkel, William T., and Linda S. Carpenter. "A Cautionary Note on the Application of Family Therapy Principles to Organizational Consultation." *Journal of the American Orthopsychiatric Association* 57(1) (1986): 111-15.

Napier, Augustus Y., with Carl A. Whitaker. *The Family Crucible.* New York: Harper & Row, 1978.

Nee, Watchman. *Spiritual Authority.* New York: Christian Fellowship Publishers, 1972.

Neill, Stephen, ed. *The Layman in Christian History.* London: SCM Press, 1963.

Newbigin, Lesslie. "Cross-Currents in Ecumenical and Evangelical Understandings of Mission." *International Bulletin of Missionary Research* 6 (October 1982): 146-155.

Niebuhr, H. Richard. *The Purpose of the Church and Its Ministry.* New York: Harper & Row, 1956.

O'Connor, Elizabeth. *Eighth Day of Creation: Gifts and Creativity.* Waco, Tex.: Word, 1971.

Ogden, Greg. *The New Reformation: Returning the Ministry to the People of God.* Grand Rapids: Zondervan, 1990.

Packer, J. I. "God." In *The New Dictionary of Theology,* edited by Sinclair Ferguson, DavidWright, and J. I. Packer. Downers Grove, Ill.: InterVarsity, 1988.

Pattison, E. Mansell. *Pastor and Parish: A Systems Approach.* Philadelphia: Fortress Press, 1977.

Rademacher, William J. *Lay Ministry: A Theological, Spiritual, and Pastoral Handbook.* NewYork: Crossroad, 1991.

Rappaport, Julian. "In Praise of Paradox: A Social Policy of Empowerment Over Prevention." *American Journal of Community Psychology* 9(1) (1981): 1025.

Real, Terry. "The Therapeutic Use of Self in Constructionist/Systemic Therapy." *Family Process* 29 (September 1990): 255-72.

Redekop, John. "Christian Labour: A Place for Christians?" *Faith Today* (September-October 1989): 18-23.

Reiss, Ira. L. *Family Systems in America.* 3rd ed. New York: Holt, Rinehart and Winston, 1980.

Ridderbos, Herman. *Paul: An Outline of His Theology.* Grand Rapids: Eerdmans, 1977.

Robinson, Jerry, and Roy Clifford. *Leadership Roles in Community Groups.* Urbana: College of Agriculture, University of Illinois, 1975.

Robinson, John A. T. *The Body: A Study in Pauline Theology.* London: SCM Press, 1977.

Rowthorn, Anne. *The Liberation of the Laity.* Wilton, Conn.: Morehouse-Barlow, 1986.

Rudge, Peter F. *Ministry and Management.* London: Tavistock Publications, 1968.

Satir, Virginia. *Peoplemaking.* Palo Alto, Calif.: Science and Behavior Books, 1972.

_____. *Conjoint Family Therapy.* rev. ed. Palo Alto, Calif.: Science and Behavior Books, 1983.

Schaef, Anne Wilson, "Is the Church an Addictive Organization?" *Christian Century* (-10 January 1990): 18-21.

Schaef, Anne Wilson, and Diane Fassel. *The Addictive Organization.* San Francisco: Harper & Row, 1988.

Schein, Edgar H. *Organizational Culture and Leadership: A Dynamic View.* San Francisco: Jossey-Bass, 1991.

Schoberg, Gerry, and R. Paul Stevens. *Satisfying Work: Christian Living from Nine to Five.* Wheaton, Ill.: Harold Shaw, 1989.

Schweizer, Eduard. "Soma." In *Theological Dictionary of the New Testament,* vol. 7. Edited by G. Kittel. Translated and edited by Geoffrey W. Bromiley. Grand Rapids: Eerdmans, 1971.

Segal, L. "The Myth of Objectivity." In *The Dream of Reality: Heinz Von Foerster's Constructivism.* New York: W. W. Norton, 1986.

Shawchuck, Norman. *How to Be a More Effective Church Leader.* Glendale Heights, IL.: Organization Resources Press/Spiritual Growth Resources, 1981.

_____. "Are You a Flexible Leader?" *Leadership* (Spring 1981): 89-93.

Snyder, Howard A. *The Radical Wesley and Patterns for Church Renewal.* Downers Grove, Ill.: InterVarsity, 1980.

Spidlik, Tomas. *The Spirituality of the Christian East: A Systematic Handbook.* Kalamazoo: Cistercian Publications, 1986.

Stelck, Brian, and R. Paul Stevens. "Equipping Equippers Cross-Culturally: An Experiment in the Globalization of Theological Education." *Missiology*, forthcoming.

Stevens, R. Paul. *Married for Good: The Lost Art of Staying Happily Married*. Downers Grove, Ill.: InterVarsity, 1986.

_____. *Liberating the Laity*. Downers Grove, Ill.: InterVarsity, 1985.

_____. *The Equipper's Guide to Every Member Ministry*. Downers Grove, Ill.: InterVarsity, 1992.

_____. "Systemic Equipping: Beyond the Packaged Program." *Pastoral Sciences: Interdisciplinary Issues in Psychology and Theology* 10 (1991): 61-75.

_____. *Disciplines of the Hungry Heart: Christian Living Seven Days a Week*. Wheaton, Ill.: Harold Shaw, 1993.

_____. "Breaking the Gender Impasse." *Christianity Today* (22 January 1992): 28-31.

_____. "The Mystery of Male and Female." *Themelios* 17 (April-May 1992): 20-24.

_____. "Marketing the Faith: A Reflection on the Importing and Exporting of Western Theological Education." *Crux* XXVIII (June 1992): 6-18.

Stott, John. *One People*. Old Tappan, N.J.: Fleming H. Revell, 1982.

Tannenbaum, Robert, and Warren Schmidt. "How to Choose a Leadership Pattern." *Harvard Business Review* 51 (March-April 1956): 162-180

Tannenbaum, Robert, Irving R. Weschler, and Fred Massarik. *Leadership and Organization: A Behavioral Science Approach*. New York: McGraw-Hill, 1959.

Terry, George R. *Principles of Management.* 3rd ed. Homewood, Ill.: Richard D. Irwin, 1960.

Thornton, L. S. *The Common Life in the Body of Christ.* 2nd ed. Westminster: Dacre Press, 1944.

van Wyk, Kenneth. *A Model for Equipping Church Laity for Ministry.* Garden Grove, Calif.: Crystal Cathedral, 1981.

Vogel, Exra F., and Norman W. Bell. "The Emotionally Disturbed Child as the Family Scapegoat." In *A Modern Introduction to the Family.* rev. ed. Edited by N. W. Bell and E. F. Vogel. New York: Macmillan, 1968.

Voltz, Carl A. *Pastoral Life and Practice in the Early Church.* Minneapolis: Augsburg, 1990.

von Bertalanffy, Ludwig. *Perspectives on General System Theory: Scientific-Philosophical Studies.* New York: George Braziller, 1975.

_____. *General System Theory.* New York: George Braziller, 1968.

von den Blink, A. J. "Family Systems Theory: A Way to Assess Pastoral CounselingOrganizations." *Journal of Pastoral Psychotherapy* 1 (Spring-Summer 1988): 33-47.

Warkentin, Marjorie. *Ordination: A Biblical-Historical View.* Grand Rapids: Eerdmans, 1982.

Wenham, Gordon. "Grace and Law in the Old Testament." In *Law, Morality, and the Bible*, edited by Bruce Kaye and Gordon Wenham. Downers Grove, Ill.: InterVarsity, 1978.

Williams, Dan. *Seven Myths about Small Groups.* Downers Grove, Ill.: InterVarsity, 1991.

World Council of Churches. *The Church for Others and the Church for the World.* Geneva, Switzerland: World Council of Churches, 1967.

Wynne, Lyman C., Susan H. McDaniel, and Timothy T. Weber. *Systems Consultation: A New Perspective for Family Therapy.* New York: Guilford Press, 1986.

Yoder, John Howard. *The Fullness of Christ: Paul's Vision of Universal Ministry.* Elgin, Ill.: Brethren Press, 1987.

The Alban Institute:
an invitation to membership

The Alban Institute, begun in 1979, believes that the congregation is essential to the task of equipping the people of God to minister in the church and the world. A multi-denominational membership organization, the Institute provides on-site training, educational programs, consulting, research, and publishing for hundreds of churches across the country.

The Alban Institute invites you to be a member of this partnership of laity, clergy, and executives—a partnership that brings together people who are raising important questions about congregational life and people who are trying new solutions, making new discoveries, finding a new way of getting clear about the task of ministry. The Institute exists to provide you with the kinds of information and resources you need to support your ministries.

Join us now and enjoy these benefits:

CONGREGATIONS, The Alban Journal, a highly respected journal published six times a year, to keep you up to date on current issues and trends.

Inside Information, Alban's quarterly newsletter, keeps you informed about research and other happenings around Alban. Available to members only.

Publications Discounts:

☐ 15% for Individual, Retired Clergy, and Seminarian Members
☐ 25% for Congregational Members
☐ 40% for Judicatory and Seminary Executive Members

Discounts on Training and Education Events

Write our Membership Department at the address below or call us at (202) 244-7320 for more information about how to join The Alban Institute's growing membership, particularly about Congregational Membership in which 12 designated persons receive all benefits of membership.

 The Alban Institute, Inc.
4125 Nebraska Avenue, NW
Washington, DC 20016

253
ST845 E

LINCOLN CHRISTIAN COLLEGE AND SEMINARY

87043

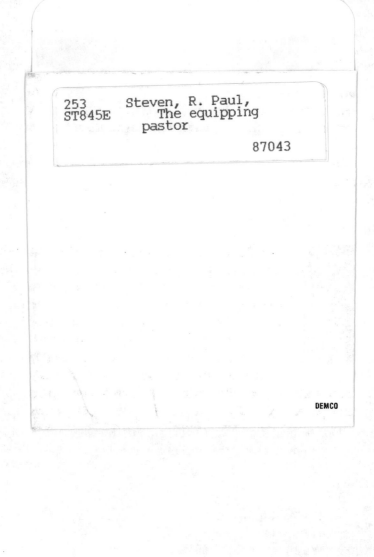

253
ST845E   Steven, R. Paul,
            The equipping
        pastor

                        87043

                                    DEMCO